Accounting Made Easy™
An Introductory Financial Accounting Course

FIRST EDITION

Neville Joffe
Author

AME | Learning

ISBN: 978-0-9733051-5-9

Publisher: AME Learning Inc.
Senior Editor: Anita Joshua
Production Coordinator: Anand Karat
Production Editor: Vicky Elliott
Cover Design: Charles Maynard
Interior Design: Krista Donnelly
Cover and Content Images: © iStockphoto.com

Printed and bound in Canada

This book is written to provide accurate information concerning the covered topics. It is not meant to take the place of professional advice.

For more information contact:

AME Learning Inc.
9251 Yonge Street, Suite 306
Richmond Hill ON CANADA L4C 9T3
Phone: 905.731.2408 or 1.888.401.3881
Fax: 905.731.8120
Email: info@amelearning.com
www.amelearning.com

ACKNOWLEDGEMENTS

We wish to extend a sincere thank you to the many people who participated in the design and completion of this book and the online program. Thank you for helping to make this first edition a reality.

CONTENT REVIEWERS AND CONSULTANTS

A special thank you to the following reviewers and consultants:

Delano Antoine
Professor, School of Marketing and e-Business, Seneca College

Dennis Wilson
Former Professor, Business Studies, Centennial College

Guy Baker
Professor and Hospitality Coordinator, School of Tourism, Seneca College

David Schlanger
Professor, Management, Entrepreneurship & Strategy, Ryerson University

Jim Whiteway
Professor of Business Sales, Loyalist College

Lloyd Lewis
Former Professor, Seneca College

Robert Savard
Former Professor, Concordia University

Rupert Rode
Chartered Accountant

Scott Duncan
President, Scott Duncan & Associates

Philip Becker
Chartered Accountant, Fruitman & Kates

AME | Learning

Table of Contents

introduction

Accounting Made Easy™
Introduction

About the Author

Neville Joffe created the AME™ program after spending more than 25 years in the manufacturing industry. His maverick style of leadership embraced numerous philosophies such as *Quality Circle*, the *Theory of Constraints*, *Just In Time* inventory systems, and many more. These processes were adopted in an attempt to seek new and innovative ways to improve productivity and profitability.

Eventually Neville discovered that the one key factor that was required to make all these philosophies effective was to ensure that his peers and employees understood the financial impact of their decisions.

Non-financial employees had problems relating to accounting principles because they had never been exposed to business finance. However, once they understood logic, purpose and context, they were more receptive to learn the subject matter. Teaching accounting/bookkeeping in the traditional manner did not bring value to the non-financial people, but understanding the concept of accounting and its connection to their own financial well being was far more valuable. Neville realized that there was a desperate need for another teaching method. He took a sabbatical during which time he developed a training tool that has since been used to train non-financial managers in corporations.

Corporate clients of the AME system include well known companies such as Hallmark Cards, Campbell's Soup, ACNielsen, Burger King, Bata Shoes, Royal Bank and Boston Pizza, in addition to many government institutions. Attendees at almost every corporate workshop commented that they wished they had learned accounting the AME way at college or that they had learned more in the one-day course than they learned during six months at college. As a result, the AME System was developed for the college market, both as a classroom and online program.

The AME™ teaching system has won several awards including the *Otter Award* (Canadian Society for Training and Development) for the best training program in Canada. The system has also been awarded with a patent in several countries.

Message to Students

This accounting course will teach you an essential life skill in both your personal life and business career that you will use forever regardless of your job. Having a job to earn an income is one thing, but building wealth is different. To build financial security you must understand the basic skills that this course will offer you.

Here are some more examples of why this course is important for you:

1. *Sales profession:* You will be ahead of your competition if you are able to chat about gross margins, the financial benefits of helping customers maintain low inventory levels, or how your sales methods are helping your company's profits.

2. *Human resource professional:* Imagine holding a discussion with the financial controller of your company about how certain training initiatives will improve liquidity and profitability ratios.

3. *Warehouse manager:* You will need to understand the impact of inventory control, cash flow, procurement methods and the financial impact on the organization.

4. *Accounts receivable clerk:* You will need to understand the connection between your role when allowing credit terms to a customer in relation to cash flow, discounting and its impact on margin, as well as credit risk and how to communicate these topics with a financial controller.

5. *Fast food business franchisee:* Many small businesses fail because owners do not understand the business elements of the operation. You will stand a far better chance of success when you can make appropriate demands of your bookkeeper and understand the meaning of subjects such as operating profit, cash flow and bank involvement. You will also learn to understand how to manage and control your business by being able to read key financial ratios and performance metrics.

Regardless of your job, when you can speak the language of accounting and connect the financial numbers to your performance, you will earn respect from your peers and employer.

There are two distinct types of accounting students in college: those students who wish to study accounting as a career and those students that either have to complete the subject as part of their course or simply wish to have more business know-how. This course is designed for the benefit of everyone.

The Meaning of Accounting

A ccounting is about tracking how much you are worth. Imagine owning a yacht, nice cars, a beautiful home and tickets to travel the world - you must understand how to measure your wealth and how to sustain it.

Most people associate accounting with calculators, computers and long lists of numbers. That may be true to some degree when you are a practicing bookkeeper or accountant. However, understanding accounting principles is not primarily about numbers. It's actually about logic - a way of thinking. Here is an example of the logic behind one of the principles that you will learn in this course - the concept of net worth.

Which scenario would you prefer?

Scenario #1

Assets	
Cash	$3,000
Value of home	80,000
Automobile	15,000
Contents of home	6,000
Total Assets	**$104,000**

Scenario #2

Assets	
Cash	$5,000
Value of home	100,000
Automobile	20,000
Contents of home	8,000
Total Assets	**$133,000**

It would appear, on first impression, that Scenario #2 is more favourable. However, there is some crucial information missing. We must not look only at what we own, but must also consider how much we owe. In examining these scenarios again, which one would you prefer?

Scenario #1

Assets		Liabilities	
Cash	$3,000	Bank loan	$0
Value of home	80,000	Credit card account	2,000
Automobile	15,000	Mortgage on home	60,000
Contents of home	6,000	Automobile loan	5,000
Total Assets	**$104,000**	Student loan	5,000
		Total Liabilities	**$72,000**
		Net Worth	**$32,000**

Scenario #2

Assets		Liabilities	
Cash	$5,000	Bank loan	$8,000
Value of home	100,000	Credit card account	4,000
Automobile	20,000	Mortgage on home	80,000
Contents of home	8,000	Automobile loan	5,000
Total Assets	**$133,000**	Student loan	10,000
		Total Liabilities	**$107,000**
		Net Worth	**$26,000**

Net Worth

An explanation of Net Worth is that if you chose to *cash out* (sell all your assets according to the value on your balance sheet) and pay everything that you owe, the remaining cash **represents how much you are worth.**

Assets = all that you OWN

Liabilities = all that you OWE

Value of Assets = $200,000

Value of Liabilities = $150,000

Net Worth = $50,000

The amount you are worth and the records used to track this amount is the key underlying principle of what accounting is all about, in both your personal and business economic life.

To increase Net Worth you must ensure that your expenses do not exceed your revenue. If you do not maintain a record of your revenue and expenses, you will never know what activities caused your Net Worth to increase or decrease.

This principle remains the same in business.

The AME™ Method

The AME™ learning system rapidly converts the theoretical and abstract nature of accounting into a practical and concrete discipline, using unique, patented proprietary tools.

It is a fact that we tend to remember 20% of what we hear, 30% of what we see and 90% of what we do. AME demystifies accounting by using colour-coded diagrams to help you remember the accounting process from a uniform, consistent and logical point of view. The program is an interactive simulation, which reduces the learning curve to literally hours.

The program first teaches key concepts and principles using personal financial statements before progressing to more advanced business subject matter.

You will use this combined textbook/workbook in class and will be required to access the online program prior to attending class. This preparatory work online is crucial. When you log on, you will be provided with important configuration instructions, which we have included for your review in this textbook:

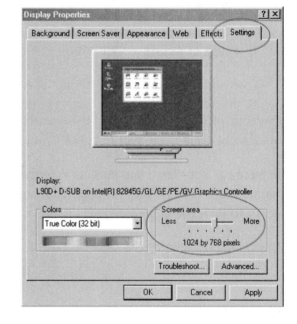

1. **Optimal screen setting:** You need to set your screen resolution to allow for full screen coverage. Right click on your desktop, select **Properties** and the **Settings** tab, move the slide over to **1024 x 768**, click on **Apply.**

2. **Sequential nature of the course:** You must complete the course sequentially, because the curriculum has been specifically designed to help you understand each learning outcome in context. However, once you have completed a section you will have the option to redo or review.

3. **Sound:** This course is supported with sound so you will either need speakers or a headset.

4. **PDF support material:** The entire course is supported with downloadable PDF files that summarize each of the key learning outcomes. Click on this icon when prompted at the end of the section:

Functionality

Bookmarking: When you log out of the program, the program does not automatically save where you left off. You therefore need to bookmark the slide you are on before logging off.

Forward button

Back button

Redo button

Spacebar: After completing T-Account entries, you can press the spacebar instead of using the mouse each time to move forward.

There are various **tools** that you will be working with:

1. Virtual, colour-coded balance sheet and income statement *boards* (diagrams)

2. Virtual *money tray* from which you will drag *tokens* to and from the boards

3. T-Accounts - electronic worksheets that require you to enter data from time to time. There are two sides to each account as per the illustration below - increase and decrease. (T-Accounts get their name from their "T" shape.)

4. Dragging a token *onto* the board corresponds to an *increase* on the T-Account and dragging a token *off* the board corresponds to a *decrease* on the T-Account.

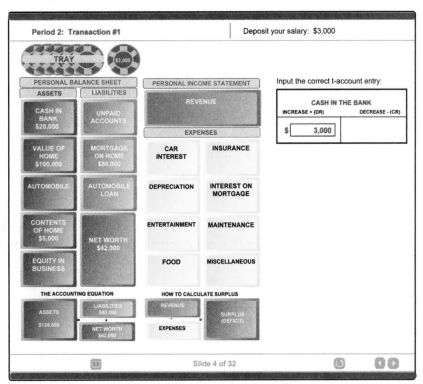

Chapter 1

Chapter 1
Personal
SECTION 1

Section 1

▶ The Concept of Money and Value
▶ The Role of the Balance Sheet
▶ The Income Statement
▶ The Accounting Equation - Part I

The Concept of Money and Value

Other than cash in your bank account, every other financial aspect of your life relates to values and not to cash.

For example:

Relating to the things that you own, which are called assets:

- A house has *value* but is *not actually cash.*

- An automobile has *value* but is *not actually cash.*

- An entertainment system has *value* but is *not actually cash.*

In other words, at some time during your past these assets were either purchased with cash (or you may have borrowed the money) but now *represent a value.* When you sell these assets one day they will then be *converted into cash.*

Relating to the things that you owe, which are called liabilities:

- The amount of "money" you owe a friend is not cash, it is simply an IOU (I Owe You).

- The amount of "money" that you owe against your credit card account is not cash, it is simply how much you owe (also an IOU).

However, when you pay your friend or the credit card company, you will be required to pay them with cash. Until that happens the amount that you owe is simply a *value.* **Accounting** is the process with which we record these values, whether they represent real cash or simply a value.

Remember that it is quite possible to have a high Net Worth with no cash in the bank.

Example:

Assets (what you own):		Liabilities (what you owe):	
Cash	$2,000	*Value of* loan from the bank	$6,000
Value of home	100,000	*Value of* loan from a friend	2,000
Value of Automobile	20,000	*Value of* credit card balance	2,000
Value of furniture	6,000	Total value of liabilities	$10,000
Value of computer	2,000		
Total value of assets	**$130,000**	**Assets - Liabilities = Net Worth**	**$120,000**

The Role of the Balance Sheet

The balance sheet is used to record what you own (assets) and what you owe (liabilities). The difference between what you own and what you owe represents your Net Worth. In other words, if you sold all your assets and used the cash to pay your debts, the amount remaining would be your Net Worth.

Example: Note that there is only $7,000 cash in the bank. At this point in time, if you needed to pay everything that you owe ($10,000) you would need to sell some of your assets. The value of your assets will convert into cash, which will be used to pay what you owe. Although you may think you are only worth the $7,000 you have in the bank, in reality your true value (or Net Worth) is $36,500.

Scenario #1: Net Worth is equal to assets less liabilities.

BALANCE SHEET			
Assets		**Liabilities**	
Daily banking account	$7,000	Unpaid accounts	$500
Savings account	500	Mortgage on home	100,000
Value of home	120,000	Loan from bank	5,000
Automobile	10,000		
Contents of home	4,500	**Total Liabilities**	**$105,500**
Total Assets	**$142,000**	**Net Worth**	**$36,500**

Scenario #2: Notice that the cash balance has decreased, giving the impression that you are poorer when in fact your Net Worth is HIGHER.

BALANCE SHEET			
Assets		**Liabilities**	
Daily banking account	$1,000	Unpaid accounts	$5,000
Savings account	8,000	Mortgage on home	100,000
Pension savings	10,000	Loan from bank	0
Value of home	120,000		
Automobile	10,000		
Contents of home	4,500	**Total Liabilities**	**$105,000**
Total Assets	**$153,500**	**Net Worth**	**$48,500**

Scenario #3: You have a bank overdraft, meaning that you have a negative bank balance, but your Net Worth is significantly higher than when you had more cash.

BALANCE SHEET				
Assets		**Liabilities**		
Daily banking account	-$2,000	Unpaid accounts	$10,000	
Savings account	0	Mortgage on home	80,000	
Pension savings	10,000	Loan from bank	0	
Value of home	180,000	Car Loan	6,000	
Automobile	10,000	Family Loan	7,000	
Contents of home	5,000			
Investments	20,000	Total Liabilities	$103,000	
Total Assets	$223,000	Net Worth	$120,000	

Scenario #4: The owner of this balance sheet has a lot of cash, a nice home and fancy cars. However, when assessing the owner's Net Worth it is apparent that he is not worth very much. He has borrowed a significant amount from the bank for his house and car and he even borrowed money from his family.

BALANCE SHEET				
Assets		**Liabilities**		
Daily banking account	$50,000	Unpaid accounts	$15,000	
Savings account	0	Mortgage on home	220,000	
Pension savings	3,000	Loan from bank	50,000	
Value of home	250,000	Car Loan	40,000	
Automobile	50,000	Family Loan	10,000	
Contents of home	12,000			
Investments	5,000	Total Liabilities	$335,000	
Total Assets	$370,000	Net Worth	$35,000	

The owner in Scenario #3, with the negative cash balance, is actually worth the most.

The Income Statement

The Income Statement is basically used as a *temporary notepad* to record transactions relating to revenue and expenses. The sole purpose of this statement is to determine the change in your Net Worth (revenue minus expenses).

If you did not want to use a formal income statement, you could just record every transaction on the balance sheet. Since an increase in Net Worth is called *revenue* and a decrease in Net Worth is called an *expense*, you could just record every revenue or expense amount directly under Net Worth on the balance sheet. For example:

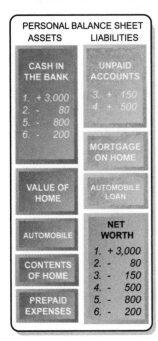

1.   Deposit your salary cheque of $3,000.

2.   Pay cash for your $80 telephone bill for the month.

3.   Receive a bill for $150 for car maintenance.

4.   Receive a bill for $500 for insurance.

5.   Pay cash of $800 for your monthly rent.

6.   Spend $200 on groceries.

... but very soon you would run out of space to record the transactions (and you wouldn't know the details of any of the transactions).

Instead you could make note of revenue or expenses on a separate piece of paper:

Using a formal income statement allows you to keep a clean record of all the changes to your Net Worth throughout the accounting period (a period is usually one month or one year). It also allows you to review your records at any time to see what caused the changes in Net Worth.

The Accounting Equation - Part I

The Accounting Equation (why should the balance sheet balance?):

	Assets	Liabilities
	$100	- $70
Net Worth		= 30

	Assets	Liabilities
	$100	$70
Net Worth		+ 30
TOTAL	$100	$100

If Assets **minus** Liabilities = Owner's Equity, then mathematically...   ⟶

Assets must equal Liabilities **plus** Owner's Equity

Newton's 3rd Law: Every action has an equal and opposite reaction, transaction and financial consequence. In accounting terms, there is always a *double entry* of the same value for every transaction. This means that each transaction is entered twice, once to the debit of one account and once to the credit of another account. The logic of the double entry is based on the Accounting Equation, which is:

Assets = Liabilities + Net Worth

In the absence of a logical opposite entry the balance sheet will not balance.

Original balance sheet:

	Assets	Liabilities
	100	70
Net Worth		30
	100	100

Logical

Deposit salary:

	Assets	Liabilities
	110	70
Net Worth		30
	110	100

110 ≠ 100 (not logical)

	Assets	Liabilities	
	110	70	
Net Worth		40	*Increase Net Worth*
	110	110	

110 = 110 (logical)

Pay cash expenses:

	Assets	Liabilities
	90	70
Net Worth		30
	90	100

	Assets	Liabilities	
	90	70	
Net Worth		20	*Decrease Net Worth*
	90	90	

Exercises: Section 1

Exercise #1

Complete the T-Accounts on the opposite page for the following transactions and calculate Net Worth.

The opening balances are:

Cash	$3,000
Home	100,000
Contents of Home	3,000
Mortgage	70,000
Net Worth	36,000

Transactions:

Revenue

1. Deposit your salary $2,000
2. Deposit interest earned on savings 300

Expenses (all cash)

3. Food 300
4. Entertainment 200
5. Clothing 100
6. Repairs to home 500
7. Electricity and gas 100

This is a summary of the process, when ending a period, to see if you are richer or poorer:

1. Add the revenue that is recorded on the income statement (how much you earned).

2. Add all the expenses that are recorded on the income statement.

3. If your revenue amounted to more than your expenses you have a surplus. If your expenses were more than your revenue you have a deficit. You then calculate the surplus or deficit and write it at the bottom of the income statement. A surplus will make you *richer*, which means that your Net Worth goes up. A deficit will make you *poorer*, which makes your Net Worth go down.

4. Update Net Worth by adding the surplus to the amount of Net Worth you started with at the beginning of the period, or deduct the deficit from the starting Net Worth amount.

5. You need to ensure that you completed all the entries with a double entry. To check if you did this properly, do the following:

   a. Add up the value of all assets.

   b. Add up the value of all liabilities.

   c. If you did all your double entries then...

   d. The total of all Assets will be equal to Liabilities + Net Worth.

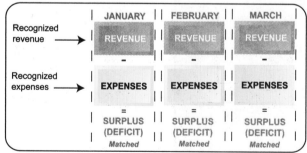

8

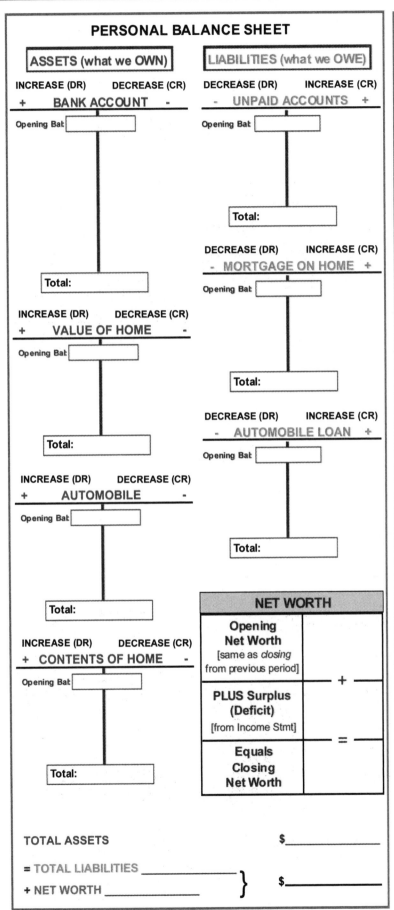

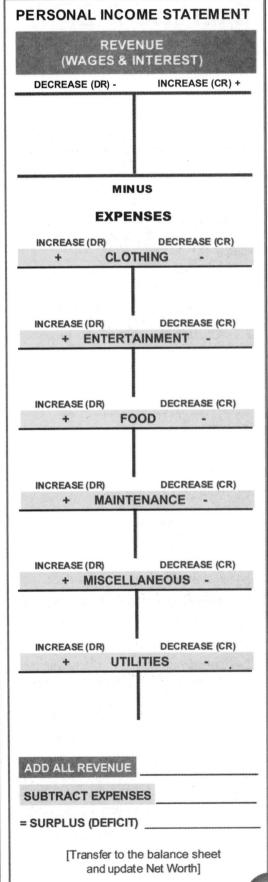

PERSONAL BALANCE SHEET

ASSETS (what we OWN)

INCREASE (DR)   DECREASE (CR)
+   BANK ACCOUNT   -

Opening Bal:

Total:

INCREASE (DR)   DECREASE (CR)
+   VALUE OF HOME   -

Opening Bal:

Total:

INCREASE (DR)   DECREASE (CR)
+   AUTOMOBILE   -

Opening Bal:

Total:

INCREASE (DR)   DECREASE (CR)
+ CONTENTS OF HOME -

Opening Bal:

Total:

LIABILITIES (what we OWE)

DECREASE (DR)   INCREASE (CR)
-   UNPAID ACCOUNTS   +

Opening Bal:

Total:

DECREASE (DR)   INCREASE (CR)
-   MORTGAGE ON HOME   +

Opening Bal:

Total:

DECREASE (DR)   INCREASE (CR)
-   AUTOMOBILE LOAN   +

Opening Bal:

Total:

NET WORTH

Opening Net Worth [same as *closing* from previous period]	
PLUS Surplus (Deficit) [from Income Stmt]	+
Equals Closing Net Worth	=

TOTAL ASSETS $_____

= TOTAL LIABILITIES _____

+ NET WORTH _____ } $_____

PERSONAL INCOME STATEMENT

REVENUE (WAGES & INTEREST)

DECREASE (DR) -   INCREASE (CR) +

MINUS

EXPENSES

INCREASE (DR)   DECREASE (CR)
+   CLOTHING   -

INCREASE (DR)   DECREASE (CR)
+   ENTERTAINMENT   -

INCREASE (DR)   DECREASE (CR)
+   FOOD   -

INCREASE (DR)   DECREASE (CR)
+   MAINTENANCE   -

INCREASE (DR)   DECREASE (CR)
+   MISCELLANEOUS   -

INCREASE (DR)   DECREASE (CR)
+   UTILITIES   -

ADD ALL REVENUE _____

SUBTRACT EXPENSES _____

= SURPLUS (DEFICIT) _____

[Transfer to the balance sheet and update Net Worth]

9

Exercise # 2

1. Explain the role of the Balance Sheet.

_____

_____

_____

_____

_____

_____

2. Explain the role of the Income Statement.

_____

_____

_____

_____

_____

_____

3. Explain the meaning of ASSETS.

_____

_____

4. Explain the meaning of LIABILITIES.

_____

_____

5. Explain the meaning of Net Worth.

    _____

    _____

6. *Newton's Third Law* is:
    a. Everything that goes up, must come down.
    b. The law of relativity.
    c. For every action there is an equal and opposite reaction.

7. Every financial transaction must be entered in pairs.
    a. True
    b. False

8. Every increase MUST include another increase for the other entry.
    a. True
    b. False

9. Every decrease MUST include another decrease for the other entry.
    a. True
    b. False

10. The combinations of increases and decreases vary according to the transactions.
    a. True
    b. False

Notes

AME | Learning

Chapter 1
Personal
SECTION 2

Section 2

▶ Interest versus Debt Reduction (mortgage payments)
▶ The Accounting Equation - Part II

Mortgage Payments

All the cash you spend is not necessarily for expenses. Let's say that you have a mortgage payment of $800 to be made each month. There are two parts to the payment:

1.   The first payment, in the amount of $700, corresponds to the interest portion only (an expense); and

2.   The second payment, in the amount of $100, will be used to reduce the amount owing to the mortgage company (principal).

Transaction #1:
Pay the interest portion in the amount of $700. (Remember *Newton's Third Law?* There are two sides to the transaction). Net worth decreased, which is called an **expense**.

Transaction #2:
Pay the *principal* of $100. Net Worth does **not** change and therefore there is no need to record this transaction on the income statement.

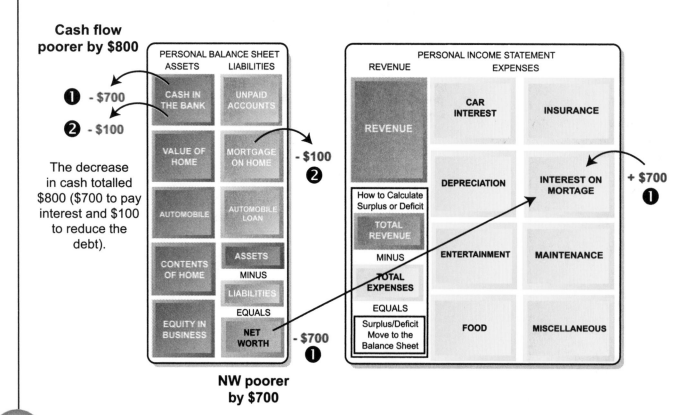

The transactions would appear on the T-Accounts as follows:

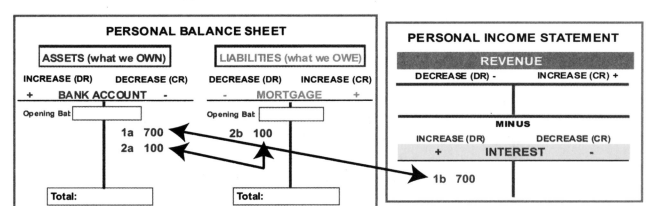

A reduction in mortgage principal is the same concept as reducing a loan from a friend.

1. Borrow $100 from a friend. You are richer in cash, but there is no change to Net Worth.

2. Repay your friend. You are now poorer with the loss of cash, but there is still no change to Net Worth.

When you pay debt you are cash flow poorer, not Net Worth poorer.

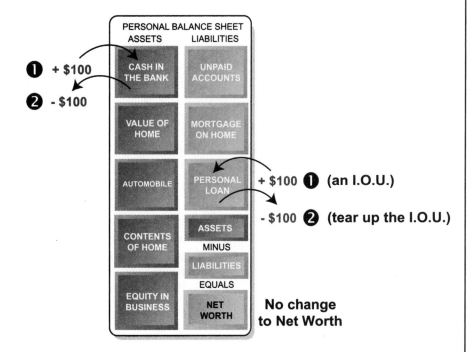

The Accounting Equation - Part II

If you imagine the accounting equation as a scale, with each side in balance, the left side of the scale would include assets and the right side would include liabilities and net worth.

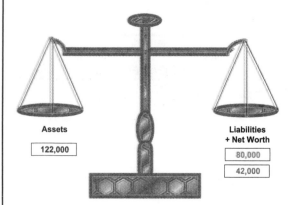

The scale must always be in balance.

Assets = Liabilities + Net Worth

[$122,000 = $80,000 + $42,000]

Example:

When cash increases by depositing a salary cheque in the amount of $3,000, the scale goes out of balance.

To get the scale back in balance you must increase Net Worth.

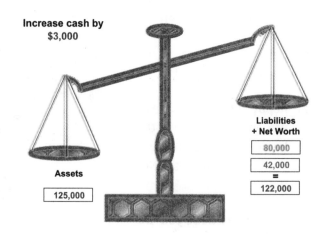

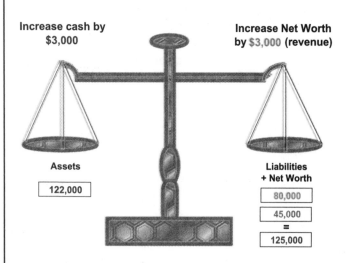

An increase to Net Worth (recording the revenue side of the transaction) brings the scale back into balance.

Exercises: Section 2

Exercise #1

Complete the T-Accounts on the opposite page for the following transactions and calculate Net Worth.

The opening balances are:

Daily banking account	$1,000
Automobile	13,000
Computer	1,000
Credit card	5,000
Automobile loan	5,000
Student loan	3,000
Net Worth	2,000

Transactions:

1. Deposit salary cheque 2,000
2. Pay cash for entertainment expenses 500
3. Pay interest on your student loan 100
4. Reduce the principal on your student loan 300
5. Pay interest on an overdue credit card balance 200
6. Pay interest on your automobile loan 300
7. Reduce the principal on your automobile loan 1,500
8. Pay telephone bill for the month 100

When you have finished entering the transactions, calculate Net Worth:

➲ Deduct Expenses from Revenue = Surplus (Deficit)
➲ Transfer the Surplus (Deficit) to Net Worth on the balance sheet
➲ Total all Assets and all Liabilities
➲ The total of all Assets should equal Liabilities plus Net Worth

Once you have completed the worksheets, transfer the totals to the financial statements over the page.

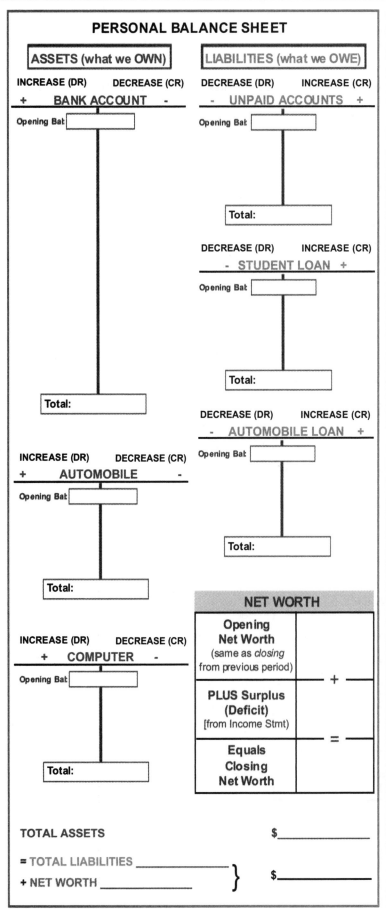

PERSONAL BALANCE SHEET

ASSETS (what we OWN)

INCREASE (DR)   **DECREASE (CR)**
+   BANK ACCOUNT   -

Opening Bal:

Total:

INCREASE (DR)   **DECREASE (CR)**
+   AUTOMOBILE   -

Opening Bal:

Total:

INCREASE (DR)   **DECREASE (CR)**
+   COMPUTER   -

Opening Bal:

Total:

LIABILITIES (what we OWE)

DECREASE (DR)   **INCREASE (CR)**
-   UNPAID ACCOUNTS   +

Opening Bal:

Total:

DECREASE (DR)   **INCREASE (CR)**
-   STUDENT LOAN   +

Opening Bal:

Total:

DECREASE (DR)   **INCREASE (CR)**
-   AUTOMOBILE LOAN   +

Opening Bal:

Total:

NET WORTH

Opening Net Worth (same as *closing* from previous period)	**+**
PLUS Surplus (Deficit) [from Income Stmt]	
Equals Closing Net Worth	**=**

TOTAL ASSETS $_____

= TOTAL LIABILITIES _____
+ NET WORTH _____   } $_____

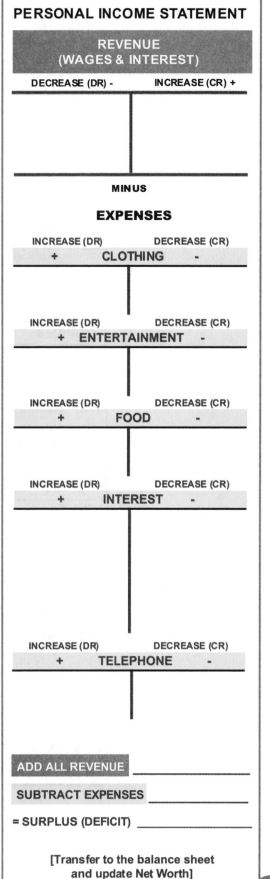

PERSONAL INCOME STATEMENT

REVENUE (WAGES & INTEREST)

DECREASE (DR) -   **INCREASE (CR) +**

MINUS

EXPENSES

INCREASE (DR)   **DECREASE (CR)**
+   CLOTHING   -

INCREASE (DR)   **DECREASE (CR)**
+   ENTERTAINMENT   -

INCREASE (DR)   **DECREASE (CR)**
+   FOOD   -

INCREASE (DR)   **DECREASE (CR)**
+   INTEREST   -

INCREASE (DR)   **DECREASE (CR)**
+   TELEPHONE   -

ADD ALL REVENUE _____

SUBTRACT EXPENSES _____

= SURPLUS (DEFICIT) _____

[Transfer to the balance sheet and update Net Worth]

19

Complete the following financial statements based on the results of the transactions you just recorded - enter the account names and amounts.

BALANCE SHEET	
Assets	
Total Assets	
Liabilities	
Total Liabilities	
Net Worth	
Opening Net Worth	
Plus Surplus (Deficit)	

INCOME STATEMENT

Revenue	
Expenses	
Total Expenses	
Surplus (Deficit)	

Exercise #2

Explain in detail why the opening cash balance was $1,000 and the period ended with no cash while there was a surplus of revenue over expenses.

_____
_____
_____
_____
_____
_____
_____
_____
_____
_____
_____
_____
_____
_____
_____
_____
_____
_____
_____
_____
_____
_____
_____
_____
_____
_____

Exercise #3

The following illustration represents how the bank calculates monthly payments. Section A includes *Assumptions*, which is the amount borrowed (principal of $4,000), the rate of interest (10% per annum) and the number of months over which the loan will be paid (10 months).

A				
Assumptions				
$4,000 loan				
10% interest → per annum				
10 months				

B	C	D	E	F
Month (end of)	Debt payment	Outstanding balance	Interest for the month (based on outstanding amount)	Total outflow
Opening		$4,000		
January	$400	$3,600	$33	$433
February	400	$3,200	$30	$430
March	400	$2,800	$26	$426
April	400	$2,400	$23	$423
May	400	$2,000	$20	$420
June	400	$1,600	$16	$416
July	400	$1,200	$13	$413
August	400	$800	$10	$410
September	400	$400	$6	$406
October	400	$0	$3	$403
Total	**$4,000**		**$180**	**$4,180**

- Column B represents the month in which the payment is made.
- Column C represents the amount of principal that is being reduced each month.
- Column D represents how much of the debt is outstanding each month.
- Column E represents the monthly interest payment.
- Column F calculates the total amount to be paid (debt repayment of $400 plus the interest).

Complete the following table:

Assumptions				
$9,000 loan				
10% interest → on the outstanding amount (per annum)				
12 months				

Month	Debt payment	Outstanding balance	Interest per month	Total cash outflow
Opening		$9,000.00		
January				
February				
March				
April				
May				
June				
July				
August				
September				
October				
November				
December				
Total				

Exercise #4

Unless there are special circumstances, whenever you purchase a product with credit terms or borrow money an interest and principal factor will always apply. List some examples of items that would include principal and interest payments:

_____

_____

_____

_____

_____

_____

_____

_____

_____

_____

Notes

AME | Learning

Chapter 1
Personal
SECTION 3

Section 3

▶ Buying Assets (Cash vs. Net Worth)
▶ Book Value versus Net Worth

Buying Assets

Buying or selling assets (according to the value stated on the balance sheet) has **no** impact on Net Worth.

Example: purchase a new car for $10,000. Pay $3,000 cash and take a loan from the bank for the remaining $7,000. The transactions are:

1. **Pay $3,000 cash**

Assets

You get the front of the car for $3,000 cash.

When paying cash for the car, on asset is exchanged for another asset (cash for a car), with **no change** to Net Worth.

2. **Bank loan of $7,000**

Assets   **Liability**

Taking a loan for the balance owing gives you the back of the car.

When you borrow money to buy a car, you increase the asset and increase the liability, with **no change** to Net Worth.

You now own a $10,000 car, which makes you feel richer, but there has been no change to your Net Worth.

In fact, the only way you can become richer or poorer is if revenue exceeds expenses or vice versa (except for capital, which we will discuss later on).

The transactions would appear on the T-Accounts as follows:

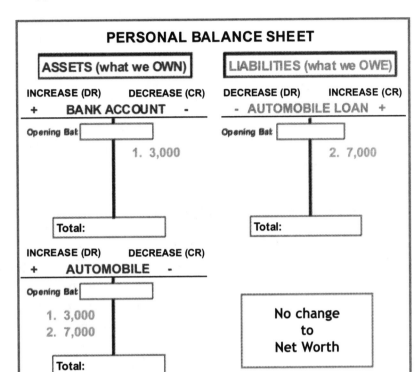

NOTE: These transactions have been reduced to their purest form - Net Worth will decrease when purchasing an asset (such as a car) due to depreciation. Depreciation is an expense, which certainly does reduce Net Worth, however, we have not determined what type of vehicle was purchased. It could have been a valuable antique vehicle, for which the value may increase rather than decrease Net Worth. Each of these principles is being addressed on its own merits.

Recording a purchase as opposed to an expense is a matter of *materiality*. We will discuss this in more detail later on in this textbook.

Book Value vs. Net Worth

When calculating personal Net Worth, there are no rules regarding how you value your assets. They are essentially valued according to their *market value* (the value of the asset on the market if it were sold immediately).

Example 1:

On your personal financial statements you may choose to depreciate furniture over a 5-year period. The *book value* (the amount after depreciation) of the furniture would then be $1,000, but the market value may be $1,200. In this case you would value the furniture on your statements at $1,200, regardless of the depreciation policy that you have determined.

In business there are very strict rules with regard to valuing assets. The outcome of this example would be the opposite in that the book value of the asset would be recorded on the balance sheet.

Example 2:

If you purchase shares in a public company such as *IBM* or *Toyota*, the value of the shares (on the asset side of your balance sheet) will change almost daily. You should increase or decrease the value of these shares every time you decide to update your net worth. An increase is called a **gain** and a decrease is called a **loss** on investments. Gains are not considered regular income.

The *book value* of your net worth and the *market value* of your net worth may be different.

Exercises: Section 3

Exercise #1

Complete the T-Accounts on the opposite page for the following transactions and calculate Net Worth.

The opening balances are:

Daily banking account	$2,000
Contents of home	5,000
Student loan	4,000
Net Worth	3,000

Transactions:

1.	Pay cash to purchase a new stereo	500
2.	Deposit your salary cheque	2,500
3.	Record interest received on daily banking account	100
4.	Record the transfer of funds from your daily account to your savings account (to get higher interest)	600
5.	Sell an old stereo for cash	100
6.	Pay the principal owing on your student loan for the month	300
7.	Pay the interest owing on your student loan for the month	700
8.	Pay for other miscellaneous living expenses	1,000
9.	Buy furniture using your credit card	500

When you have finished entering the transactions, calculate Net Worth:

➲ Deduct Expenses from Revenue = Surplus (Deficit)
➲ Transfer the Surplus (Deficit) to Net Worth on the balance sheet
➲ Total all Assets and all Liabilities
➲ The total of all Assets should equal Liabilities plus Net Worth

Once you have completed the worksheets, transfer the totals to the financial statements over the page.

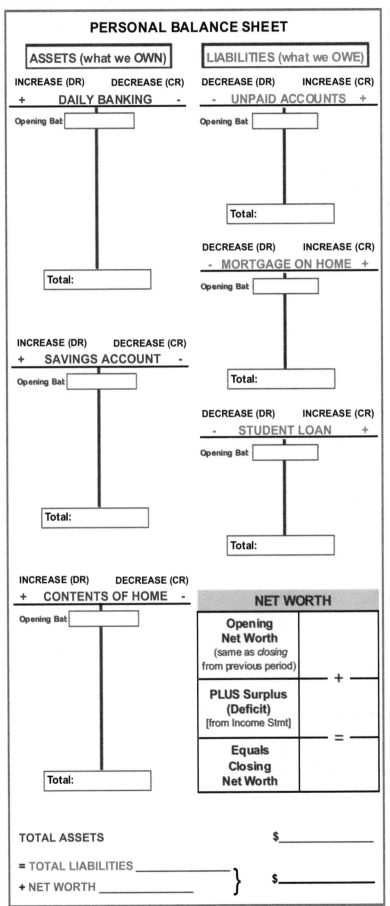

PERSONAL BALANCE SHEET

ASSETS (what we OWN)

INCREASE (DR)   DECREASE (CR)

+   DAILY BANKING   **-**

Opening Bal

Total:

INCREASE (DR)   DECREASE (CR)

+   SAVINGS ACCOUNT   **-**

Opening Bal

Total:

INCREASE (DR)   DECREASE (CR)

+   CONTENTS OF HOME   **-**

Opening Bal

Total:

LIABILITIES (what we OWE)

DECREASE (DR)   INCREASE (CR)

-   UNPAID ACCOUNTS   **+**

Opening Bal

Total:

DECREASE (DR)   INCREASE (CR)

-   MORTGAGE ON HOME   **+**

Opening Bal

Total:

DECREASE (DR)   INCREASE (CR)

-   STUDENT LOAN   **+**

Opening Bal

Total:

NET WORTH

Opening Net Worth (same as *closing* from previous period)	**+**
PLUS Surplus (Deficit) [from Income Stmt]	**=**
Equals Closing Net Worth	

TOTAL ASSETS $_____

= TOTAL LIABILITIES _____

+ NET WORTH _____   } $_____

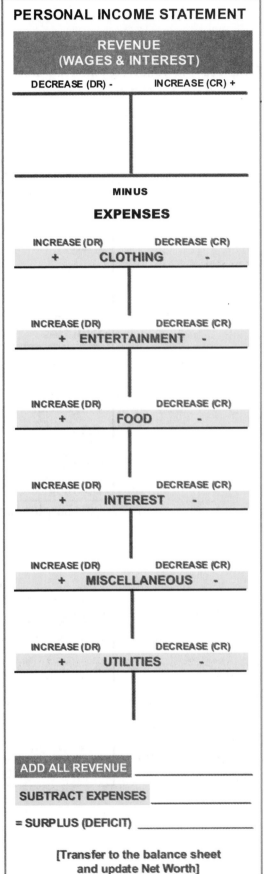

PERSONAL INCOME STATEMENT

REVENUE (WAGES & INTEREST)

DECREASE (DR) -   INCREASE (CR) +

MINUS

EXPENSES

INCREASE (DR)   DECREASE (CR)

+   CLOTHING   **-**

INCREASE (DR)   DECREASE (CR)

+   ENTERTAINMENT   **-**

INCREASE (DR)   DECREASE (CR)

+   FOOD   **-**

INCREASE (DR)   DECREASE (CR)

+   INTEREST   **-**

INCREASE (DR)   DECREASE (CR)

+   MISCELLANEOUS   **-**

INCREASE (DR)   DECREASE (CR)

+   UTILITIES   **-**

ADD ALL REVENUE _____

SUBTRACT EXPENSES _____

= SURPLUS (DEFICIT) _____

[Transfer to the balance sheet and update Net Worth]

31

Complete the following financial statements based on the results of the transactions you just recorded - enter the account names and amounts.

BALANCE SHEET	
Assets	
Total Assets	
Liabilities	
Total Liabilities	
Net Worth	
Opening Net Worth	
Plus Surplus (Deficit)	

INCOME STATEMENT

Revenue	
Expenses	
Total Expenses	
Surplus (Deficit)	

Exercise #2

Explain in detail why Net Worth changed by an amount that differs to the amount of the change in cash in the daily banking account.

_____

_____

_____

_____

_____

_____

_____

_____

_____

_____

_____

_____

_____

_____

_____

_____

_____

_____

_____

_____

_____

_____

_____

_____

_____

_____

_____

_____

_____

_____

Exercise #3

Complete the following Accounting Equation exercise. Using the opening balances provided in the first balance sheet for each transaction, enter the correct updated amounts in the blank balance sheet (*Answers*):

1. **Borrow $4,000 from the bank**

   Opening Balances

Assets		Liabilities	
Cash	5,000	Bank loan	0
Value of home	80,000	Credit card account	3,000
Automobile	20,000	Mortgage on home	50,000
Contents of home	6,000	Automobile loan	5,000
Investment	8,000	Student loan	6,000
		Total liabilities	**64,000**
		Net Worth	55,000
Total Assets	**119,000**	**Liabilities + Net Worth**	**119,000**

   Answers

Assets		Liabilities	
Cash		Bank loan	
Value of home		Credit card account	
Automobile		Mortgage on home	
Contents of home		Automobile loan	
Investment		Student loan	
		Total liabilities	
		Net Worth	
Total Assets		**Liabilities + Net Worth**	

2. **Sell investments for the same value as recorded under Assets**

   Opening Balances

Assets		Liabilities	
Cash	1,000	Bank loan	0
Value of home	80,000	Credit card account	3,000
Automobile	20,000	Mortgage on home	50,000
Contents of home	6,000	Automobile loan	5,000
Investment	8,000	Student loan	6,000
		Total liabilities	**64,000**
		Net Worth	51,000
Total Assets	**115,000**	**Liabilities + Net Worth**	**115,000**

   Answers

Assets		Liabilities	
Cash		Bank loan	
Value of home		Credit card account	
Automobile		Mortgage on home	
Contents of home		Automobile loan	
Investment		Student loan	
		Total liabilities	
		Net Worth	
Total Assets		**Liabilities + Net Worth**	

3. **Pay $1,000 to reduce an outstanding automobile loan**

Opening Balances

Assets		Liabilities	
Cash	3,000	Bank loan	0
Value of home	80,000	Credit card account	3,000
Automobile	20,000	Mortgage on home	50,000
Contents of home	6,000	Automobile loan	5,000
		Student loan	6,000
		Total liabilities	**64,000**
		Net Worth	45,000
Total Assets	**109,000**	**Liabilities + Net Worth**	**109,000**

Answers

Assets		Liabilities	
Cash		Bank loan	
Value of home		Credit card account	
Automobile		Mortgage on home	
Contents of home		Automobile loan	
		Student loan	
		Total liabilities	
		Net Worth	
Total Assets		**Liabilities + Net Worth**	

4. **Buy a motorcycle for $6,000 - pay a $1,000 deposit and borrow $5,000 from the bank**

Opening Balances

Assets		Liabilities	
Cash	2,000	Bank loan	1,000
Value of home	80,000	Credit card account	3,000
Automobile	20,000	Mortgage on home	50,000
Contents of home	4,000	Automobile loan	5,000
Motor cycle	-	Student loan	6,000
		Total liabilities	**65,000**
		Net Worth	41,000
Total Assets	**106,000**	**Liabilities + Net Worth**	**106,000**

Answers

Assets		Liabilities	
Cash		Bank loan	
Value of home		Credit card account	
Automobile		Mortgage on home	
Contents of home		Automobile loan	
Motor cycle		Student loan	
		Total liabilities	
		Net Worth	
Total Assets		**Liabilities + Net Worth**	

Exercise #4

For the following transactions, mark with "x" whether there would be an increase, decrease or no change to the bank balance and Net Worth.

	Transaction	Bank Balance			Net Worth		
		Increase	Decrease	No change	Increase	Decrease	No change
1	Salary deposit						
2	Pay cash for food						
3	Buy a new car - take a loan						
4	Sell stereo for cash						
5	Pay student loan interest						
6	Reduce student loan principal						
7	Buy a new computer for cash						
8	Deposit a bank loan						
9	Pay entertainment expenses						
10	Record interest on your savings						

Exercise #5

For the following transactions, mark with "x" whether there would be an increase, decrease or no change to the bank balance and Net Worth. Enter the new cash balance and Net Worth balance with each transaction.

	Transaction	Amount	Bank Balance				Net Worth			
			Increase	Decrease	No change	Cash Balance	Increase	Decrease	No change	Net Worth
	Opening balances					$1,000				$3,000
1	Sell your car for cash	$3,000								
2	Borrow cash from a friend	1,000								
3	Fix your computer - pay cash	500								
4	Record interest paid on car loan	200								
5	Pay back a loan to a family member	1,000								
6	Pay back some of your car loan	300								
7	Lend your friend some cash	500								
8	Deposit a student loan	5,000								
9	Your friend pays back some of the loan	200								
10	Deposit your salary from a summer job	3,000								

Chapter 1
Personal
SECTION 4

Section 4

- ▸ Credit Cards
- ▸ Matching Principle
- ▸ Prepaid Expenses
- ▸ Depreciation
- ▸ Capital
- ▸ Increases and Decreases in Cash

Credit Cards

Credit cards first appeared in the late '40s when banks began giving out paper certificates that could be used as cash in local stores. The Franklin National Bank in New York issued the first real credit card in 1951.

A credit card gives you the power to buy goods or services now and pay for them later. It represents approval by a bank, or company, to use their money. Credit card issuers are usually banks, even though the card may bear another company's name or logo. The amount of money you can use on your card and the amount of interest you will pay for late payment will largely depend on your **creditworthiness**. In other words, if you consistently pay your bills on time and have sufficient earnings each month to support the payments, the credit card company will usually allow more and more credit on the card for you to borrow. If, however, you fail to pay on time, all the credit privileges may be taken away - making it difficult to get credit from any other bank or company.

When you apply for a credit card, the bank (who gives you the credit on the card) will want to make sure that when you charge a purchase to the card you will keep your promise and pay them back when due. If you keep your promise and pay by the due date, there is no charge to you. If, however, you pay late you will need to pay very high interest rates for the unpaid portion of the debt while affecting your ability to borrow money in the future.

An example of a credit card expense would be charging your monthly grocery bill of $500.

This is your balance sheet before you charge the groceries to your credit card: ⟶

BALANCE SHEET	
Assets	
Daily Banking Account	2,000
Savings Account	500
Automobile	10,000
Contents of Home	4,000
Total Assets	**16,500**
Liabilities	
Unpaid Accounts	0
Mortgage on home	0
Student Loan	15,000
Total Liabilities	**15,000**
Net Worth	
Opening Net Worth	1,500
Plus Surplus (Deficit)	0
Closing Net Worth	**1,500**

This is how the credit card expense will be recorded on the balance sheet:

Increase Unpaid Accounts (liability)
Decrease Net Worth

Take a look at the balance sheet now: ————————→

Your Net Worth decreased as soon as you incurred the debt. In other words you **recognized** that Net Worth decreased even though the cash balance in your bank account did not change.

This is called an accrual, which means that you must **recognize** a change in Net Worth at the time in which it happens, regardless of when the payment is made.

You will see the importance of this method of accounting as this curriculum rolls out.

BALANCE SHEET	
Assets	
Daily Banking Account	2,000
Savings Account	500
Automobile	10,000
Contents of Home	4,000
Total Assets	**16,500**
Liabilities	
Unpaid Accounts	500
Mortgage on home	0
Student Loan	15,000
Total Liabilities	**15,500**
Net Worth	
Opening Net Worth	1,500
Plus Surplus (Deficit)	(500)
Closing Net Worth	**1,000**

> 📌 **A definition of ACCRUAL ACCOUNTING is:**
>
> **Recognizing revenue and expenses in the time period in which they occur, regardless when the payment is made.**

So far you have learned that there are two ways in which your Net Worth can decrease:

❶ Decrease cash by $500, or

❷ Increase debt by $500 (credit card)

In both cases you have *recognized* that Net Worth decreased *the moment you incurred the expense* (when your debt increased).

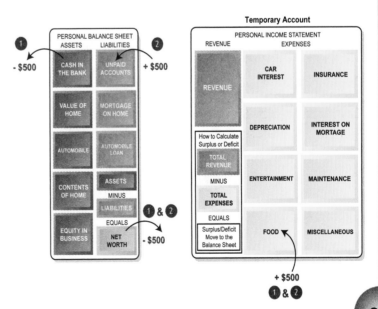

Accounting Periods

For accounting purposes, although you can keep changing numbers continuously, it is more convenient to consider the changes in separate periods. Companies normally use one year as their accounting period, however, they sub-divide the year into months. This allows for more control over the spending of money.

For your personal balance sheet and personal income statement, consider using monthly periods, because you receive your bills on a monthly basis:

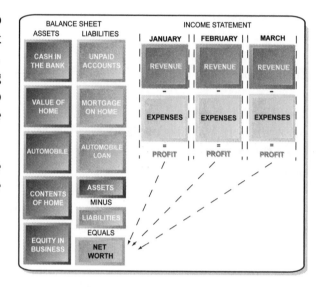

- Your cell phone company bills you each month

- Your internet provider bills you each month

- Your credit card company bills you each month

If you use a month as your accounting period you can look back at previous months (periods) and guess what your expenses and income will be in the coming months. You can also estimate the surplus or deficit you generate each month. If you are saving for a major purchase - a car, a new computer, an expensive entertainment system - you will know when you will have enough money to buy the desired item, or at least have the down payment.

The Matching Principle

Here are some examples of the matching principle:

Illustration #1:

Deposit $5,000 in salary.

Cash increased by $5,000 with an increase to Net Worth. Therefore the temporary record will reflect a revenue entry.

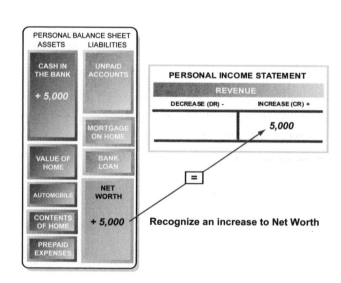

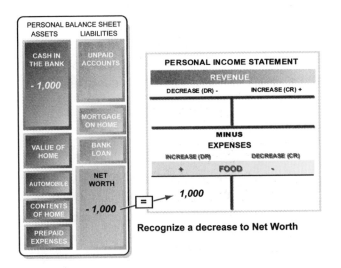

Recognize a decrease to Net Worth

Illustration #2:

Pay $1,000 in cash for food expenses.

Cash and Net Worth decreased. Therefore the temporary record reflects an expense entry.

Illustration #3:

Record a $500 credit card bill for gas expenses.

Debt increased and Net Worth decreased. Therefore the temporary record reflects an expense entry.

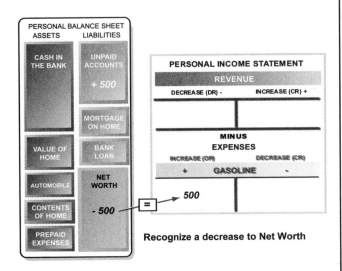

Recognize a decrease to Net Worth

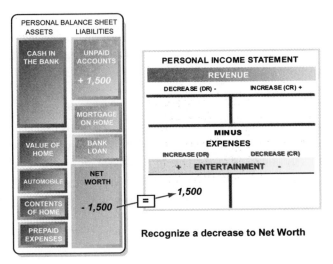

Recognize a decrease to Net Worth

Illustration #4:

Record a $1,500 credit card bill for entertainment expenses.

Debt increased and Net Worth decreased. Therefore the temporary record reflects an expense entry.

Imagine depositing your salary in January to the amount of $3,000, but charging $2,000 worth of expenses (food, entertainment, gas, etc.) to your credit card for payment in February. Would it be true to then say that your Net Worth increased in January by $3,000? Of course not. So, you need to match what you earn each month with your expenses for that month. The credit card expenses would be **recognized** in January when they they were incurred and not in February when they were paid.

This is called the **accrual** method of accounting.

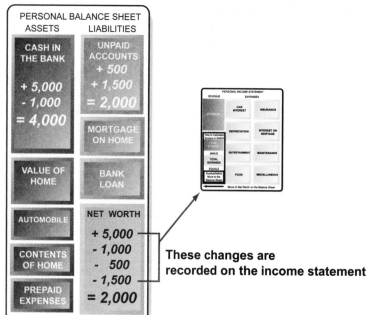

Review the illustration: You will note that cash increased by $4,000, which may leave you with the impression that your Net Worth increased by that amount. In fact, your Net Worth only increased by $2,000 because the revenue and expenses were **matched** in the same time period, without regard for when the expenses were actually paid.

These changes are recorded on the income statement

Prepaid Expenses

It is common practice to pay for various expenses in advance. Some examples are insurance, rent and garden services. These prepayments are not considered as an expense **at the time they are paid**. Here's the logic:

Let's say that you hire a gardening service that costs $600 per year ($50 per month). The service provider requests you to prepay the full $600 in January. If you were to cancel the contract with the company the next morning you would receive all the cash back, because the money does not belong to them - they have not yet provided the service. In effect, you have simply given them an interest free loan. Therefore, if you were to cancel the contract in 6 months, you would get back $300 and so on.

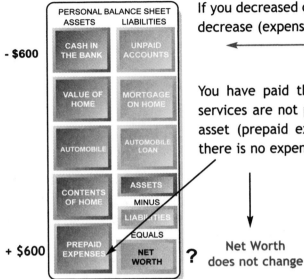

- $600

+ $600

If you decreased cash without another entry, your Net Worth would also decrease (expense), but this is not true.

You have paid the $600 in advance, but they owe you cash if the services are not provided. As a result, this payment is considered an asset (prepaid expense) because your Net Worth does not change - there is no expense until the services are provided.

? Net Worth does not change

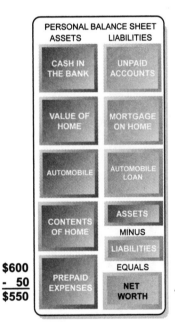

As each month goes by the value of the prepaid expense will decrease together with your Net Worth. In other words, you are recognizing the expense in the month in which it is used and not when it is paid.

So, after the first month's service is provided, you will recognize $50 as an expense for that month (which decreases Net Worth) and they now owe you $550.

$600
- 50
$550

- $50 (expense)

Another example - prepaid insurance:

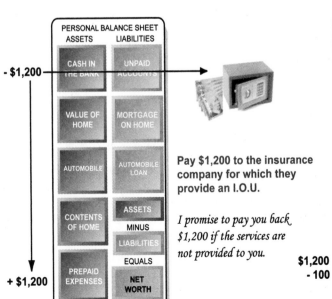

- $1,200

+ $1,200

Pay $1,200 to the insurance company for which they provide an I.O.U.

I promise to pay you back $1,200 if the services are not provided to you.

$1,200
- 100

- 100 (expense)

After the services are provided for the first month, the insurance company is allowed to take $100, thus reducing the value of the I.O.U.

You will now recognize the expense (recognize a decrease to Net Worth).

43

In business it is common practice to pay for various expenses in advance such as insurance, rent and web-hosting services. The same principle applies whereby the money is owed back to the business if the service is not provided.

There are only three ways to recognize an expense:

1. Pay as the expense occurs.

2. Pay before the event and recognize the expense when the event occurs (prepaid expense).

3. Pay after the event occurs (Unpaid Accounts).

In all three circumstances, you need to *recognize* the change to Net Worth.

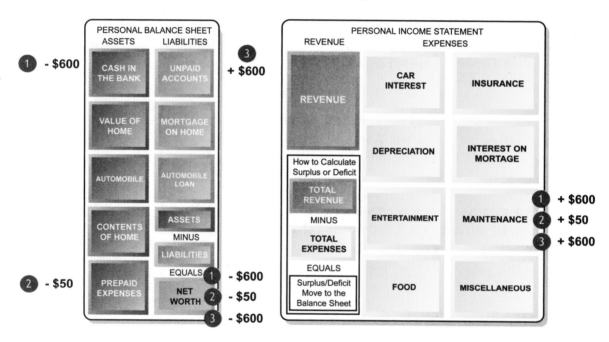

The recognition of prepaid expenses is a typical month-end or year-end adjustment.

There are two types of adjustments:

1. Adjusting the value of assets or liabilities that impact Net Worth.

2. Adjusting one account to another, which has no impact on Net Worth.

Given that this concept is more important in the business world, it will be covered in more detail in the business section of this textbook.

AME | Learning

Depreciation

Do you think that if you were to sell your assets you would get the same value as you paid for them?

As you now know, if you buy an asset your Net Worth will not change and if you sell an asset, *for the value that is recorded on your balance sheet*, your Net Worth will not change.

The big question is this: *What is the **true** value of your assets and what is your actual Net Worth?* We all know how much our liabilities are, but we don't really know the true value of our assets until we sell them. So in reality, we don't know our Net Worth unless we sell all our assets, pay off our liabilities and see how much cash is left.

The process of accounting (in both our personal lives and in business) helps us record the value of our assets as accurately as possible. This is not always easy. Before continuing, let's first define the word **asset** and how an asset is different from an expense.

In simple terms, an asset is something of value that can be sold for cash (there are some exceptions to this statement) and an expense is something that cannot be converted to cash and makes you poorer.

Some examples: **Assets** - TV, video camera, furniture, car, house, etc. and **Expenses** - gas, food, movie tickets, insurance, etc.

Sometimes the difference is not quite so clear. One person may consider DVD's an expense because they may believe that once they are opened, they have no value. Another person could logically argue that even though you paid, say, $30 for the DVD, someone may be willing to pay $10 in 6 month's time. It's often a question of judgement. However, on the personal side, we need to use common sense and ask ourselves how much we think the asset is really worth. Expressed another way, we want to determine if the asset is **material**, relative to Net Worth, or how important it is to record the item as part of Net Worth.

Let's use wealthy movie stars as an example. They earn millions of dollars and have beautiful homes, fancy cars, etc. The value of a $200 DVD player is not too important to them when they may have $20 million worth of other assets. In other words, relative to all the other valuable assets that the movie star owns, the DVD in not material. If however, it was your DVD and you only had a total of $1,000 worth of assets, the DVD would be material. The DVD would represent a significant portion of your assets.

If you think that an item purchased will have any material value at the end of the year, then you would need to record the full value that you paid for it and then decrease its value to how much you think you would get for it at the end of the year. In other words, you need to **adjust** the value of your assets on the balance sheet according to their **realistic value**.

The reduction of the value of your assets, that makes you poorer, is called **depreciation** expense.

Both assets and expenses start out the same way - you usually use cash (or your credit card) to buy an asset or pay for an expense. The assets shown on your personal balance sheet (cell phone, entertainment system, computer, vehicle, etc.) will all last for more than one year. Eventually, they will wear out or become obsolete and outdated.

Keeping in mind that an asset lasts more than a year, it is not reasonable to include assets on the income statement. If you include an asset on the income statement the results for the period will indicate that you became poorer for the full amount of the asset. There is still some value in the asset that will decrease over a period of more than one year.

It is not reasonable either to show the asset on your balance sheet forever. Since the asset deteriorates, or eventually has no value, it should disappear from the balance sheet at some point.

The solution is depreciation, which allows you to include a portion of the asset cost as an expense each period on the income statement.

As an example of this principle let's consider a cell phone that cost $100.

Cell Phone:

> Cost = $100
> Expected Life = 2 years

Your cell phone will last for two years before it is worn-out or becomes obsolete and worthless. (Two years is an *accounting estimate* - the cell phone may last for only one year or for more than three years.) However, it is an asset and so it should be included on the balance sheet.

Your cash decreased when you bought the cell phone, with no change to Net Worth (at that time). However, the cell phone will lose some of its value soon after buying it - if you assume that the phone will last for two years then the asset will decrease by 1/2 of its value each year: $100/2 = $50 per year.

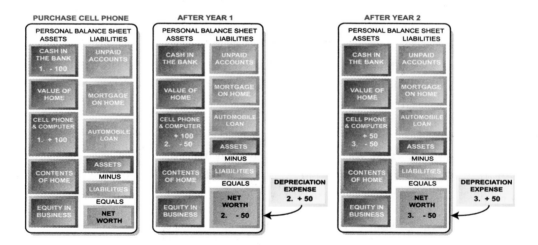

Therefore $50 is removed from the balance sheet in period 1 and included on the income statement in period (year) 1 and $50 is removed from the balance sheet in period 2 and included on the income statement in period 2, leaving no value at the end of year 2.

Part of the cost (one-half, if the cell phone lasts two years) is removed from the asset account (cell phone) each period. Since the basic accounting equation has to remain in balance, the same amount is removed from Net Worth (*see the illustration on the previous page*).

Cash does not decrease when you record depreciation - the value of the asset goes down, and so does Net Worth. Cash decreases when you buy the asset, **not** when you record depreciation.

Let's examine the balance sheet and income statement, for each of 3 periods, when depreciating a computer over 3 years:

Depreciation of Computer		
Period	Balance Sheet	Income Statement
Date of Purchase (Period 0)	On the date of purchase, 3/3 of the cost is shown on the Balance Sheet. $1,200	On the date of purchase, no part of the cost is shown on the income statement. $0
Period 1	At the end of Period 1, 2/3 of the cost is shown on the balance sheet. $1,200 - $400 = $800	During Period 1, one-third of the cost is transferred to the income statement, making you poorer. $400
Period 2	At the end of Period 2, 1/3 of the cost is shown on the balance sheet. $800 - $400 = $400	During Period 2, one-third of the cost is transferred to the income statement, making you poorer again. $400
Period 3	At the end of Period 3, 1/3 of the cost is shown on the balance sheet. $400 - $400 = $0 At this time, we are assuming the computer will not be worth anything.	During Period 3, the remaining one-third of the cost is transferred to the income statement. $400

If you were to assess your Net Worth at the end of the 3-year period, you will have adjusted it to exclude the value of the computer. You would record the depreciation on the balance sheet and income statement each period.

Some assets can also increase in value (*appreciate*). Some examples include:

· Cash investments
· RRSP stocks
· Home
· Antiques
· Jewellery

When these assets increase in value so does Net Worth, which will probably fluctuate from year-to-year. It is prudent to maintain a separate record of this change to Net Worth from your regular monthly income and expenses. Remember that, to a large extent, you can neither control the value of these investments, nor can you be living off the profits that could be made from them on a month-to-month basis. It is therefore important to monitor monthly revenue and expenses separately to ensure that you are managing your personal finances in a responsible manner.

Materiality

When maintaining your personal financial statements there are no strict rules with regard to how you should record the depreciation of your assets. In fact some assets that you buy may be regarded as an expense (such as a toaster, an inexpensive watch or golf clubs).

The question is: how important is the value of the items that you bought *relative* to the value of the rest of your assets? A high-end digital camera might be worth a considerable amount to you relative to all your other assets.

The same high-end digital camera may be considered *immaterial* relative to the millions of dollars worth of assets of a company. This is called **The Rule of Materiality**.

Capital

There are several ways to increase Net Worth:

1. Ensuring that revenue (the amount of money earned) exceeds expenses (the amount of money spent).

2. Selling assets for more than you paid for them, winning the lottery, finding cash, or just receiving a gift, are all cases of *newfound money*. This is not considered regular revenue, but it does increase your Net Worth. This newfound wealth is called **capital**.

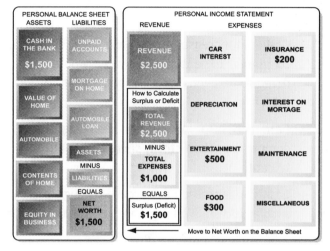

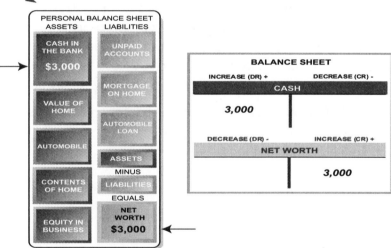

Part of the accounting function is to manage your economic life by recording your monthly revenue matched to your monthly expenses, to ensure that you do not spend more than you earn. Newfound cash such as gifts or lottery winnings are not part of everyday activities so they are recorded directly in the Net Worth section.

It is also important to separate these records, because by pooling all your revenue together (including profit that is made on the sale of mutual funds, or the sale of your old car) you are clouding your ability to manage your economic life.

Increases and Decreases in Cash

It should now be apparent that an increase or decrease in cash does not necessarily mean that Net Worth has increased or decreased. There are essentially 3 ways of increasing or decreasing your cash position:

1. Cash can increase or decrease through everyday activities of earning money and spending money on regular expenses. Ideally you would want to increase your cash position by ensuring that your revenue exceeds your expenses. In other words, this is **cash generated from day-to-day activities**.

2. Cash can also increase or decrease by **investing** or **selling** investments you make in other companies called *stock*, *shares* and *Mutual Funds*. Investments can also include buying a property to rent out.

3. Cash can increase or decrease through borrowing or paying back loans or through capital deposits such as lottery winnings, gifts and other amounts that simply increase or decrease your Net Worth. This is called **financing**.

You should always strive to **ensure that your cash increases through day-to-day activities**, which will ultimately increase your wealth. If you have to rely on your investments to increase your wealth you could be in for a nasty surprise. It is therefore important to maintain an income statement each month to ensure that your revenue exceeds expenses. If you can successfully increase your wealth through investments, then it should be monitored separately from your day-to-day activities.

These same principles apply to a business (to be addressed later on in this textbook).

AME | Learning

Exercises: Section 4

Exercise #1

Accruals

Complete each entry for the following transactions using the balance sheet worksheet provided on the facing page. Use a '+' sign for an increase and a '-' for a decrease. **For example:**

Pay $100 cash for an expense

Cash	- 100
Net Worth (expense)	+ 100

Once you have recorded all the entries, complete the balance sheet by adding up assets, liabilities and Net Worth.

Transactions:

1.	Deposit your salary *(this transaction has been done for you)*	$2,000
2.	Pay cash for entertainment	300
3.	Reduce car loan debt	1,000
4.	Deposit wages from part-time job	1,000
5.	Buy clothing - charge to your credit card	100
6.	Pay cash for interest on car loan	200
7.	Buy a TV and bill it to your credit card	500
8.	Pay for car repairs with your credit card	400

Important!

Once you have completed the exercise, review the balance sheet with this in mind: what caused the changes to Net Worth?

Now move to Exercise #2 on the next page.

BALANCE SHEET

ASSETS

CASH

Opening: $ 0

1. + 2,000

Closing: $

CONTENTS OF HOME

Opening: $ 3,000

Closing: $

CAR

Opening: $ 6,000

Closing: $

TOTAL ASSETS $

LIABILITIES

CREDIT CARD DEBT

Opening: $ 0

Closing: $

CAR LOAN

Opening: $ 3,000

Closing: $

TOTAL LIABILITIES $

NET WORTH

Opening: $ 6,000

New Balance 8,000

New Balance _____

New Balance _____

New Balance _____

New Balance _____

New Balance _____

LIABILITIES + NET WORTH $

Exercise #2

More Accruals

Complete each entry for the same transactions as in Exercise #1 using the balance sheet worksheet provided on the facing page (using the '+' and '-' signs).

This time, record any revenue or expenses under the columns provided to explain the reason for the increase or decrease to Net Worth. Update Net Worth, once all the transactions have been entered, by subtracting the total expenses from total revenue to determine the surplus amount with one summary entry. Transfer this surplus to Net Worth on the balance sheet and complete the balance sheet.

Transactions:

1.	Deposit your salary	$2,000
2.	Pay cash for entertainment	300
3.	Reduce car loan debt	1,000
4.	Deposit wages from part-time job	1,000
5.	Buy clothing - charge to your credit card	100
6.	Pay interest on car loan	200
7.	Buy a TV and bill it to your credit card	500
8.	Pay for car repairs with your credit card	400

Important!

Review the balance sheet and the table you completed with regards to the changes in Net Worth. Now you know what caused these changes in Net Worth.

Instead of filling out the tables, as you did in this exercise, you would record the revenue and expenses on an income statement to determine the changes to Net Worth. This is the primary purpose of an income statement.

BALANCE SHEET

ASSETS

LIABILITIES

CASH
Opening: $ 0

Closing: $

CONTENTS OF HOME
Opening: $ 3,000

Closing: $

CAR
Opening: $ 6,000

Closing: $

TOTAL ASSETS $

CREDIT CARD DEBT
Opening: $ 0

Closing: $

CAR LOAN
Opening: $ 3,000

Closing: $

TOTAL LIABILITIES $

NET WORTH

Opening Net Worth: $ 6,000

+

Surplus: $

=

Closing Net Worth: $

LIABILITIES + NET WORTH $

List the reasons for INCREASES to Net Worth (i.e. Salary)		List the reasons for DECREASES to Net Worth (i.e. Expenses)	
Item	Amount	Item	Amount
Total: _____		**Total:** _____	

Difference = Surplus

$

Revenue - Expenses

Exercise #3

Complete the following calculation for Net Worth versus cash in the bank (*we have provided an example*):

#	Description of Transaction	1st Transaction: account name and increase or decrease	2nd Transaction: account name and increase or decrease	Bank balance: increase, decrease or no change	Accounting Equation: will the balance sheet be in balance after this transaction
	Buy a computer for cash.	Cash - decrease	Computer asset - increase	decrease	Yes
1	Receive a bill for expenses.				
2	Pay a credit card bill.				
3	Charge a new TV to your credit card.				
4	Deposit your salary cheque.				
5	Receive interest on your savings account.				
6	Pay cash for insurance.				
7	Receive electricity bill for power used in January - to be paid in February.				
8	Buy a used car for cash.				
9	Sell your stereo for cash.				
10	Borrow cash from a friend.				
11	Pay back a loan.				

Exercise #4

Circle the correct answer.

1. If your bank account increases you are definitely richer.
    a. True
    b. False

    Explain your answer:

    _____

    _____

2. You receive a bill for $300 for repairs to your car in January. You do not have to pay the bill until February. You are poorer in:
    a. January when the expense is incurred
    b. February when the bill is paid

    Explain your answer:

    _____

    _____

3. Your salary for January is $700. It's 5:00 pm on Friday, January 31st and the bank is closed. You deposit the cash into your bank account on Monday, February 3rd. In which month were you made richer?
    a. January when you earned the salary
    b. February when you deposited the cash

    Explain your answer:

    _____

    _____

4. Considering questions 2 and 3 above, what was the change to Net Worth in January?
    a. Increase
    b. Decrease
    c. No change

    Explain your answer:

    _____

    _____

5. Considering questions 2 and 3 on the previous page, what was the change to Net Worth in February?
    a. Increase
    b. Decrease
    c. No change

    Explain your answer:

    _____

    _____

6. A balance sheet that balances is a true reflection of how much you are worth.
    a. True
    b. False

    Explain your answer:

    _____

    _____

7. The balance sheet will remain in balance immediately after entering an expense on the income statement.
    a. True
    b. False

    Explain your answer:

    _____

    _____

8. The balance sheet will remain in balance immediately after entering revenue on the income statement.
    a. True
    b. False

    Explain your answer:

    _____

    _____

9. The balance sheet will remain in balance immediately after entering the purchase of an asset when paying cash for the asset.
    a. True
    b. False

    Explain your answer:

    _____

    _____

10. The balance sheet will remain in balance immediately after entering the purchase of an asset when charging it to your credit card.
    a. True
    b. False

    Explain your answer:

    _____

    _____

Exercise #5

Effects of transactions on account balances

1. **Complete the table below** by indicating the effect on assets, liabilities, etc. (*we have provided an example*).

Transaction	Assets	Liabilities	Revenue	Expenses	Net Worth
Buy an asset using store credit	*Increase*	*Increase*	*No Effect*	*No Effect*	*No Effect*
a. Incur expense on credit					
b. Withdraw cash for food					
c. Pay credit card bill with cash					
d. Pay balance of the outstanding store credit					
e. Pay part of your vehicle loan					
f. Pay your credit card balance					
g. Pay loan principal					
h. Record and pay loan interest					
i. Sell computer equipment for cash					
j. Trade your entertainment system for a computer of the same value					

2. Which of the following transactions increases Net Worth?
   a. Getting a student loan
   b. Paying off a loan
   c. Recording interest received
   d. Recording wages earned

3. Which of the following transactions decreases Net Worth?
   a. Buying food at a restaurant
   b. Paying off the bank loan
   c. Paying insurance on your car
   d. Recording wages earned

4. Which of the following transactions has no effect on Net Worth?

    a. Buying a new computer

    b. Selling your *PS2* to a friend

    c. Buying a phone card

    d. Purchasing a surround sound system

5. Give three examples of transactions that change Net Worth.

    (1)_____

    (2)_____

    (3)_____

6. Give three examples of transactions that <u>do not</u> change Net Worth.

    (1)_____

    (2)_____

    (3)_____

7. Explain why you do not use an income statement entry when you buy or sell assets.

    _____

    _____

    _____

8. List 2 reasons why it is beneficial to compare your income statements from period to period.

    (1)_____

    (2)_____

9. Does reducing your debt:

    a. Make you richer

    b. Make you poorer

    c. Have no affect on Net Worth

10. Explain why you do not use an income statement entry when you borrow money or reduce debt.

_____

_____

_____

_____

_____

_____

_____

11. Why is it easy for many people to find themselves in financial *hot water* before they know it?

_____

_____

_____

_____

_____

_____

Exercise #6

For each item below indicate whether there is an increase in cash (cash in) or a decrease in cash (cash out), or the transaction has no effect on cash.

When applicable, indicate if the item is revenue or an expense (*we have provided an example*).

Description	Cash In	Cash Out	Not a Cash Entry	Revenue	Expense
Buy a motorcycle - pay now		✓			
1. Buy an entertainment system using store credit					
2. Buy earphones using your credit card					
3. Payment of credit card balance					
4. Record wages earned and received					
5. Buy clothing for cash					
6. Car maintenance and fuel on credit card					
7. Paid credit card balance					
8. Buy CDs on credit card					
9. Miscellaneous expenses - pay cash					
10. Earn wages - not received until next week					
11. Pay outstanding credit card bill with a cheque					
12. Pay for your internet connection with a cheque					
13. Add a new scanner to your computer equipment - pay by debit card					
14. Sell your entertainment system for cash					
15. Buy a new entertainment system using your credit card					
16. Trade old computer for a gently used *XBox*					
17. Purchase a new computer system on store credit					
18. Use debit card to buy lunch					

Exercise #7

Complete the T-Accounts on the opposite page for the following transactions and calculate Net Worth.

The opening balances are:

Daily Banking Account	$1,000
Personal Assets	4,000
Credit Card Debt	1,000
Student Loan	2,000
Net Worth	2,000

Transactions:

1.	Deposit your salary	$2,000
2.	Buy a new bike and charge it to your credit card	500
3.	Prepay your car insurance for one year	600
4.	Recognize prepaid insurance for one month as an expense	50
5.	Charge a meal to your credit card (pay next month)	50
6.	Sell some old furniture for cash	200
7.	You forgot to make a credit card payment - pay the interest	100
8.	Pay some of your credit card debt	400
9.	Depreciate some of your personal assets	800
10.	An Aunt left some money for you in her will - deposit the cash	5,000

When you have finished entering the transactions, calculate Net Worth:

➲ Deduct Expenses from Revenue = Surplus (Deficit)
➲ Transfer the Surplus (Deficit) to Net Worth on the balance sheet
➲ Total all Assets and all Liabilities
➲ The total of all Assets should equal Liabilities plus Net Worth

PERSONAL BALANCE SHEET

ASSETS (what we OWN)

INCREASE (DR) DECREASE (CR)

+   DAILY BANKING   -

Opening Bal:

Total:

INCREASE (DR) DECREASE (CR)

+   PREPAID EXPENSES   -

Opening Bal:

Total:

INCREASE (DR) DECREASE (CR)

+   PERSONAL ASSETS   -

Opening Bal:

Total:

LIABILITIES (what we OWE)

DECREASE (DR) INCREASE (CR)

-   CREDIT CARD DEBT   +

Opening Bal:

Total:

DECREASE (DR) INCREASE (CR)

-   OTHER DEBT   +

Opening Bal:

Total:

DECREASE (DR) INCREASE (CR)

-   STUDENT LOAN   +

Opening Bal:

Total:

NET WORTH

Opening Net Worth (same as *closing* from previous period)	
PLUS Surplus (Deficit) [from Income Stmt]	+
Equals Closing Net Worth	=

TOTAL ASSETS $_____

= TOTAL LIABILITIES _____

+ NET WORTH _____   } $_____

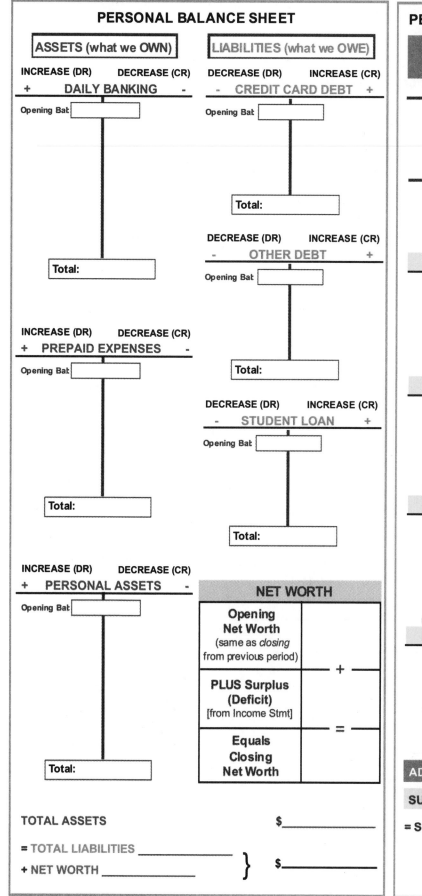

PERSONAL INCOME STATEMENT

REVENUE (WAGES & INTEREST)

DECREASE (DR) -   INCREASE (CR) +

MINUS

EXPENSES

INCREASE (DR)   DECREASE (CR)

+   DEPRECIATION   -

INCREASE (DR)   DECREASE (CR)

+   FOOD   -

INCREASE (DR)   DECREASE (CR)

+   INSURANCE   -

INCREASE (DR)   DECREASE (CR)

+   INTEREST   -

ADD ALL REVENUE _____

SUBTRACT EXPENSES _____

= SURPLUS (DEFICIT) _____

[Transfer to the balance sheet and update Net Worth]

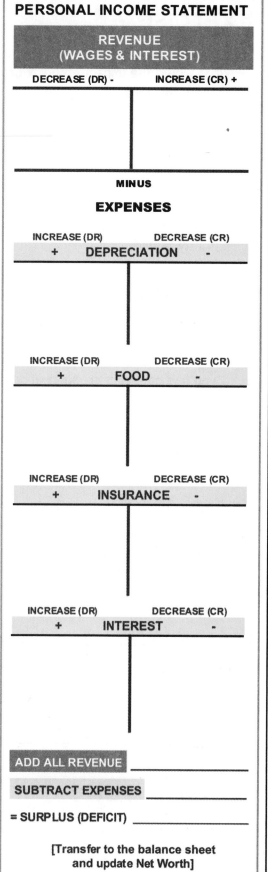

Exercise #8

1. What would the impact on Net Worth have been, had you chosen to record the total amount of prepaid insurance as an expense for this month?

   _____

   _____

   _____

2. How would this have impacted the remaining months of this year with regard to managing your monthly budget?

   _____

   _____

   _____

3. If you had paid your credit card on time, what difference would it have made to your Net Worth this month?

   _____

   _____

   _____

4. What would the impact on Net Worth have been, had you chosen to ignore the meal charged to your credit card for this month and instead recorded it as an expense next month when paid? How would this have impacted your monthly budget?

   _____

   _____

   _____

   _____

   _____

5. If you had recorded the money from your Aunt as revenue, your Net Worth would still have increased by the same amount. Why was it important to record it as capital directly to your Net Worth account rather than revenue?

_____

_____

_____

_____

_____

_____

6. Explain in detail why your Net Worth differed from the change in cash.

_____

_____

_____

_____

_____

_____

_____

_____

_____

_____

_____

_____

_____

Exercise #9

Explain the Matching Principle in your own words and provide 3 examples that do not involve cash.

_____

_____

_____

_____

_____

_____

_____

_____

_____

_____

_____

_____

_____

_____

_____

_____

_____

_____

_____

_____

Exercise #10

Record the account name for each transaction and whether it increased (inc) or decreased (dec) and the change in cash or Net Worth, if any (*we have provided an example*).

	Transaction	Part 1: Acount Name Inc or Dec	Part 2: Acount Name Inc or Dec	Bank Balance: Inc, Dec or No Change	Net Worth: Inc, Dec or No Change
	Deposit your salary	Cash - Inc	Revenue - Inc	Inc	Inc
1	Pay cash expenses				
2	Charge a meal to your credit card				
3	Pay cash for interest				
4	Pay your credit card bill				
5	Prepay last month's rent				
6	Borrow cash from the bank				
7	Win the lottery				
8	Order a new car for delivery in two months time				
9	Pay back your student loan				
10	Borrow cash from a friend				

Exercise #11

For the following transactions, mark with "x" whether there would be an increase, decrease or no change to the bank balance and Net Worth.

	Transaction	Bank Balance			Net Worth		
		Increase	Decrease	No change	Increase	Decrease	No change
1	Salary deposit						
2	Buy food - charge to credit card						
3	Buy a used car - pay cash for the desposit						
4	Sell furniture for cash						
5	Pay student loan interest						
6	Reduce student loan principal						
7	Buy a new computer - use store credit						
8	Deposit a bank loan						
9	Prepay your insurance for one year						
10	Record interest on your savings						
11	Deposit cash gifts received for your birthday						
12	Lend cash to a friend - pay back next month						
13	Depreciate the value of your assets						
14	Recognize prepaid insurance for one month						
15	Cancel insurance - receive refund for balance of prepayment amount						

Exercise #12

Critical Thinking

John graduated from college two years ago, and shortly thereafter, started his new career with an entry level position at a top rated employer offering numerous employee benefits. As he approaches the two-year mark in his job, John starts thinking about his personal financial position.

John is single and lives in a small apartment close to his work. John likes to go to local spots for entertainment. There is a grocery store and a number of retail outlets nearby. He rarely needs to work outside the premises, and when that is necessary, his employer pays the necessary expenses. John is working under a second one-year contract with his employer. John's employer has indicated that John would be hired full-time if he successfully completes the second one-year contract.

John's current benefits include enhanced health care with drug benefits, a dental plan, and a stock-option plan that allows John to buy company stock at a discount (when hired fulltime). If hired fulltime, John will have to join the union, and will be required to join a defined contribution pension plan. The union negotiated a three-year contract last month. The union wage is 5% more than he is currently earning, and will increase by 2% in each of the next two years.

John **owns** the following:

Auto	$3,000	Value shown is amount for which the car can be sold in the current market. An old car, but still in good working condition.
Furniture	$8,200	Value shown is cost, two years ago.
TV and Stereo	$3,500	Value shown is cost, two years ago.
Clothes	$5,000	Value shown is cost.
Jewellery (watch, chain and ring)	$2,000	Value shown is cost.

John **owes** the following amounts:

Lender	Principal	Interest Owing	Total	Monthly Payments	Maximum Credit	Interest Rate
Visa	$3,200	$1,400	$4,600	200	$10,000	19.75%
Mastercard	1,652	430	2,082	130	4,000	18.50%
Amex	1,576	536	2,112	120	5,000	18.50%
Home Improvement Co.	1,950	236	2,186	165	3,000	28.80%
Acme Finance - Car Loan	6,500	2,300	8,800	250		9.75%
College Finance Corporation - Student Loan	4,000	1,502	5,502	125		11.25%
Total	$18,878	$6,404	$25,282	$990		

John approached his bank and learned that he could borrow enough from the bank to pay off all his debts. The loan would have to be paid over five years in equal monthly installments. The current bank loan rate for unsecured loans is 8.25%. Under these conditions, monthly payments would amount to $450. The bank would also require John to purchase life insurance because the loan would be unsecured. Cost of this insurance would be $25 per month.

John's income and expenses are:

Monthly Gross Income	$4,700
Less taxes and other deductions	1,700
Net Income	**$3,000**
Monthly cash outlays	
Rent	$1,200
Food	600
Car insurance	150
Home insurance	50
Gas	120
Car maintenance	140
Clothes (on average)	50
Home phone	25
Cell phone	60
Internet	50
Entertainment	250
Monthly debt payments	990
Total Cash Outlay	**$3,685**
Monthly Cash Short	**($685)**

John is concerned that he is increasing his debt by $685 every month and has asked you for your advice.

[Answers to this exercise are to be handed in separately.]

Practical Insights

Practical Insights

CHEQUES

What is a cheque?

Sending cash in an envelope to someone can be risky. What if it got lost or stolen? It's also a nuisance to have to keep going to the bank to draw cash to pay bills. To reduce this risk, you can write an instruction to the bank to pay an amount of money out of your bank account to another person. Of course you need to have enough cash (funds) in the account for the bank to do this.

The cheque needs to be signed by you to authorize the payment. At the end of the month, the bank will send you a list (bank statement) of all the payments that were made from your bank account and all deposits made into the account to make sure that they are all correct. (Banks do make mistakes.) Never issue a cheque if you are not quite sure that you have sufficient money in your account. A bank will charge you a fee for a **returned cheque** (which is bad for your reputation).

Cheques must be written **accurately**. There are several details that are very important such as the date, matching the numbers to the written amount, the name of the person you are paying (Payee) and your signature authorizing the payment - see opposite page.

Notice the *cheque stub*. This is the part of the cheque book that is used to record the details of the cheque, which you will then enter into your financial records. Remember that you give the actual written cheque to the person to whom you are paying, so you need to record the details of the cheque for your own records.

1 Cheque number

2 Personal information

3 Date

4 Name of person or company being paid (Payee)

5 Dollar amount owing Payee

6 Dollar amount written in full

7 Bank information

8 Signature line

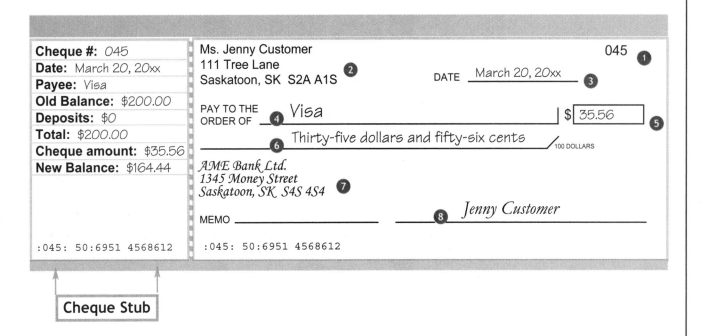

Cheque Stub

RETURNED CHEQUES

There can be several reasons why a bank would return a cheque to you and not clear it for payment. Usually, there are technical errors such as incorrect date format, payee and amount details, signature, alterations, damage, or there is simply an insufficient balance in your account. Returned cheques are costly, frustrating and can be embarrassing. Here are some useful tips when writing cheques.

Q: *Could the incorrect date on my cheque cause it to be returned?*

A: Absolutely. All cheques must be written in this format - "DD/MM/YY", for example, August 17, 2008 should be filled in as: 17/08/08.

If you need to post-date your cheques (a date later than the date on which you are writing the cheque), ensure that the party presenting the cheque does so on or after the date of the cheque. Otherwise, the cheque will not be honoured.

Note: All cheques expire automatically after six months from the date of issue.

Q: *Do I have to write out the amount completely?*

A: You have to write the amount in both words and numbers and they both must match.

Q: *If there are two signatories on file (meaning that 2 people need to sign the cheque), would my signature alone be enough?*

A: On every cheque you write, all signatures have to correspond with the bank's records. For instance, if you share an account with your significant other and you are both joint signatories on the cheques, then you would both have to sign the cheque, as it is on file. If your cheque is missing a signature, or if the signature(s) is not the same as the bank's records, it will be returned.

Q: *What if I need to change the details on the cheque?*

A: At any time if you need to alter any detail on the cheque, for example, the date, simply sign in full next to the alteration. Otherwise, your cheque will be returned.

Q: *There is a small tear on the cheque. Can it still be presented to the bank?*

A: No. Cheques which are damaged in any way cannot be presented to the bank. Damaged cheques may make automated processing impossible.

Q: *Can I re-present a cheque once it has been returned to me?*

A: You may do so only if your payee has informed the bank to allow the cheque to be re-presented for clearance. Otherwise, cheques returned due to technical errors cannot be presented again.

Q: *How can I ensure I have sufficient funds in my account before I write a cheque?*

A: Here are three quick and easy ways to ensure you have sufficient funds in your account before issuing a cheque:

1. With *Internet Banking* services available with most commercial banks, you can access your account any time and anywhere around the world. You can check your account balance as well as transfer funds from one account to another. This means you can manage your account(s) more effectively and conveniently.

2. Use an *ATM* to check your balance. Check your account balance, deposit cash/cheques and perform fund transfers.

3. You may also wish to set up a *Standing Instruction* with your bank branch to transfer money automatically from your savings account to your chequing account to ensure that there are sufficient funds in your account.

You should know that banks charge a fee for returned cheques. This fee can be avoided by being responsible when writing cheques.

Source: **http://www.englishdaily626.com/letters.php?037**

Ethical Issues

BORROWING MONEY

Question:

May someone borrow money from an individual even though they may have no foreseeable way of repaying the loan and are only relying on "borrowing from Peter to pay Paul" or on some miracle to provide the money?

Answer:

Knowing how you are going to pay back borrowed money is a vital part of both business and domestic life. When you take a loan from anyone you must do so only when you know how you will pay back the loan - on time! It is a wonderful thing to have faith that you will somehow find a way, but not at the expense of others.

Borrowing money without anticipating how you will repay the loan is reckless behaviour and will backfire on you. At some point in the future when you need a loan you will be unable to get one since you will have lost your credibility. Remember too that creating debt without knowing how to pay it back can be very stressful.

BANK ACCOUNT

There are various types of bank accounts, for example

Money Market Accounts: Most institutions offer an interest-bearing account, called a *money market account*, that allows you to write cheques. This type of account usually pays a higher rate of interest than a chequing or savings account. Money market accounts often require a higher minimum balance to start earning interest, but they frequently pay higher rates for higher balances. Withdrawing funds from a money market account may not be as convenient as doing so from a chequing account. Each month you are limited to a certain number of transactions at no charge. As they do with chequing accounts, most institutions apply fees on money market accounts.

Savings Accounts: With savings accounts you can make withdrawals, but you do not have the flexibility of using cheques to do so. As with a money market account, the number of withdrawals or transfers you can make on the account each month is limited.

Many institutions offer more than one type of savings account, for example, passbook savings and statement savings. With a passbook savings account you receive a record book in which your deposits and withdrawals are entered to keep track of transactions on your account; this record book must be presented when you make deposits and withdrawals. With a statement savings account, the institution regularly mails you a statement that shows your withdrawals and deposits for the account.

As with other accounts, institutions may assess various fees on savings accounts, such as fees for a minimum balance.

Basic or No-Frill Banking Accounts: Many institutions offer accounts that provide you with a limited set of services for a low price (often referred to as *basic* or *no frill* account). Basic accounts give you a convenient way to pay bills and cash cheques for less than what you might pay without an account. They are usually chequing accounts, but they may limit the number of cheques you can write and the number of deposits and withdrawals you can make. Interest generally is not paid on basic accounts. Compare basic and regular chequing accounts for the best deal in low fees or low minimum balance requirements.

The right type of account depends on how you plan to use the account. If you need to reach your money quickly and easily a savings or chequing account may be the best choice. You will probably find that a chequing account is best for you if you plan to write several cheques each month (to pay bills for example).

Remember, bank account features and fees vary from one institution to the next. If you have questions, you should ask a representative of the institution about any bank account features and fees *before* you open an account.

This information was extracted from the http://www.foreignborn.com/self-help/banking/3-acct_types.htm website. Surf the site for more information.

INTEREST vs. PRINCIPAL

When you buy an asset such as a car or some type of service (e.g. student loan for education) it is important to ensure that the lender provides you with a breakdown of how much interest you will be paying versus the principal amount being paid.

For example, if you establish that the interest is 8% and you know that you could refinance the loan with another institution for say 6%, then it would pay to change lenders. Some lenders, if you have a good credit history (you always pay your debts on time), will reduce your interest payments (it may even be worth it to pay for any minor penalties in order to move your account to them). This has less of a negative impact on your Net Worth.

The important lesson here is to first understand the accounting principle, which will then help you make the right decision.

CREDIT CARDS

In today's fast-paced world, having a credit card is practically a necessity. Eating in restaurants, buying items online and making large purchases (TVs, entertainment centres, etc.) is usually done with a credit card these days. While you can certainly live a full life without them, credit cards make certain things much easier.

Most people understand that if you want to purchase something and don't have the money, you can simply whip out your favourite credit card and the item is yours (assuming the credit card company gave you enough credit). That's enough for most people to know about credit cards. However, for discriminating consumers, it's valuable to know that there are many different types of credit cards, each with its own benefits.

Balance-transfer and *low-interest* credit cards are typical. You may know what these are simply by their names. Some credit cards are more complicated. Some credit card companies give you airline miles whenever you purchase something - if you accumulate enough airline miles with your credit card purchases, you can travel for free. Other credit cards offer rewards for your purchases in the form of gas rebates and store discounts.

There are also credit cards available for those with bad credit. These cards are usually called *prepaid credit cards* or *secured credit cards*. Typically, they require some type of collateral before they approve you for an account. That is, the credit card company may want you to deposit $1,000 before they issue you a secured credit card.

When the time comes for you to choose a credit card, review your spending habits over the past twelve months. Also, review what purchases you decided against simply because you didn't have the money. Keep these things in mind when you receive your credit card because you don't want to get into too much debt.

Remember, there is a credit card that is right for your unique needs. The trick is in finding the right card for you.

Take a look at: http://www.chargecards.ca (for Canada) or http://www.bychargecards.com (for U.S.A.). These sites will provide information about most credit cards on the market.

Notes

Chapter 2

Introduction to Business

Introduction to Business

- ▶ Accounting in Business
- ▶ Types of Accountants
- ▶ Fields of Accounting
- ▶ Forms of Organizations
- ▶ Stakeholders

- ▶ Ethics in Accounting
- ▶ Benefits of a Good Accounting System
- ▶ GAAP
- ▶ Triple Bottom Line
- ▶ Types of Business Models

Accounting in Business

What is an entrepreneur (en·tre·pre·neur)? The name comes from the Old French, *"entreprendre"*, which means to undertake.

Entrepreneur is defined as:
- ⇨   A person who organizes, operates and assumes the risk for a business venture.
- ⇨   A risk-taker who has the skills and initiative to establish a business.

Are you an entrepreneur? There are certain traits and attitudes that make some people more suited to running a successful small business than others, such as:

- ▶   primarily motivated by an overwhelming need for achievement
- ▶   capacity or ability to lead
- ▶   influence ability in others to some purpose
- ▶   optimist - very few pessimists are entrepreneurs

According to studies conducted by the Bank of Montreal, Institute for Small Business, "The Six Success Factors" for starting a small business are self-motivation, business and industry knowledge, organization and management capabilities, marketing skills, customer/vendor relations and vision.

People keen to start their own businesses sometimes forget about the managerial and administrative skills necessary to run a business. If you're going to start a successful small business, you need to have or develop expertise in money management, managing people, directing business operations, and directing sales and marketing operations. A sound knowledge of finances and cash flow management will help you learn how to manage these aspects of starting a small business.

Investing the time to learn the skills you need before you start your own business is especially wise because once you've decided to put your energy into starting a business, you're going to want it to develop into a successful, thriving enterprise. Sadly, there's a large percentage of small businesses started each year that survive less than two years.

Types of Accountants

One of the first decisions to be made in starting up a business is choosing the right accountant to assist with business decisions. The different types of accountants that are available are:

Chartered Accountant (Canada) or Certified Public Accountant (U.S.A.)

Chartered Accountants (CA's) and Certified Public Accountants (CPA's) are the authorities for *Generally Accepted Accounting Principles* (GAAP) in Canada and the U.S.A.

All CA's must work in public practice (accounting firms) as part of their lengthy training. Many work with smaller CA firms that specialize in consulting to small businesses.

To become a CA or CPA you must have successfully completed an undergraduate degree and specific business courses. In addition, you need work experience in a recognized training office. Finally, you must pass a three-day evaluation called the *Uniform Final Examination* to demonstrate professional competence by responding to business simulations of the kinds of challenges you're likely to face as a newly qualified CA or CPA.

Certified General Accountant

CGA's are professional accountants "working in industry, commerce, finance, government and public practice."[1]

Like CA's, many CGA's own their own accounting firms and provide tax and financial advice to individuals and to businesses of all sizes.

To become a CGA, you must earn an undergraduate degree from a post-secondary educational institution and complete the *CGA Program of Professional Studies*. The CGA program combines weekly assignments, optional lectures, national examinations and mandatory practical work experience. It is delivered through distance education so you can continue working full time while you are studying.

Unlike CA's, CGA's may work in a variety of industries, not only in public accounting firms. The minimum period of practical experience is two years, although many CGA's have six or more years of experience by the time they earn their CGA designation.

Certified Management Accountant

CMA's are "strategic financial management professionals" who combine accounting and business expertise with professional management skills to provide leadership, innovation and an "integrating perspective to organizational decision-making."[2]

Choosing the right type of accountant: An accountant who operates a small practice is more likely to offer lots of personal advice relating to a small business. Large accounting firms are usually better suited to large companies.

Fields of Accounting

The accounting discipline has many applications:

Public Accounting

Public accounting means an accountant serves various organizations for a fee. His/her responsibilities include auditing to ensure that the client's financial position truly reflects the economic events that occurred during the reported period. It also ensures that they are fairly represented in accordance with GAAP. Some public accountants specialize in various subspecialties such as tax, international accounting, forensics, business advisory services, mergers and acquisitions, etc.

---

[1] http://www.cga-canada.org/eng/about/corporate/corporate.htm

[2] http://www.cma-canada.org/cmacan/CMAContent.asp?QuickLinkID=1&WebPageID=11&CategoryID=1

Managerial Accounting

Managerial accounting is when an accountant serves the needs of internal users and generally works for one organization. The accountants' responsibilities include roles such as preparing financial statements for the organization, ensuring that all the policies and procedures are adhered to, control cash flow, do costings, prepare and maintain budgets, negotiate with banks and other creditors, etc.

Consulting

Some accountants do not practice technical accounting at all, but use their accounting knowledge and expertise to consult for various businesses. These roles could include Information Technology (IT), financial advising, investment advice, to mention but a few.

Forms of Organizations

Proprietorship

A small business that is owned by one person is generally structured in the form of a proprietorship. Some examples of typical proprietorship businesses are: bookkeeping services, gardening, painting or maintenance businesses, small grocery stores, etc. Usually only a small amount of money is invested by the owner in such a business.

A sole proprietorship is an unincorporated business owned by one person, and usually operated by that person. From an accounting perspective, the financial affairs of the business are *separate* from the financial affairs of the owner. From a legal perspective a sole proprietorship is *not a separate entity from its owner*. This means that the assets and liabilities of the business legally belong to the proprietor, even though the financial activities are recorded separately. If the business is unable to pay its debts, creditors of the business can force the owner to sell his or her personal assets to pay the business debts.

In other words, the owner will receive all the profits, suffer the losses and be personally liable for all financial obligations of the business.

Partnership

A partnership is a business owned by two or more persons called *partners*. Like a proprietorship, the only special legal requirement that must be met in order to start a partnership, is registering the business name and obtaining a business license. To run a business together, the partners need an oral or written agreement that usually indicates how profits and losses are to be shared. A partnership, like a proprietorship, *is not legally separate from its owners*, therefore each partner's share of profits is reported and taxed on that partner's tax return. Partners are usually subject to *unlimited liability*.

There are two types of partnerships that limit liability. A **limited partnership** includes a general partner(s) with unlimited liability and a limited partner(s) with liability restricted to the amount invested. A **limited liability partnership** restricts a partner's liability to their own actions and the actions of individuals under their control. This protects an innocent partner from the negligence of another partner, yet all partners remain responsible for partnership debts.

Co-Operative

A co-operative is an enterprise or organization that is owned or managed jointly (together) by those who use its facilities or services. An example would be a group of farmers who wish to sell their products through one distributor. The cost of maintaining the distribution business is shared by all the farmers.

Corporation

A corporation is a business that is a separate legal entity from its owners. The corporation is responsible for its own activities and is liable for its own debts. It can enter into contracts, buy and sell products or assets. It can also be sued! A corporation functions through its managers and/or owners who act as legal agents for the corporation. Owners and managers are not personally liable for the activities of the corporation or its debts. The owners of the business (shareholders) are legally distinct from the business and their financial risk is limited to the amount that they have invested in the form of shares. **However, this does not mean that owners or managers who act on behalf of a corporation are not financially accountable**. There are a number of rules that govern the behaviour of officers of the corporation, such as responsible accounting and cash management.

The ownership of a corporation is divided into units called shares. For example: if the assets are worth $100,000 and the liabilities $60,000, the Owners' Equity is equal to $40,000. In other words, if the corporation were to sell all their assets for $100,000 and use some of the cash to pay the liabilities of $60,000, the remaining $40,000 cash is essentially the Net Worth of the business and belongs to the owner(s). If there were two equal shareholders, each shareholder would be paid $20,000. If there were twenty equal shareholders, each shareholder would be paid $2,000. In other words the Owners' Equity is divided amongst the shareholders in proportion to the number of shares they own.

The assets less the liabilities results in the **book value** of the shares, also referred to as *net realizable value*. The **market value** of the shares, however, is dependent upon what a buyer is willing to pay for them. This will be discussed further in the section relating to analyzing financial statements.

Non-Profit Organizations

These types of organizations include non-profit and government organizations. Unlike profit businesses, they may pay-out (re-distribute) any profits made back into the community by providing services. Examples of non-profit organizations include religious places of worship, community care centres (*Salvation Army*), charitable organizations (*Cancer Society*), hospitals, the Red Cross, etc. They do not have an identifiable owner but need financial statements as they are accountable to donors, sponsors, lenders, tax authorities, etc. Accounting records provide key information pertaining to their activities to enable them to operate as permitted financially.

How do you know which entity to use?

If you were a non-profit organization, it would be very clear how you should register your business. However, your accountant will provide you with sound advice depending on your business. He/she would probably tell you to use a proprietorship if you are operating a low risk business that you operate yourself, such as a screen printing business in your garage. If you wish to be in the business of computer consulting services or perhaps manufacturing some type of life saving equipment, your accountant will probably advise you to incorporate your business because if you are sued for damages, it will be the company that will be sued and not you personally. Partnerships on the other hand are usually used for professionals such as lawyers.

Stakeholders

There are many stakeholders that rely on accurate information about an organization to enable them to make appropriate decisions. These stakeholders can be divided into 2 categories.

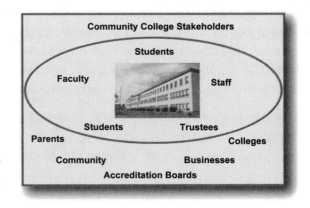

1. *Internal* stakeholders are those people who own the business and work in the business.

2. *External* stakeholders are all those people or organizations that are *outside* the business such as suppliers, banks, external accountants, etc.

Typically, external stakeholders need financial statements to ensure that the investment they make in the business, whether it relates to cash loans or supplying product or services on credit, is protected. If a business is poorly operated or is not operating profitably, then an external stakeholder has the choice of supplying or not supplying the business. They want to ensure that they get back loans or get paid for services they render to the business. There are also indirect external users - the tax authorities will also want to look at financial statements to ensure that the business is paying the appropriate taxes. Indirect external users also include customers, trade unions, etc.

Internal stakeholders rely on financial statements to enable them to help manage the business better. In other words, they will assess how the business is operating by examining the financial results each month, which can change the way they do business. Financial statements to an internal stakeholder have the same purpose as a scoreboard to a player in a game.

Here is an example of how stakeholders are affected: You may remember the NHL hockey strike in 2004. The players (internal stakeholders) went on strike over money and other issues. The players were not the only stakeholders who were affected by not playing hockey. No hockey games resulted in no business for the external stakeholders such as hotdog vendors (and the factories that make the hotdogs, napkins, ketchup, plastic cutlery), restaurants and all food suppliers, beer breweries and even the beer tax paid to the government, advertisers, and all other suppliers of materials and services surrounding hockey. The list of those affected goes on and on.

Ethics in Accounting

As described above, stakeholders place significant trust in the accuracy of financial records to enable them to make careful and sensible decisions about the business. For that reason, one of the accountant's responsibilities is to ensure that they accurately report the financial status of the business. The standards by which these actions are judged as being honest versus dishonest, right or wrong, fair or unfair, are also known as **ethics**.

There are various professional accounting bodies that have strict rules governing the behaviour of their members. There are many cases on record that have resulted in jail sentences for violating these rules. Two of the most infamous examples relate to *Enron* and *Worldcom*. The senior executives were found guilty of various offences including: using company funds for their own personal use and covering up certain negative financial information, in addition to all other types of activities that were not regarded as legal or moral by the shareholders and government authorities.

Typical of the codes of ethics for accountants:

- Acting with trustworthiness, integrity and objectivity

- Participation in or providing services to, any activity that the member is aware of, or which a reasonably prudent person would believe to be unlawful.

- A member shall not engage in a discriminatory practice on a prohibited ground of discrimination, as those terms are defined in the Canadian Human Rights Act.

- A member shall not criticize another professional colleague without first submitting this criticism to that colleague for explanation.

- Members shall act in the interest of their clients, employers, and interested third parties, and shall be prepared to sacrifice their self-interest to do so. Members shall honour the trust bestowed upon them by others, and shall not use their privileged position without their principal's knowledge and consent. Members shall avoid conflicts of interest.

- A member shall not disclose or use any confidential information concerning the affairs of any client, former client, employer or former employer.

- A member shall, when engaged to audit or review financial statements or other information, be free of any influence, interest or relationship in respect to the client's affairs, which impairs the member's professional judgment or objectivity, or which, in the view of a reasonable observer, may have that effect.

- A member shall not, without an employer's or client's consent, use confidential information relating to the business of the member's employer or client to directly or indirectly obtain a personal advantage. Members shall not take any action, such as acquiring any interest, property or benefit, in connection with which unauthorized use is made of confidential knowledge of an employer's or client's affairs obtained in the course of his or her duties.

· Members shall strive to continually upgrade and develop their technical knowledge and skills into the areas in which they practise as professionals. This technical expertise shall be employed with due professional care and judgment.

· Members shall adhere to acknowledged principles and standards of professional practice.

· Members shall not be associated with any information that the member knows, or ought to know, to be false or misleading, whether by statement or omission.

· Members shall always act in accordance with the duties and responsibilities associated with being members of the profession and shall carry on work in a manner that will enhance the image of the profession and the Association.

Ethics items included in month-to-month discussions include:

· Ethical issues related to cash discounts

· Ethical issues related to the operation of petty cash found

· Ethical issues involved in the manipulation of amortization to manage earnings

· Ethics - insider trading

There is often a fine line between the law and ethics. A behaviour can be quite legal, but immoral. For example, a manager may want to employ his nephew in a company he works at. He decides to pay his nephew a much higher salary than others in a similar position in the business. While this practice may not be illegal, it is certainly immoral and unethical. Many organizations create their own set of rules pertaining to ethics and morals. An internationally recognized code of conduct is the *4-way test*. (You can find more information on this process on the internet at the following address: http://www.rotary.org/aboutrotary/4way.html)

The 4-Way Test

From the earliest days of *Rotary* organizations (a major national and international service club), *Rotarians* were concerned with promoting high ethical standards in their professional lives. The 4-Way Test is one of the world's most widely printed and quoted statements of business ethics. It was created in 1932 by Rotarian, Herbert J. Taylor (who later served as Rotary International President) when he was asked to take charge of a company that was facing bankruptcy. This 24-word test for employees to follow in their business and professional lives became the guide for sales, production, advertising, all relations with dealers and customers, and the survival of the company. Adopted by Rotary in 1943, this simply philosophy has been translated into more than one hundred languages and published in thousands of ways. It asks the following four questions:

Of the things we think, say or do:

1. Is it the TRUTH?

2. Is it FAIR to all concerned?

3. Will it build GOODWILL and BETTER FRIENDSHIPS?

4. Will it be BENEFICIAL to all concerned?

24 words

The Benefits of a Good Accounting System

Imagine playing a sport such as hockey, baseball or golf without a scoreboard or scorecard. It would be difficult to measure your performance. In fact you would be confused as you played the game because you would never know whether you were winning or losing.

Financial records are the scoreboard of a business. A business owner or manager needs regular financial statements (records) to help him or her make appropriate management decisions in the business based upon the information provided by the accountant. A good accounting system will accurately record the business sales matched against the various expenses to assess if the business is making a profit. A good system will also provide a balance sheet to inform the reader how much the assets are worth, how much the business owes in the form of liabilities and the Net Worth of the business (Owner's Equity). The financial records will also inform the reader where cash came from and how the cash was used.

Different types of businesses require different types of information. For example, a simple business such as a consulting service will require less information than a complicated manufacturing business that calculates the value of inventory, etc. Whatever the business type, a manager requires the services of an accountant to help sort the information and financial data into a format that can be used. Depending on the size of a business there is often a requirement for many people to complete different types of information.

For example: An accounting clerk (also known as a bookkeeper) ensures that all the transactions are properly recorded into the correct categories. The bookkeeper also ensures that all the supporting documents (**source documents**) are correctly filed for easy access at a later time. The bookkeeper ensures that all the day-to-day financial transactions are maintained. There are often other people who will work with the bookkeeper such as an Accounts Receivable Clerk, an Accounts Payable Clerk and a Payroll Clerk.

An accountant, on the other hand, is a professional who develops and maintains the accounting system, interprets the data and prepares various management reports and supervises all the clerks to ensure that the information is correct. The accountant will also ensure that the financial records are being represented according to moral and ethical standards as defined in GAAP (Generally Accepted Accounting Principles).

Generally Accepted Accounting Principles (GAAP)

GAAP is a combination of authoritative standards (set by policy boards) and the accepted ways of doing accounting. It is the common set of accounting principles, standards, and procedures - the rules that companies are expected to follow. Financial statements must be prepared using GAAP principles, however GAAP is only a set of standards and can therefore still be manipulated by accountants.

A commonly used definition of GAAP is: *Generally Accepted Accounting Principles, which are conventions, rules, and procedures that serve as the norm for the fair presentation of financial statements.*

Here is an interesting perspective on GAAP: *What is the Net Worth of your business and are your financial statements reporting the truth?*

Financial statements are used to accurately record the various events that both internal and external stakeholders can use for their own purposes. The accuracy of financial statements is important to assist managers to measure their company's performance so that they can make strategic decisions relating to products, sales prices and policies, marketing, budgeting and a host of other issues that influence business results.

One of the key principles of accounting is to match revenue to the related expenses in the same period. Not all revenue and expenses relate to cash. Here are two examples of breaking GAAP rules:

1. Let's say that you recognize all your revenue ($1,000) in the month of January, which are paid to you in cash, but fail to record $600 worth of expenses charged to your credit card in the same month. Instead you record the expense in the month of February when the credit card is due to be paid. Your financial statements will reflect that you made a profit of $1,000 in January, which in fact is not true and is not reported in accordance with GAAP rules.

2. Let's say that a customer gives you $200 in January as a deposit for cutting their lawn, which you will only start cutting in March. GAAP rules would dictate that the $200 is regarded as a liability because you must give the money back if you do not deliver the service to the customer. GAAP rules will be broken if you consider the $200 deposit as a revenue in January, meaning that you made a profit and subsequently were made richer in the month of January. You would only become richer in the month of March when you have earned your right to the money.

We will address GAAP throughout the balance of this course.

GAAP.....

GAAP rules are complex and plentiful - following are some of the more important rules to be aware of:

The Business Entity Concept

This concept provides that the accounting for a business or organization be kept separate from the personal affairs of its owner, or from any other business or organization. This means that the owner of a business should not place any personal assets on the business balance sheet. The balance sheet of the business must reflect the financial position of the business alone. Also, when transactions of the business are recorded, any personal expenditures of the owner are charged to the owner and are not allowed to affect the operating results of the business.

The Continuing Concern Concept

The Continuing Concern Concept assumes that a business will continue to operate, unless it is known that such is not the case. The values of the assets belonging to a business that is alive and well are uncomplicated. For example, a supply of files with the company's name printed on them would be valued at their cost. This would not be the case if the company was going out of business. In that case, the files would be difficult to sell because the company's name is on them. When a company is going out of business, the values of the assets usually suffer because they have to be sold under unfavorable circumstances.

The Objectivity Principle

The Objectivity Principle states that accounting will be recorded on the basis of objective evidence. It means that different people looking at the evidence will arrive at the same values for the transaction. Or, this means that accounting entries will be based on fact and not on personal opinion. The source document for a transaction is always the best objective evidence obtainable. The source document shows the amount agreed to by the buyer and the seller, who are usually independent and unrelated to each other.

The Time Period Concept

The time period concept provides that accounting take place over specific time periods known as fiscal periods. These fiscal periods are of equal length, and are used when measuring the financial progress of a business.

The Principle of Conservatism

The principle of conservatism provides that accounting for a business should be fair and reasonable. Accountants are required to make evaluations, to deliver opinions, and to select procedures.

The Revenue Recognition Convention

The revenue recognition convention provides that revenue be taken into the accounts (recognized) at the time the transaction is completed. This just means recording revenue when the bill for it is sent to the customer. If it is a cash transaction, the revenue is recorded when the sale is completed and the cash received. But when we speak about building a large project such as a dam, it takes a construction company a number of years to complete such a project. The company does not wait until the project is entirely completed before it sends its bill. Periodically, it bills for the amount of work completed and receives payments as the work progresses. Revenue is taken into the accounts on this periodic basis. It is important to take revenue into the accounts properly.

The Matching Principle

The Matching Principle states that each expense item related to revenue earned must be recorded in the same accounting period as the revenue it helped to earn. If this is not done, the financial statements will not measure the results of operations fairly.

The Cost Principle

The cost principle states that the accounting for purchases must be at their cost price. This is the figure that appears on the source document for the transaction in almost all cases. The value recorded in the accounts for an asset is not changed until later if the market value of the asset changes. It would take an entirely new transaction based on new objective evidence to change the original value of an asset. There are times when the above type of objective evidence is not available. For example, a building could be received as a gift. In such a case, the transaction would be recorded at fair market value which must be determined by some independent means.

The Consistency Principle

The Consistency Principle prevents people from changing methods for the sole purpose of manipulating figures on the financial statements. The consistency principle requires accountants to apply the same methods and procedures from period to period. When they change a method from one period to another they must explain the change clearly on the financial statements. The readers of financial statements have the right to assume that consistency has been applied if there is no statement to the contrary.

The Materiality Principle

The Materiality Principle requires accountants to use Generally Accepted Accounting Principles except when to do so would be expensive or complicated, and where it makes no real difference if the rules are ignored. If a rule is temporarily ignored, the net income of the company must not be significantly affected, nor should the reader's ability to judge the financial statements be impaired.

The Full Disclosure Principle

The Full Disclosure Principle states that any and all information that affects the full understanding of a company's financial statements must be included with the financial statements. Some items may not affect the ledger accounts directly. These would be included in the form of accompanying notes. Examples of such items are outstanding lawsuits, tax disputes, and company takeovers.

Triple Bottom Line

Traditionally, organizations measured the success of their business using just one yardstick - **profitability** - this was the only bottom line of an organization. Today for an organization to succeed and sustain its growth strategies it is necessary that they take two other crucial elements into consideration - the **environment** (controlled wastage/pollution, etc.) and the **society** (employee health, safety, community contributions to improve living standards, etc.).

Astonishingly, when these two aspects are viewed seriously by an organization, it has proven to improve the profitability of the business in the long run.

SUSTAINABILITY

ECONOMIC
Corporate
Growth

SOCIAL
Employee
Safety

ENVIRONMENT
Wastage,
Pollution

For an organization to sustain its growth strategies, it has to be successful in all three areas - economic, social and environmental. These three aspects are called the **Triple Bottom Line** of an organization.

Triple bottom line reporting describes the company's approach to managing the three dimensions of the triple bottom line. Unlike the traditional statutory reporting of just financial statements to shareholders and management, TBL reporting of information goes beyond this by including the relationship and impact the company has on its stakeholders (shareholders, investors, suppliers, customers, employees, communities, local authorities, trade unions and business partners).

Some of the benefits of TBL reporting are:

a.   Enhanced corporate reputation

b.   Improved relations with stakeholders

c.   Community support to operate

d.   Creating a brand that attracts and retains high caliber employees

e.   Helping achieve a differentiated position among competitors

f.   Increasing accountability and transparency within an organization

A recent survey by KPMG has shown that 45% of the world's top 250 organizations publish a separate TBL corporate report that includes all their economic, social and environmental performance. The report concludes that: "Good environmental stewardship and social responsibility are clear examples of good management and there is no disputing the clear link between good management and business performance."

[*Source:* KPMG Global Sustainability Services 2002. KPMG International of Corporate Sustainability Reporting 2002.]

Types of Business Models

Service Industry

▶ Consulting
▶ Legal
▶ Financial Services
▶ Gardening Services
▶ Teaching
▶ Insurance

Merchandise

▶ Retail
▶ Restaurants
▶ Wholesale (distribution)
▶ Pharmacy

Manufacturing

▶ Computers and parts
▶ Cars
▶ Paper
▶ Furniture
▶ Food

Each of these business models would use different financial statement layouts depending on the needs of the organization. For example: A small consulting firm would use a very simple income statement and balance sheet compared to a complex manufacturing company (that also buys and sells product). The manufacturing company will require a more detailed set of financial statements due to the amount of information a manager will need to know in order to operate the business effectively.

The lessons you will experience in this textbook will begin with a simple service business that is very similar to personal financial statements. You will then learn about a manufacturing business and a merchandise business.

Chapter 3
Linking Personal to Business

Linking Personal to Business

▶ Owner's Equity vs. Net Worth
▶ Financing a Business
▶ Current vs. Long-Term Liabilities
▶ Bank Loan Interest and Debt Repayment

Owner's Equity vs. Net Worth

If the owners of a business were to sell all the assets of the business (according to the value on the balance sheet) and use the cash to pay all debts, the cash remaining would be the Net Worth of the business.

There are different terms for the Net Worth of a business (assets minus liabilities):

⇨ In a Proprietary business it is known as **Owner's Equity**.

⇨ In a Corporation it is called **Shareholders' Equity**, because if all the assets of the company were cashed in and some of the cash was used to pay liabilities, the remaining cash would belong to the owners (in proportion to the amount of shares they own).

⇨ Some Government institutions refer to Net Worth as the **Accumulated Surplus and Deficit Account**.

⇨ Some organizations call it the **Capital Account**.

Essentially these terms all mean the same thing: the Net Worth of the business.

Connecting Personal to Business

Notice how similar the business financial statements are to the personal financial statements.

Other than the account names the business statements are exactly the same.

Sequence of Assets and Liabilities

The assets of a business are listed in sequence according to their level of liquidity (the ease at which the asset can be converted to cash). In other words, cash is the most liquid asset and is therefore listed first on the balance sheet, followed by savings accounts, accounts receivable (the amount of money owed by customers to the business) and so on. Fixed assets, such as buildings and machinery, are the least liquid and are therefore listed last.

Liabilities are also listed in sequence in much the same way. Those that are payable within the shortest amount of time are listed first (e.g. telephone, rent, etc.) and those debts that are not due for a long time (e.g. loans payable within two years) are listed last.

Owner's Equity in a Corporation

Let's say that Jack and Mary start a new company and each deposit $5,000 into the new business, totalling to a $10,000 investment. The cash they deposit is in the form of SHARES which are recorded in the **capital account**. They can arbitrarily divide the Capital Account into as many or as few shares as they wish. For this example they create 5,000 shares. Each share will therefore be worth $2.00. Jack and Mary each own 2,500 shares (see *figure A*).

Year One:

The company makes a profit of $1,000 in the first year of operation. The owners decide not to draw the profit out for themselves but **retain** it in the company (see *figure B*).

Year Two:

The company makes a profit of $5,000. This time the owners decide to pay $2,000 of the profits to the owners. This payment is called a **dividend** (in publicly traded companies, this is referred to as *declaring a dividend*). Each of the owners will receive $1,000, being in proportion to their 50/50 stock holding. They retain the balance of $4,000 in the company (see *figure C*).

Year Three:

The company suffers a loss of $2,000. Retained Earnings will decrease due to the loss on the Income Statement (see *figure D*).

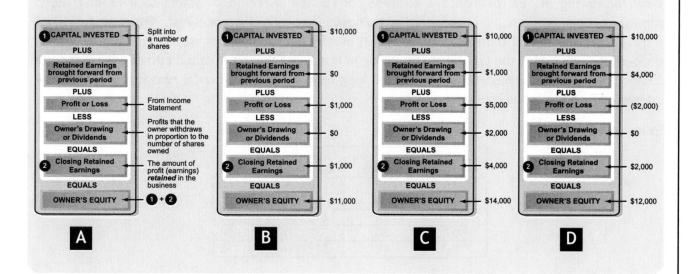

Financing a Business

When financing a *proprietary* business the sole owner provides all the cash to set up the business. This investment is recorded directly in the Owner's Equity account.

When financing a *corporation* the financial structure is set up differently. Remember that the owners and the corporation are regarded as separate legal entities to the business, so the owner can in fact lend money to the corporation just like a bank or any other lender.

There are many ways of financing a business. For the purposes of this course we will address the most common method. There are two parts to an owner's investment in the company:

1. Capital stock (shares) - this is the money invested directly into a company by its shareholders (owners). If there is one owner, then he/she will own 100% of the shares and will receive all the profits. If one owner owns 40% of the shares and another owns 60% of the shares, then they will split the profits (or the amount they would get for the business if they were to sell it) in proportion to the amount of shares they own. The only way to *cash out* the capital stock is to sell the shares.

2. Owners can also lend money to the company. These loans are treated like any other loan and can be paid back to the owner like any other lender. These are called **shareholder loans** and are recorded as a liability.

Borrowing Money

As a general rule, banks will not lend more money than the owner's investment in the business. In fact they would like the owner to have more risk than the bank.

When borrowing money to finance a business, or for the purchase of assets such as machinery, furniture, computers, etc., the loan is usually payable over more than one year. For example, when buying a car the capital (borrowed amount) will usually be payable over, say, 5 years. The loan is divided into two parts: the amount that is owing in the next 12 months (called **current debt**) and the balance owing after the next 12 months (called **long term debt**). *The specific reasons for this will be addressed later on in the course.*

Examples:

Loan amount	Months for repayment	Current	Long Term
$40,000	60	$10,000	$30,000
$20,000	48	$5,000	$15,000
$30,000	24	$15,000	$15,000
$60,000	36	$20,000	$40,000
$10,000	12	$10,000	$0

Here is an example of the set-up for a proprietary business:

1. Deposit $120,000 in personal cash into the business.

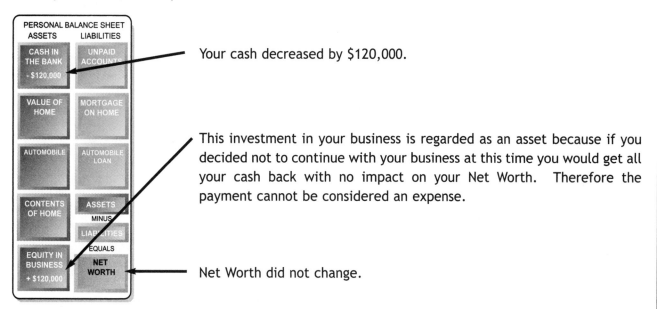

Your cash decreased by $120,000.

This investment in your business is regarded as an asset because if you decided not to continue with your business at this time you would get all your cash back with no impact on your Net Worth. Therefore the payment cannot be considered an expense.

Net Worth did not change.

Although your personal Net Worth has not changed, you now have fewer tangible assets that the bank will consider as collateral. Tangible assets are those assets that you can physically touch and feel, such as cash, cell phones, computers, etc. When you invested in the business you converted a tangible asset (cash) into an intangible asset (your equity in the business). The bank will not consider intangible assets for collateral purposes. (Other intangible assets in your personal life might include a loan to a friend, which is considered as an asset to you, but not to the lender.)

You now have a **business** balance sheet that is *separate* from your **personal** balance sheet. All the financial and moral principles that apply to your personal life also apply to a business.

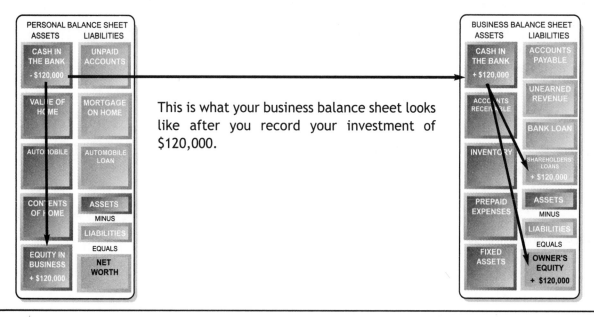

This is what your business balance sheet looks like after you record your investment of $120,000.

2. Invest $1,000 in share capital.

Simply deduct $1,000 in cash from your personal balance sheet and add it to cash in your business. The other side of the transaction is to increase Owner's Equity directly.

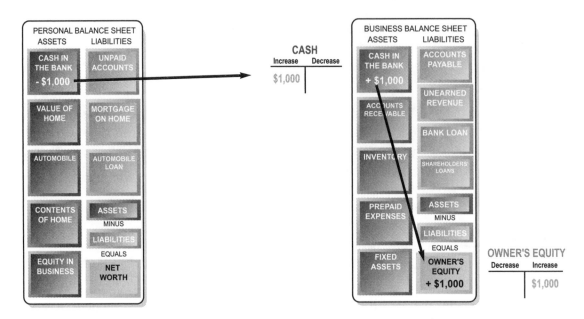

3. Record a bank loan of $60,000.

After the deposit of the bank loan, your business balance sheet will look like this: ⟶

You may feel good with the extra cash, but remember you also owe the $60,000.

Note that the Owner's Equity on the business balance sheet did not change with this transaction. There was an addition to assets and liabilities only.

In every case, Net Worth has not changed because of the transfer between your personal and business financial statements. You just feel poorer because the business now has all your cash, but it is **your** business so your personal Net Worth has not changed.

Share Capital can only be converted to cash if you sell all or part of your business. **Shareholders' Loans are treated as any other loan.**

BUSINESS Balance Sheet	
Assets	
Cash	$181,000
Accounts Receivable	0
Inventory	0
Prepaid Expenses	0
Fixed Assets	0
Total Assets	**$181,000**
Liabilities	
Accounts Payable	$0
Unearned Revenue	0
Bank Loan	60,000
Shareholders' Loans	120,000
Total Liabilities	**$180,000**
Opening Owner's Equity	**$0**
Share Capital	1,000
Owner's Equity	**$ 1,000**
Liabilities + O/E	**$181,000**

Current Liabilities vs. Long-Term Liabilities

Current assets are those assets that will likely convert to cash such as accounts receivable, inventory and prepaid expenses.

Current liabilities are amounts owing in the next 12 months. The balance amounts that are owing after 12 months are called long-term liabilities or long-term debt. *For example:* if you were to borrow $100,000 from the bank, payable over a 5-year period, $20,000 would be regarded as current debt and the balance of $80,000 would be regarded as long-term debt.

When paying down debt, the current debt will always remain unchanged until the long-term portion has been paid.

Examples:

If you borrowed 24,000 over a 2-year period, you would need to pay back $1,000 per month for 24 months. This means that the current liability is $12,000 and the long-term liability is $12,000.

Current Debt	Long-Term Debt
$12,000	$12,000

After you pay $1,000 for your first instalment, $12,000 will still be owing over the next 12 months (current debt). Therefore the current debt remains unchanged while the long-term debt is reduced by $1,000.

Current Debt	Long-Term Debt
$12,000	$11,000

After you pay $1,000 for your second installment, $12,000 is still the amount of current debt owing. However, long-term debt is reduced by another $1,000.

Current Debt	Long-Term Debt
$12,000	$10,000

Current debt can only be reduced once the long-term debt has been eliminated.

The importance and relevance of separating current and long-term debt will be explained in the Financial Analysis chapter of this textbook.

Bank Loan Interest and Debt Repayment

The cash that is used to finance a business is used to buy assets or pay wages before you start collecting revenue, etc.) One way to finance a business is to borrow money from a bank or other lending institution and pay interest for the use of the money.

Let's say the bank loaned you $4,000 and has requested you to pay it back in equal monthly instalments for the next 10 months. This is called **amortizing** the loan (over 10 months). The interest payable will be 10% of the **unpaid** amount each month.

When you borrow money, the lender will require that you pay them as follows: one part is the return of the money that you borrowed with no impact to equity (also called debt repayment or principal repayment) and the other part is the **interest** that you pay for the **use** of the money, which decreased equity. Interest rates will largely depend on the **credit risk**. In other words, if you have a poor credit history you will pay more interest. Usually the interest payable is on the outstanding balance of the unpaid portion of the debt.

If you examine this chart, you will see that in the month of June, for example, only $1,600 remains unpaid and the interest owing will have reduced to $16 per month instead of $33 (which had to be paid in January when the outstanding amount was $3,600). The quicker the debt is reduced, the lesser the interest expenses. Remember that it is the interest that makes you poorer, not the debt reduction.

The calculation for June, for example, is:

Loan outstanding from May ($2,000) x interest per annum (10%) = $200 per annum ÷ 12 months (remember the 10% interest relates to a full year) = $16.66 (*rounded to $16 on this chart*).

The illustration represents how the bank calculates your monthly payments. Section A includes *Assumptions*, they are the amount that you borrowed (principal of $4,000), the rate of interest (10% per annum) and the number of months over which the loan will be paid (10 months).

A
Assumptions
$4,000 loan
10% interest ← per annum
10 months

B	C	D	E	F
Month (end of)	**Debt payment**	**Outstanding balance**	**Interest for the month** (based on outstanding amount)	**Total outflow**
Opening		$4,000		
January	$400	$3,600	$33	$433
February	400	$3,200	$30	$430
March	400	$2,800	$26	$426
April	400	$2,400	$23	$423
May	400	$2,000	$20	$420
June	400	$1,600	$16	$416
July	400	$1,200	$13	$413
August	400	$800	$10	$410
September	400	$400	$6	$406
October	400	$0	$3	$403
Total	**$4,000**		**$180**	**$4,180**

➲ Column B represents the month in which you are making the payment.

➲ Column C represents the amount of principal that is being reduced each month.

➲ Column D represents the amount of debt outstanding each month.

➲ Column E represents the monthly interest payment. (Notice that the interest payment is decreasing each month because the interest is calculated on the outstanding/unpaid portion of the debt.)

➲ Column F calculates the total amount that you have to pay, which is the debt repayment of $400 (in principal) plus the interest.

Remember that debt reduction has no impact on Net Worth (Owner's Equity), but the interest portion does reduce Net Worth.

Notes

AME | Learning

Exercises: Chapter 3

Exercise #1

Amanda has decided to invest in a new service business. She will be running a home staging business for people wishing to prepare their homes for selling. Amanda starts this business using a simple proprietorship business format.

Complete the T-Accounts on the opposite page for the following transactions to set up this service business.

Transactions:

1.	Amanda deposits her own cash in the business in the form of Owner's Equity	$10,000
2.	Borrow cash from the bank	5,000
3.	Buy computers and furniture with cash	8,000
4.	Record cash sales	20,000
5.	Payroll - cash	12,000
6.	Advertising expenses - pay next month	1,000
7.	Record entertainment expenses charged to credit card	300
8.	Pay cash for office supplies	500
9.	Record depreciation of assets	600
10.	Record interest to be paid on bank loan (accounts payable)	100
11.	Prepay insurance for one year	6,000
12.	Pay principal portion of bank loan	500
13.	Pay accounts payable	1,000
14.	Recognize prepaid insurance for this month	500
15.	Draw cash from the business for personal use	2,000

After you have entered all the transactions, update Owner's Equity on the balance sheet.

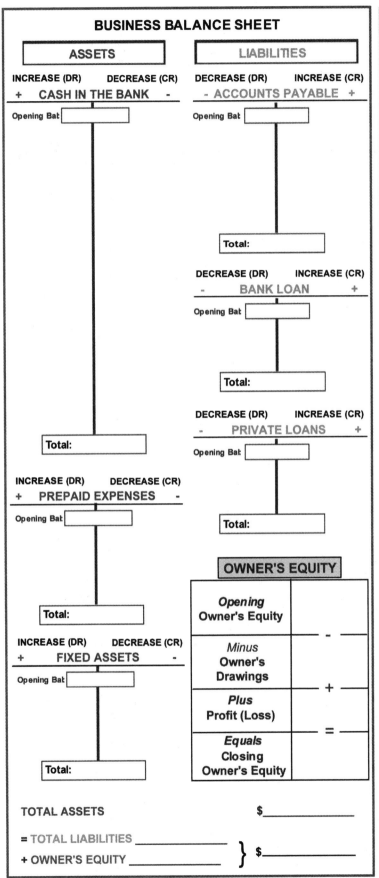

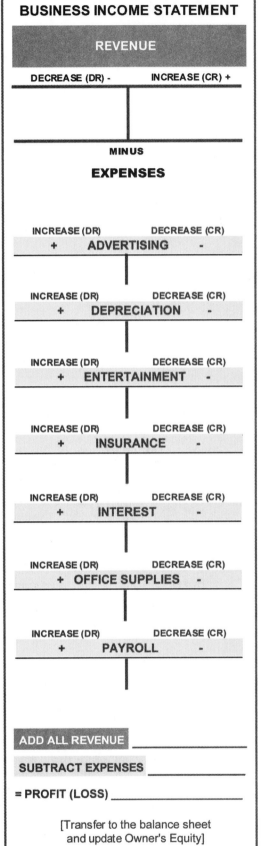

BUSINESS BALANCE SHEET

ASSETS

INCREASE (DR) +	CASH IN THE BANK	DECREASE (CR) -

Opening Bal:

Total:

INCREASE (DR) +	PREPAID EXPENSES	DECREASE (CR) -

Opening Bal:

Total:

INCREASE (DR) +	FIXED ASSETS	DECREASE (CR) -

Opening Bal:

Total:

LIABILITIES

DECREASE (DR) -	ACCOUNTS PAYABLE	INCREASE (CR) +

Opening Bal:

Total:

DECREASE (DR) -	BANK LOAN	INCREASE (CR) +

Opening Bal:

Total:

DECREASE (DR) -	PRIVATE LOANS	INCREASE (CR) +

Opening Bal:

Total:

OWNER'S EQUITY

Opening Owner's Equity	
Minus Owner's Drawings	-
Plus Profit (Loss)	+
Equals Closing Owner's Equity	=

TOTAL ASSETS $_____

= TOTAL LIABILITIES _____

+ OWNER'S EQUITY _____ } $_____

BUSINESS INCOME STATEMENT

REVENUE

DECREASE (DR) -		INCREASE (CR) +

MINUS

EXPENSES

INCREASE (DR) +	ADVERTISING	DECREASE (CR) -

INCREASE (DR) +	DEPRECIATION	DECREASE (CR) -

INCREASE (DR) +	ENTERTAINMENT	DECREASE (CR) -

INCREASE (DR) +	INSURANCE	DECREASE (CR) -

INCREASE (DR) +	INTEREST	DECREASE (CR) -

INCREASE (DR) +	OFFICE SUPPLIES	DECREASE (CR) -

INCREASE (DR) +	PAYROLL	DECREASE (CR) -

ADD ALL REVENUE _____

SUBTRACT EXPENSES _____

= PROFIT (LOSS) _____

[Transfer to the balance sheet and update Owner's Equity]

Exercise #2

1. Explain the difference between current debt and long-term debt.

    _____

    _____

    _____

    _____

    _____

    _____

    _____

    _____

    _____

    _____

    _____

    _____

    _____

2. Complete the chart: would the transaction be classified as current or long-term debt?

	Transaction	Current	Long-Term
1	Arrange a loan for $20,000 to buy a car - to be paid back over a 5-year period.		
2	Borrow $24,000 from the bank for a 6-year term.		
3	A lender offers you $36,000 to help finance some machines and requests that you pay the loan over a 3-year term.		
4	You purchase a new truck for $30,000 - the principal is to be paid over the next 5 years.		
5	Borrow $3,000 from a friend - you asked if you could borrow it for 3 years, but he insists you repay the loan within 6 months.		

3. Explain why the principal portion of a loan does not impact equity when you borrow money.

    _____

    _____

    _____

    _____

    _____

    _____

    _____

    _____

    _____

    _____

    _____

4. Explain why the interest portion of a loan decreases Owner's Equity.

    _____

    _____

    _____

    _____

    _____

    _____

    _____

    _____

    _____

    _____

    _____

Exercise #3

Current vs. Long-Term Debt

Complete the shaded areas of the chart with the current and long-term amounts owing after making payment towards a $48,000 loan.

Total Loan	$48,000
Loan payable over 48 months	
Current - owing within the next 12 months	$12,000
Long-Term - owing after the next 12 months	$36,000

Payment made	$1,000
Current amount owing	
Long-Term amount owing	

Another payment made	$1,000
Current amount owing	
Long-Term amount owing	

Another payment made	$1,000
Current amount owing	
Long-Term amount owing	

Exercise #4

Complete the chart below using the assumptions in Section A. Complete columns C, D, E and F. The transactions for January and February have been completed for you. When you are done, ensure that you calculate the totals at the bottom.

Assumptions	A
$3,600.00 loan 10% interest 12 months	

B	C	D	E	F
Month (end of)	Debt Payment	Outstanding Balance	Interest for the month (based on outstanding balance of previous month)	Total Outflow
Opening		$3,600		
January	$300	$3,300	$30.00	$330.00
February	$300	$3,000	$27.50	$327.50
March				
April				
May				
June				
July				
August				
September				
October				
November				
December				
TOTAL				

Add the totals when complete.

Notes

AME | Learning

Practical Insights

Practical Insights

MARKET VALUE OF SHARES

As you see the Stock Market Index racing upward, you realize suddenly that you need to be a part of the action. You must invest in shares. Shares can bring you big returns and also help you lose your shirt!

The key to deciding whether or not you should invest in shares - and how much - depends on your ability to carry on life when you lose your shirt. So the basic rule of thumb is that you can afford to bet as big as you can afford to lose. If you need greater clarity you need to understand your risk-quotient. Are you risk-reluctant, risk-friendly or risk-neutral? Here are a few tips to find out:

Age: Generally speaking, younger people can - and should - take greater risks. As you grow older, you should be enjoying the benefits. Ideally it is recommended that you use the 100 minus age rule for equity (stock market shares) in the entire portfolio. That is, if you are 30, then 70% of the portfolio should be in equity (shares). If you are 40, then only 60% of the portfolio should be in equity. The portion towards equity should reduce with the increase in age, as one's risk appetite goes down. No need to follow this exact formula, but you get the general drift.

Personal status: If you are married you take fewer risks, as you would if you have dependents, young children and old parents. You need to re-evaluate this situation if the children leave the nest for their own jobs, or parents are no longer around.

Career status: If you are at the peak of your career and retirement is more than ten years away, you can afford to take risks. If you have just begun your career, your risk-taking ability is reasonably high as you are expecting revenue to flow in.

Expectations: If you want higher profits, you must be willing to lose more. Ask yourself: if your portfolio gains handsomely next month, will you invest more or reserve your profits?

There's no such thing as a *quick buck*.... here's a sad story to keep in mind:

John loves sports cars, but does not earn sufficient money in his job to buy one. He heard about some friends who were *making a killing* on the stock market. After some persuasion, his friends allowed him to join the share club. John borrowed $3,000 from family and took a loan from the bank and used various assets as collateral. Within 3 months he lost most of the $3,000 and had to tell his family that he could not pay them back. This type of story is commonplace.

Yes, there are lots of people that have made lots of money on the stock market, buying and selling shares. Conversely there are lots of people that have lost everything they have (and more). Buying and selling shares is a risky business. Even stockbrokers (the people who buy and sell shares on your behalf in exchange for commission) make mistakes and often recommend poor buying decisions. Knowing how business works and how to read financial statements will help you make better decisions and reduce your risk.

Research these words: stock market *bull* and *bear* and then remember this - *there's room for bulls, room for bears and no room for pigs!!!*

CREDIT RISK

It would be wonderful if everyone in the world was totally honest and every plan and budget worked out exactly as intended, but that's not reality. Some people are dishonest, disorganized and simply experience bad luck. In any event, a lender of money wants to ensure that they get their money back.

Credit score

A credit score is a number that lenders use if a person is given a loan or credit card to determine if that person is likely to pay the loan back on time. A credit score is a snapshot of your credit risk picture at a particular point in time. The higher your score, the lower the risk to lenders. Your credit score is generated by a mathematical formula utilizing the data from your *TransUnion*, *Equifax* or *Experian* credit reports. (These are just a few organizations that offer the service.) Lenders have been using credit scores as part of lending decisions for more than 20 years.

Factors that influence your credit score

Various factors determine your credit score, including the following:

·   Payment history

·   Outstanding debt

·   Length of credit history

·   Severity and frequency of critical credit information (bankruptcies, charge-offs and collections)

·   The amount of credit used compared to the credit available

How your credit score will affect you

Your credit score is an important indicator of your financial health. Lenders use your credit score to determine:

·   Whether or not you are a good candidate for a loan.

·   What type of interest rate you will pay.

While your credit score is a key determinant of your creditworthiness, lenders also examine the information on your credit report and your loan application. Regularly checking your credit report enables you to:

·   Be informed of the most up-to-date information in your credit history.

·   Correct any inaccuracies to ensure that your credit data is a true depiction of your credit record and to increase your chances of receiving credit under the best possible terms.

A *good* credit score

There are several types of credit scores available. Typically, the higher the score, the better. Each lender decides what credit score range it considers to be a good credit risk or a poor credit risk. For this reason, the lender is the best source to explain what your credit score means in relation to the final credit decision. After all, they determine the criteria used to extend credit. The credit score is only one component of information evaluated by lenders.

Developing a credit scoring model

A lender creates a credit scoring model by using several criteria:

▶ Selecting a large sampling of customers.

▶ Analyzing the data in their credit reports to determine which factors relate to creditworthiness.

▶ Assigning a degree of importance to each of the factors, based on how accurate a predictor it is in determining who will repay their loan on time

Here are five reasons to check your own credit risk score:

1. Many inaccuracies on credit reports result from simple clerical errors and are therefore not difficult to correct if caught.

2. To ensure that your credit information is correct, you need to check it on a regular basis. You should know that inquiries do not increase or decrease your score.

3. Identity theft is a major issue in North America. By catching signs of possible fraudulent activity early, you can likely minimize the damage to your ratings.

4. When shopping for a loan, your inquiry stays on record for up to 2 years. By examining your score, you will be able to shop for the best lender and avoid unnecessary inquiries.

5. One of the most important elements of your credit score is your payment history. Verify that your payment history is accurate so lenders can see that your payments are responsible. Of course if your payment history is bad, it will be reflected in the reports, which will result in you either not being able to secure loans, or having to pay very high interest rates for the loan.

COLLATERAL

Banks lend money to people or businesses in exchange for interest payments. The amount of interest that is paid largely depends on the amount of money that is borrowed. The larger the amount, the lower the interest.

The bank will carefully evaluate the risk of lending you money. If they think that you are a good **credit risk** (i.e. that you have a good track record of paying back debt) they will charge you a lower rate of interest than if you have poor credit. There are various businesses that offer credit reporting services that maintain a record of most business and private financial affairs. If you or a bank wish to get a credit rating on a person or a business, you will need to pay a credit bureau a fee for the report. Two examples of credit agencies are *Dunn & Bradstreet* and *Equifax*. Banks often use these credit reporting services prior to lending money.

Banks want to make sure that in the event your business fails and is forced to close, they will get back the money they loaned you. They usually request some form of collateral (assets pledged as security for a loan). In other words, you or someone else on your behalf (a co-signer) will need to sign a guarantee to the bank, which means that if you don't pay back the loan, the bank will take possession of the assets that have signed over (*pledged*) to them and will sell them on your behalf and use the cash to pay the debt.

The bank will also ensure that you have not pledged the same assets to someone else. To ensure that you are telling them the truth, the bank will perform a *Personal Property Security Act* search (PPSA). In other words, once you pledge your assets to someone in the form of security, the assets that you pledge will be registered in a computer data base that can be accessed through the government.

Here is an example: Let's say that you buy a car for $20,000, but only have $5,000 of your own cash to spend on the car. You therefore have to borrow the balance of $15,000. The bank will lend you the $15,000 and will register the car in the PPSA database. If you were to go to another bank to borrow money for some other purpose and offered the car as collateral, the second lender (if they are smart) will perform a PPSA search, in which case your car will show as being registered with the first lender and therefore cannot be used again. In plain language, the first lender has first *dibs* on the car.

A lender may also request that you sign a **promissory note**, which is a document signed by a borrower promising to repay a loan under agreed-upon terms.

DEBT TO EQUITY RATIO

Total Liabilities ÷ Owner's Equity

Some debt is fine - too much debt is dangerous. Lenders are sensitive to the amount of debt a company can withstand and will be cautious as to how much they will lend.

The debt to equity ratio should not usually exceed 0.5 to 1. In other words, for every $1 worth of debt, there should be at least $2 worth of equity. There are some exceptions to this rule depending upon the industry. For example, the property industry is more tolerant of debt than, say, manufacturing.

There is another factor that should be taken into account, which is somewhat technical, but you should be aware of it. Some analysts will separate long-term debt from short-term debt as it is assumed that the current debt is covered by the current assets. The rest of the debt will then be measured against equity, in which case 0.5 to 1 will be a bit ambitious.

Questions you should be asking if the debt to equity ratio is poor:

- The company's debt could be high because the company has been purchasing too many assets with debt.

- The company is not generating sufficient cash flow from operations (such as collecting Accounts Receivable on time or inventory levels are too high) resulting in having to borrow money to fund the cash deficiency.

- The company is operating at a loss, which decreases equity, causing the debt to equity ratio to deteriorate.

There are a number of other technical reasons why a debt to equity ratio can deteriorate, but essentially the managers of a business should ensure that they contain the debt in manageable proportions.

PLEDGE

A pledge is a promise that is made to pay back what you borrow. Sometimes a **Pledgee** (the person or business that lends the money) will insist that you sign a legal document that outlines the terms of the loan. If the document has lots of legal language, like the example below, it would be wise to have a lawyer examine it before signing.

Here is a sample of a typical **Pledge of Personal Property** as collateral security document:

```
                    PLEDGE OF PERSONAL PROPERTY

     FOR VALUE RECEIVED, the undersigned hereby deposits and
pledges with XYZ Company Inc.,[Pledgee] as collateral security
to secure the payment of: a one year loan of $10,000

     The following personal property [collateral] described as:
2003 model Honda motor vehicle serial number 17264846389376

     It is understood and agreed that:
     1. Pledgee may assign or transfer said debt and the
        pledged collateral hereunder.
     2. Pledgee shall have no liability for loss, destruction
        or casualty to the collateral unless caused by his own
        negligence.
     3. The undersigned shall pay any and all insurance it
        elects to maintain on the pledged collateral and any
        personal property, excise or other tax or levy.
     4. The undersigned warrants that it has good title to the
        pledged collateral, authority to pledge same and that
        it is free of any adverse lien, encumbrance or claim.
     5. In the event of default of payment of the debt or
        breach of this pledge agreement, the Pledgee or holder
        shall have full rights to foreclose on the pledged
        collateral and exercise its rights as a secured party
        pursuant to Article 9 of the Uniform Commercial Code;
        said rights being cumulative with any other rights the
        Pledgee may have against the undersigned.

Signed under seal this __ day of _____, 20__.

Signed

Joe Bloggs
```

Ethical issue:

Sometimes the person or organization may not register the asset with the *Personal Property Security Act*. This means that you can borrow money from another person (lender #2) using the same asset as you used as collateral for lender #1. Of course lender #2 may not know that you have already pledged the asset and will lend you money thinking that if you did not pay, they can claim the asset. This is wrong. If you do not pay lender #1 back as promised, they may take possession of your car (as illustrated on the previous page in the agreement). If you do not pay lender #2 either, lender #2 will not be able to take your car because lender #1 already has it.

It is up to you to maintain integrity when pledging assets as security for a loan.

Promissory Note:

A promissory note simply means that you make a promise in writing. A promissory note does not have to be about paying a loan. It could also relate to delivering a service on time. Signing a promissory note can actually bind you legally and you can be sued if you do not keep your commitment. Remember that if you are sued and if you lose the case, your lack of honesty will be on your record for a long time.

BUSINESS FINANCING

There are various ways to finance a new business:

▶ Through the owner(s)

▶ Commercial banks

▶ Private lenders such as friends and family

▶ "Angel" financers - these are people who may have made a lot of money and want to invest privately in small businesses

▶ Government programs

▶ Venture Capital

▶ Public offering

Each of these lenders may demand different returns on their investment or different interest rates depending on the risk.

Financing a corporation through a commercial bank:

Typically a bank will be hesitant to lend a business more than half of the owner's commitment. After all the bank does not own the business. In other words, the **debt** (bank) to **equity** (owner) should be 0.5:1.

For example, if an owner finances the business with $100,000, then the bank will likely lend up to $50,000. Of course the bank will generally require adequate collateral to ensure that they get their loan back in the event that the owner defaults on the loan.

Chapter 4

Assets, Revenue and Expense Recognition

Assets, Revenue & Expense Recognition

▸ Expenses vs. Capital Assets
▸ Current vs. Fixed Assets
▸ Prepaid Expenses
▸ Expense Recognition
▸ Unearned Revenue

Expenses vs. Capital Assets

When purchasing fixed assets, there is no change to Owner's Equity at the time of the purchase. Whether the purchase should be regarded as an asset or an expense is a question of materiality. For example: the purchase of a computer may be regarded as an asset, but a box of CD's will be regarded as an expense. How will you know in which category the asset should be recorded?

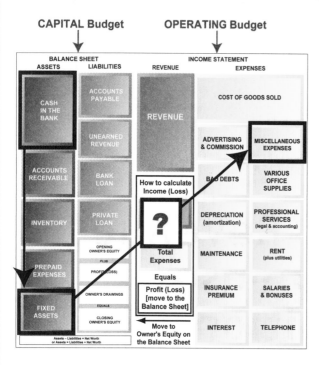

Balance sheet items (**Capital Budget** items) do not impact Net Worth (Owner's Equity) at the time of acquisition or as you are building inventory.

Income statement items (**Operating Budget** items) impact Net Worth in the time period in which the purchase occurs.

Choosing the right one is largely a matter of materiality (what is considered to be of material value to your business).

Generally speaking an asset is something that will provide value to the business for more than a year. Any item purchased that is unlikely to bring value for more than a year should be regarded as an expense. It is largely a question of good judgment, which will change according to the size of the business.

Ethical issue: If you were borrowing money from a lender and they were to assess the value of your business, you may have to face an ethical issue as to whether you are telling the truth. (Remember the GAAP definition: *What is the Net Worth of the business and are your financial statements reporting the truth?*) If you were to consider a purchase as an asset instead of an expense, it would appear that the Net Worth of the business did not change. Conversely, if you recorded the purchase as an expense, then Net Worth would change. Sometimes it is not so clear cut.

Current Assets vs. Fixed Assets

Assets are divided into two parts:

1. **Current assets** are those that will likely convert into cash within 12 months, through day-to-day operations.

2. **Fixed assets** are used to operate a business and will not likely turn into cash in 12 months, unless they are sold for reasons other than the day-to-day operations of the business.

The purpose of separating current assets from fixed assets is to enable the reader of statements to assess how much cash (also known as *liquidity*) will be generated through every day activities. The amount of cash generated in the next 12 months is compared to how much is owed within that time. Typically there should be $2.00 worth of current assets for every $1.00 worth of current liabilities.

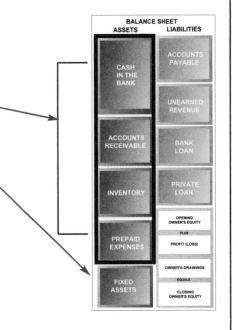

Prepaid Expenses

As discussed in Chapter 1, Section 4, some expenses (such as the first month's rent, annual insurance, deposits to lawyers, etc.) must be recognized to reflect their cost against the related revenue per month.

For example: You purchase an insurance policy for one year in the amount of $6,000 ($500 per month). If the policy is cancelled after the first month, then the refund would amount to $5,500. If the policy is cancelled after 11 months, only $500 would be refundable.

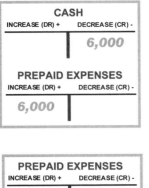

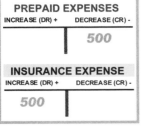

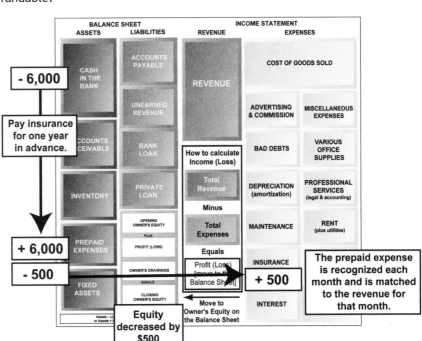

Another way of looking at this principle is to say that a prepaid expense is, in a manner of speaking, just like a promissory note signed by your vendor in which it is agreed that he or she owes you the money that you prepaid until the service has been provided in full. You have, in effect, provided your vendor with an interest-free loan (the piece of paper - a note owing to you - has value). As the service is provided, the value of the *note* decreases together with your net worth. In the language of accounting this is called an **expense**. In other words, you are **recognizing** that your Net Worth is decreasing.

The decision as to whether a prepayment should be regarded as an asset or expense is again a question of materiality. You may regard a $1,200 insurance prepayment as an asset because it is a material amount. Conversely, you may regard a deposit of $50 to attend a trade show as relatively immaterial and simply expense it immediately, regardless of when the event is to take place.

Remember that revenue must be **matched** to expenses in the same time period to assess the profitability of the business.

Non-Refundable Deposits

There is a difference between legal and accounting issues for the purpose of non-refundable deposits. Even if a prepayment is non-refundable, accrual accounting still requires that revenue is matched to the related expense in the same period to help management assess profitability. The legal obligation to refund or not to refund is a separate issue and has no bearing on the manner in which revenue and expenses are matched.

The Significance of Prepaids to Budget Control

The principle of prepaid expenses has significant importance in relation to budgets. For example: If your financial year-end is December, you have $10,000 of available budget for the month of December and you need to balance your budget, you cannot do so by prepaying your vendor $10,000 for products or services to be received in January. In this case the $10,000 payment has been prepaid in anticipation of a service to be delivered at a later date and therefore has no impact on the budget for December. This prepayment will impact the January budget (for the next year). *This is a very common mistake or misconception.*

Expense Recognition

There are three ways to recognize **expenses**:

1. Pay as you go (pay in cash)

2. Pay after the fact - in another period (Accounts Payable)

3. Pay before the fact (Prepaid Expenses)

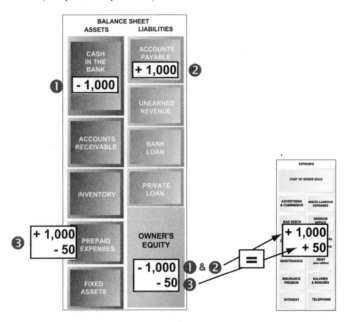

In each of these scenarios, you will notice that we are focusing on the Net Worth of the business. An increase to Net Worth is called revenue recognition (*we will address this later in the textbook*) and a decrease to Net Worth is called expense recognition.

The Matching Principle requires that revenue be matched to expenses in the same period, regardless when the cash is paid or received. This rule is part of GAAP (Generally Accepted Accounting Principles) and the *Sarbanes-Oxley Law* for publicly traded companies.

Logic: Imagine if you were to pay cash for all your expenses in January, but only receive payment for your services in February. It would appear that you had suffered a loss in January (expenses with no revenue), but made a great profit in February (revenue with no expenses). Of course this would not be true. The value of the sale in January must be matched to the value of the expenses in January to assess if you made a profit.

GAAP: *What is the Net Worth of the business and are your financial statements reporting the truth?*

Unearned Revenue

Unearned revenue is the opposite of prepaid expenses. It represents cash that has been received but not yet earned. Just as prepaid expenses may have to be paid back to you if the service is not provided, unearned revenue may have to be paid back to your customer.

Cash paid to you for services to be rendered is considered a liability. When the service is provided the liability decreases, increasing equity (which is called revenue).

For example: A health club often requires that members pay a full year's membership in advance. Using this illustration, a member pays the club $600 for the year. This amount is regarded as **unearned** when received (it is essentially being held "in trust").

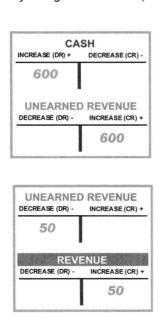

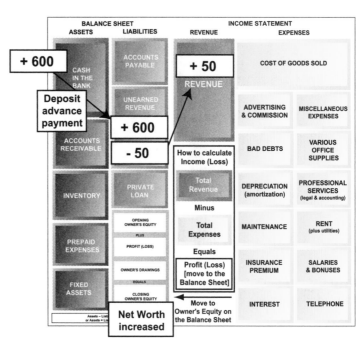

Each month the member uses the club, the club will owe the member $50 less. The health club has **recognized** the revenue for the month and will match this revenue, together with all other revenue, against various expenses to calculate the profitability for the period (the change to the Net Worth of the business).

It is quite common for businesses to maintain a separate bank account for funds that do not belong to them. Some examples are:

· Unearned revenue that can be transferred into the general chequing account when earned.
· Taxes collected on behalf of the tax authorities such as VAT, GST, etc.
· Income tax owings.

Physically transferring funds out of the general chequing account eliminates the temptation to spend cash that will need to be distributed at a later date.

Unearned revenue is a commonly used transaction that, when not fully understood, can cause business failure.

For example: Jack, who is the owner of a web design/hosting company needs cash to operate his business and cannot raise any more money from the bank or other lenders. He offers an incentive to his customers to pay him in advance in exchange for a discount. Each of Jack's 100 customers pays $600 upfront in the month of January, instead of $60 per month ($720 per year), totalling $60,000 worth of revenue in January.

Neither Jack nor his bookkeeper fully understood the accrual concept and created an invoice for each customer. According to accruals this meant that he actually *sold* the services, resulting in a significant profit in January. Jack started spending the cash at a fast rate and unfortunately ran out of money in July - he was spending with no further sales being made. (Remember that he was already paid by his customers.)

Here is a chart to illustrate the way Jack recorded his revenue and expenses versus the way he *should* have recorded them:

Scenario #1:

	Revenue	Expenses	Profit
January	$60,000	$3,000	$57,000
February	0	3,000	(3,000)
March	0	3,000	(3,000)
April	0	3,000	(3,000)
May	0	3,000	(3,000)
June	0	3,000	(3,000)
July	0	3,000	(3,000)
August	0	3,000	(3,000)
September	0	3,000	(3,000)
October	0	3,000	(3,000)
November	0	3,000	(3,000)
December	0	3,000	(3,000)
Total	$60,000	$36,000	$24,000

Scenario #2:

	Revenue	Expenses	Profit
January	$5,000	$3,000	$2,000
February	5,000	3,000	2,000
March	5,000	3,000	2,000
April	5,000	3,000	2,000
May	5,000	3,000	2,000
June	5,000	3,000	2,000
July	5,000	3,000	2,000
August	5,000	3,000	2,000
September	5,000	3,000	2,000
October	5,000	3,000	2,000
November	5,000	3,000	2,000
December	5,000	3,000	2,000
Total	$60,000	$36,000	$24,000

In *Scenario #1* Jack showed a huge profit in the month of January that, in conjunction with all the cash received, made him a little excited and sent him on a spending spree. Of course during the month of February and through to the end of the year, there was no matching of revenue to expenses resulting in recorded losses for those months.

The $60,000 received in January should have been regarded as **unearned revenue** on the liability side of the balance sheet and perhaps even deposited into a separate bank account. Jack should not have issued an invoice indicating a sale, but should have issued a cash receipt instead. Each month, Jack should have transferred $5,000 from the savings account to the daily banking account and invoiced that amount. This would have been recorded as revenue matched to the $2,000 of expenses each month (*Scenario #2*).

Furthermore, Jack would not have used the funds that had not yet been *earned* and therefore would not have run out of money.

Matching revenue earned to expenses incurred in the same period represents the fundamental principle of accrual accounting.

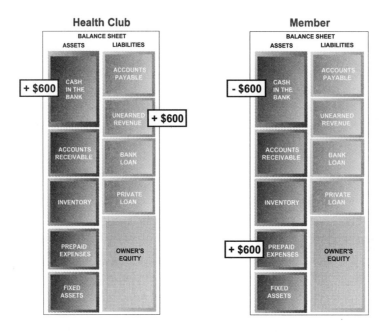

Ethical Issues

Revenue and Expense Recognition

GAAP: *What is the net worth of your business and are your financial statements reporting the truth?*

This topic would not be complete without mentioning *Enron*, which treated the entire amount of the future energy contracts it traded as revenue. Of course there were also no costs associated with the *revenue*, which boosted book profits even more. As a result, *Enron* slotted in as the fifth largest U.S. corporation on the 2001 *Fortune 500* (published in 2002) with $139 billion in revenue, even though it had recently filed for *Chapter 11* bankruptcy protection.

Given the importance of this principle, here are some more examples for you to consider.

Example #1

The owner of a small publishing firm, that sells magazine subscriptions, is very successful at soliciting customers to pay in advance. He collects $120,000 between the months of January and March, but the magazines will only be shipped between March and December. Additional financing is required from the bank to help pay for new computers and a new home for the owner.

Ethical issue: When presenting the financial statements to the bank (with the bank balance at $120,000), does the owner report that revenues are $120,000 for the months of January to March or that revenues were only $10,000 for the same period?

Example #2

 The operator of a tour business wants to sell part of her business to a friend who is not very experienced in business matters and trusts the owner's business judgment. The business is entering a busy period before the summer and $300,000 in deposits has been collected from customers, who are to take tours in two months time. It is expected that commissions and gross profit will be about $50,000 in two months.

Ethical issue: When the owner presents the current financial statements to her friend, does she present revenues of $300,000, because the cash has already been collected, or does she report zero revenues at this time and expected revenues of $50,000 in two months time?

Example #3

 You decide to start a hi-tech business that wholesales long distance telephone services. Customers can call your office to purchase long distance services in advance and dial a code to access their account when making a call. This is a very convenient service and business is booming. During the months of January to June you collect $240,000 in advance payments from customers. About $100,000 of the prepayments has already been used by the customers that signed up with you and suddenly business slows down. (It appears that your competition has gotten word of your idea and has copied you but they have more advanced software.) You need to borrow money from the bank to upgrade your system.

Ethical issue: Given that you received the cash in advance from your customers, do you report sales for the first half of the year as $240,000, or sales of $140,000 for the period?

Notes

AME | Learning

Exercises: Chapter 4

Exercise #1

Walter starts his own manufacturing business specializing in plastic containers. He sets up the business in the form of a corporation and records transactions relating to the following activities for the month of January.

Complete the T-Accounts on the opposite page for the following transactions to set up a business.

Transactions:

1.	Deposit share capital	$1,000
2.	Deposit loan from owner	100,000
3.	Borrow from the bank - 5-year term loan	50,000
4.	Buy plant and machinery with cash (fixed assets)	110,000
5.	Prepay insurance for one year	12,000
6.	Deposit cash from a customer - services to be provided *next month*	20,000

After you have entered all the transactions and updated Net Worth on the balance sheet, answer the related questions over the page.

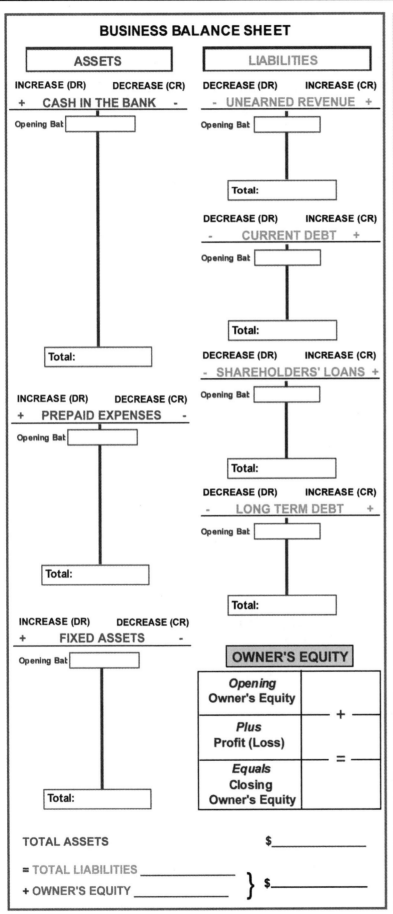

BUSINESS BALANCE SHEET

ASSETS

INCREASE (DR) DECREASE (CR)

+   CASH IN THE BANK   -

Opening Bal

Total:

INCREASE (DR) DECREASE (CR)

+   PREPAID EXPENSES   -

Opening Bal

Total:

INCREASE (DR) DECREASE (CR)

+   FIXED ASSETS   -

Opening Bal

Total:

LIABILITIES

DECREASE (DR) INCREASE (CR)

-    UNEARNED REVENUE   +

Opening Bal

Total:

DECREASE (DR) INCREASE (CR)

-    CURRENT DEBT   +

Opening Bal

Total:

DECREASE (DR) INCREASE (CR)

-    SHAREHOLDERS' LOANS   +

Opening Bal

Total:

DECREASE (DR) INCREASE (CR)

-    LONG TERM DEBT   +

Opening Bal

Total:

OWNER'S EQUITY

Opening Owner's Equity	
Plus Profit (Loss)	+
Equals Closing Owner's Equity	=

TOTAL ASSETS $_____

= TOTAL LIABILITIES _____ } $_____
+ OWNER'S EQUITY _____

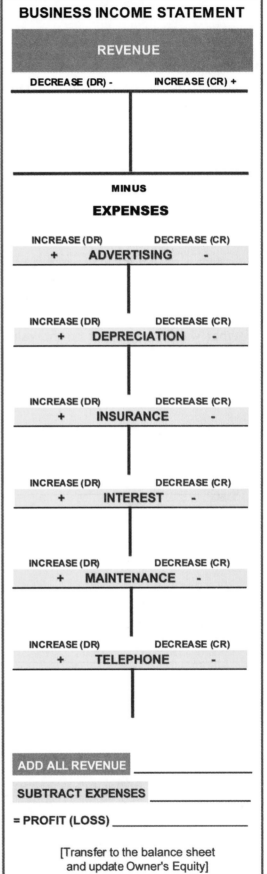

BUSINESS INCOME STATEMENT

REVENUE

DECREASE (DR) -   INCREASE (CR) +

MINUS

EXPENSES

INCREASE (DR)   DECREASE (CR)

+   ADVERTISING   -

INCREASE (DR)   DECREASE (CR)

+   DEPRECIATION   -

INCREASE (DR)   DECREASE (CR)

+   INSURANCE   -

INCREASE (DR)   DECREASE (CR)

+   INTEREST   -

INCREASE (DR)   DECREASE (CR)

+   MAINTENANCE   -

INCREASE (DR)   DECREASE (CR)

+   TELEPHONE   -

ADD ALL REVENUE _____

SUBTRACT EXPENSES _____

= PROFIT (LOSS) _____

[Transfer to the balance sheet and update Owner's Equity]

1. What would the impact on the value of the business be if Walter had recorded the prepayment as an expense for the month of January?

_____

_____

_____

_____

_____

_____

2. What would the impact on the value of the business be if Walter had recorded the customer deposit as earned revenue for the month of January?

_____

_____

_____

_____

_____

_____

3. If Walter wishes to borrow money on the strength of profitable operating results, what is the ethical problem of doing this in the eyes of a bank?

_____

_____

_____

_____

_____

_____

4. How much profit would Walter have reported for the month of January if he decided to expense all the prepaid expenses and recognize the customer's upfront payment as earned revenue? What impact would this have on the rest of the year?

_____

_____

_____

_____

_____

_____

_____

_____

_____

_____

5. If Walter recorded the transactions as described in question 4 above, which accounting principle would have been offended?

_____

_____

_____

_____

6. Explain in detail why the Owner's Equity of $1,000 did not change.

Exercise #2

ASSET vs. EXPENSE

For the transactions below select which should be assets and which should be expenses (use a ✓):

	Description	Asset	Expense
1	Buy a machine to produce widgets.		
2	Buy photocopy paper.		
3	Print new business cards.		
4	Buy a computer.		
5	Purchase a $200 upgrade for one of the computers.		
6	Buy uniforms for the staff.		
7	Pay for a $100 roof repair.		
8	Prepay $4,000 for car insurance.		
9	Prepay $100 to a hotel to secure a future stay.		
10	Pay for the last month's rent as a security deposit.		

Exercise # 3

Jenny operates a health spa. In setting up her business she invested $20,000 of her own money in the form of Owner's Equity. She also sold some spa deals in advance to corporate clients in exchange for a large discount incentive.

Record the activities for this month and answer the questions over the page after you have calculated Net Worth.

The opening balances are:

Cash	$20,000
Opening Owner's Equity	20,000

Transactions:

1.	Borrow money from the bank	$10,000
2.	Buy furniture and computers with cash	20,000
3.	Prepay annual insurance	6,000
4.	Deposit advance payments from customers - you will not provide the services until next month	3,000
5.	Sell services for cash	10,000
6.	Pay rent	1,800
7.	Pay interest on bank loan	100
8.	Record advertising expenses for this month - pay next month	500
9.	Pay wages	3,000
10.	Receive telephone bill - to be paid next month	200
11.	Repairs and maintenance - pay immediately	400
12.	Pay portion of bank loan principal	1,000

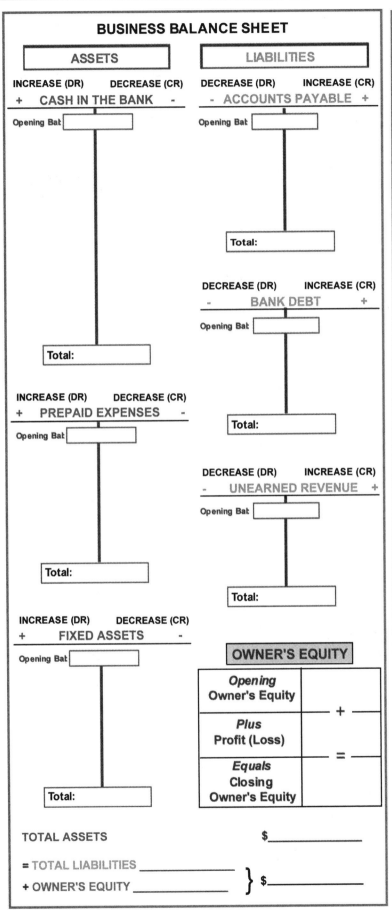

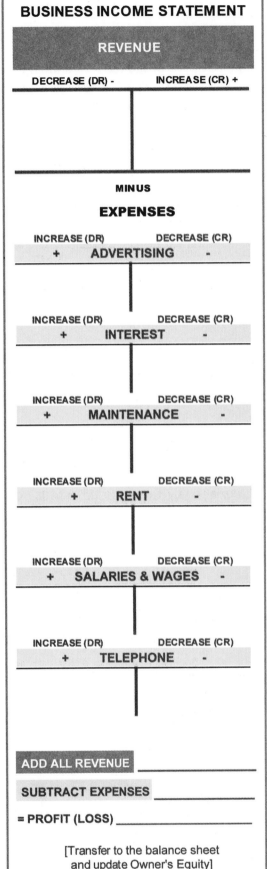

BUSINESS BALANCE SHEET

ASSETS

CASH IN THE BANK
INCREASE (DR) +   DECREASE (CR) -

Opening Bal.

Total:

PREPAID EXPENSES
INCREASE (DR) +   DECREASE (CR) -

Opening Bal.

Total:

FIXED ASSETS
INCREASE (DR) +   DECREASE (CR) -

Opening Bal.

Total:

LIABILITIES

ACCOUNTS PAYABLE
DECREASE (DR) -   INCREASE (CR) +

Opening Bal.

Total:

BANK DEBT
DECREASE (DR) -   INCREASE (CR) +

Opening Bal.

Total:

UNEARNED REVENUE
DECREASE (DR) -   INCREASE (CR) +

Opening Bal.

Total:

OWNER'S EQUITY

Opening Owner's Equity	
Plus Profit (Loss)	+
Equals Closing Owner's Equity	=

TOTAL ASSETS $_____

= TOTAL LIABILITIES _____
+ OWNER'S EQUITY _____ } $_____

BUSINESS INCOME STATEMENT

REVENUE

DECREASE (DR) -   INCREASE (CR) +

MINUS

EXPENSES

ADVERTISING
INCREASE (DR) +   DECREASE (CR) -

INTEREST
INCREASE (DR) +   DECREASE (CR) -

MAINTENANCE
INCREASE (DR) +   DECREASE (CR) -

RENT
INCREASE (DR) +   DECREASE (CR) -

SALARIES & WAGES
INCREASE (DR) +   DECREASE (CR) -

TELEPHONE
INCREASE (DR) +   DECREASE (CR) -

ADD ALL REVENUE _____

SUBTRACT EXPENSES _____

= PROFIT (LOSS) _____

[Transfer to the balance sheet and update Owner's Equity]

139

1. Regarding transaction #3 - annual insurance prepayment: How much of this prepayment should have been recognized for this month? Had you recognized this as an expense for this month, how much profit would Jenny have made versus the current result?

   _____

   _____

   _____

   _____

   _____

2. Regarding transactions #8 & #10: Since these amounts are to be paid next month, what would the profits be for this period if you had decided not to record these transactions this month?

   _____

   _____

   _____

   _____

   _____

3. Explain why the profit amount is not the same as the change to the cash balance.

   _____

   _____

   _____

   _____

   _____

Chapter 5
Building Inventory

Building Inventory

▶ Building Assets
▶ Depreciation
▶ Cost Allocation

Building Assets

Assets can be in various forms such as tangible assets (those you can touch - eg. cars, machinery, furniture, etc.) and intangible assets (those that are not physical - eg. goodwill, patents, etc.).

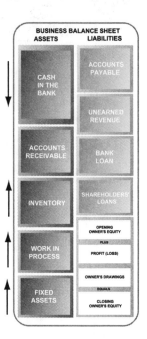

In the manufacturing industry, tangible assets include inventory used to sell to customers (*more about this later*) - assets that will be used for a long time such as machinery and equipment. Some businesses will take a long time to build assets such as electric power lines or a telephone infrastructure. While these are being built they may not be regarded as *fixed assets* (because they are not complete and bring no value) but will instead be recorded as Work in Process (WIP). Once the product is complete, the full cost of the asset will be moved into the fixed asset account.

Another example is when a consulting firm is working on a large project. The accountants may choose to regard the labour and other direct costs as WIP until they bill the customer, at which time they will decrease the WIP account and increase the Cost of Goods Sold account so that it can be *matched* to the value of the sale.

Companies within the service industry often build assets that are not tangible. Examples include web designers, software producers, computer game creators, etc. The assets that they produce are regarded as fixed assets because they will be used to generate sales. The asset can also be regarded as WIP while it is being built. (These assets will lose value over a period of time due to Depreciation.)

The building of assets is a balance sheet entry with no impact on the equity (Net Worth) of the business during the building period.

Depreciation

Depreciation in relation to building assets means that when assets are purchased for the purpose of manufacturing, the depreciation value of the asset is considered part of the manufacturing cost. For example: If a machine costs $10,000 and is expected to be used to build 10,000 products, then the depreciation of the machine can be amortized at a rate of $1.00 per unit. If the machine is expected to build 20,000 products, then the cost per unit is 50¢.

[*More about depreciation later on...*]

There are three levels to building inventory:

     1.   Raw materials

+   2.   Labour, factory overheads, depreciation, rent, insurance, etc.

=   3.   Finished goods, *at cost*, ready to sell

Here's an example of manufacturing a table:

The components are considered as inventory but cannot be called a table ...

... to convert the components into a table ready to sell you need to add labour and other manufacturing costs.

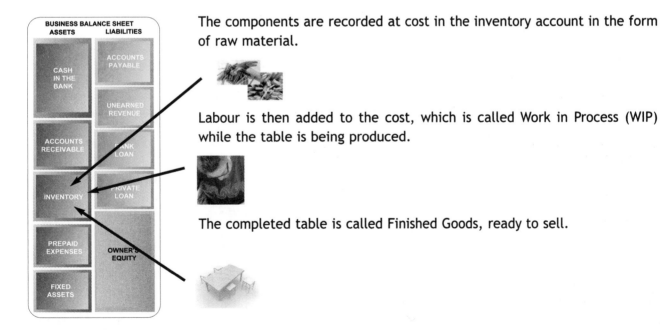

The components are recorded at cost in the inventory account in the form of raw material.

Labour is then added to the cost, which is called Work in Process (WIP) while the table is being produced.

The completed table is called Finished Goods, ready to sell.

This entire process is regarded as **inventory** (raw material). By adding labour, depreciation of machinery, rent and other manufacturing costs, the assembled product can now be called a table, with a new value ready to sell.

Allocating the amount of labour, rent and other manufacturing expenses to each product is called **Activity Based Costing** (ABC).

There are various ways in which machines can be amortized - we will discuss this later on in the textbook. However, for the purpose of manufacturing, the depreciation is allocated to the cost of building inventory and is not regarded as an expense. The amount of depreciation allocated to each product is explained in this diagram using manufactured clothing as an example.

Components (variable cost)	Cost per Shirt
Material	10.00
Sewing thread	0.30
Buttons	0.40
Lining	0.20
Label	0.10
Total variable cost per shirt	**$11.00**

Fixed manufacturing costs	
Rent	1,600
Electricity	500
Insurance	300
Maintenance	600
Manager	3,000
Depreciation of machines	2,000
Total fixed manufacturing costs	**$8,000**

# of Shirts Produced	Cost per Shirt?
3,000	
5,000	
1,000	
6,000	
2,000	
500	

Here's a quick exercise for you:
Using the numbers provided in the chart above, how much would each shirt cost, based on the production numbers provided (fill in the chart).

Cost Allocation

Only those expenses that relate directly to the manufacturing process are regarded as part of the cost of the product.

100,000 square feet

80,000 square feet in used for the manufacturing plant.

20,000 square feet in used for non-manufacturing administration such as accounting, sales and HR.

For example: 100% of *direct labour* would be regarded as part of manufacturing costs. However, not all the occupancy space (rent, property taxes, etc.) is used for manufacturing. In the example above, 20% of the space is used for administration, which means that 80% of the occupancy space would be allocated towards manufacturing and recorded in the inventory or WIP account on the balance sheet. The balance of 20% would be regarded as a direct operating expense on the income statement.

This calculation is called cost allocation.

The T-Account entries would be as follows:

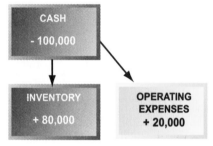

Notes

AME | Learning

Exercises: Chapter 5

Exercise #1

You start a small manufacturing business with $45,000 of your own money and a bank loan of $5,000. You purchase $30,000 worth of plant and machinery. During this period, you build a product to place in inventory so that you will have something to sell next month.

Record this month's activities and update the income and balance sheet when you are done.

Opening balances:

Bank account	$20,000
Fixed assets	30,000
Bank loan	5,000
Opening Owner's Equity	45,000

Transactions:

1. Buy raw materials - pay next month $3,000

2. Direct labour to manufacture goods - cash   3,000

3. Pay $10,000 in cash for the total rent for the month:
   (a) Allocate 70% of the rent to manufacturing
   (b) Allocate 30% of the rent to general administration expenses

4. Total insurance due is $1,000, which is to be paid next month:
   (a) Allocate 80% of the insurance to manufacturing
   (b) Allocate 20% of the insurance to non-manufacturing expenses

5. Pay cash for administrative staff   1,000

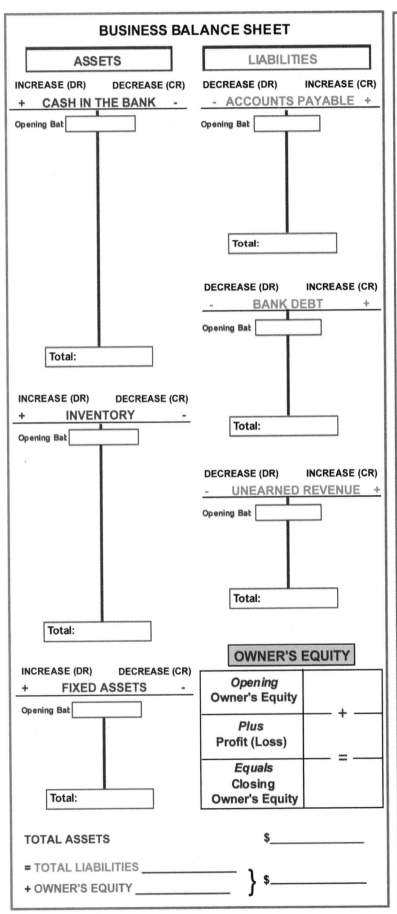

BUSINESS BALANCE SHEET

ASSETS

INCREASE (DR)   **DECREASE (CR)**
+   CASH IN THE BANK   -

Opening Bal

Total:

INCREASE (DR)   **DECREASE (CR)**
+   INVENTORY   -

Opening Bal

Total:

INCREASE (DR)   **DECREASE (CR)**
+   FIXED ASSETS   -

Opening Bal

Total:

LIABILITIES

DECREASE (DR)   **INCREASE (CR)**
-      ACCOUNTS PAYABLE   +

Opening Bal

Total:

DECREASE (DR)   **INCREASE (CR)**
-      BANK DEBT   +

Opening Bal

Total:

DECREASE (DR)   **INCREASE (CR)**
-      UNEARNED REVENUE   +

Opening Bal

Total:

OWNER'S EQUITY

Opening Owner's Equity	
Plus Profit (Loss)	+
Equals Closing Owner's Equity	=

TOTAL ASSETS $_____

= TOTAL LIABILITIES _____
+ OWNER'S EQUITY _____   } $_____

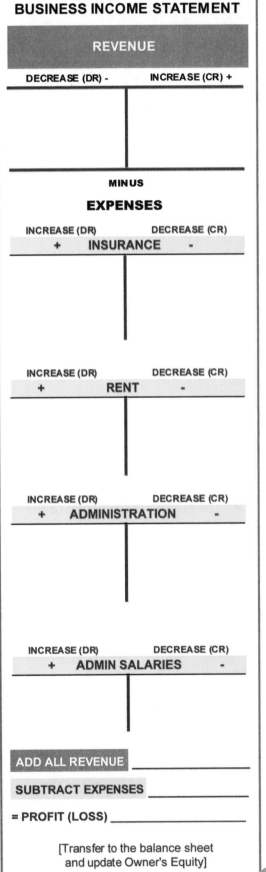

BUSINESS INCOME STATEMENT

REVENUE

DECREASE (DR) -   **INCREASE (CR) +**

MINUS

EXPENSES

INCREASE (DR)   **DECREASE (CR)**
+   INSURANCE   -

INCREASE (DR)   **DECREASE (CR)**
+   RENT   -

INCREASE (DR)   **DECREASE (CR)**
+   ADMINISTRATION   -

INCREASE (DR)   **DECREASE (CR)**
+   ADMIN SALARIES   -

ADD ALL REVENUE _____

SUBTRACT EXPENSES _____

= PROFIT (LOSS) _____

[Transfer to the balance sheet and update Owner's Equity]

Exercise #2

1. What would have happened to the cost of your product had you regarded all the rent, insurance and administrative costs as the cost of the product?

_____

_____

_____

_____

_____

2. What do you suppose might have happened to your marketing and selling efforts had you done this?

_____

_____

_____

_____

_____

3. What would have happened to the cost of your product had you decided to allocate all the rent and administration costs to administration and had not included anything in the cost of the product? Also comment on what impact this might have had on the selling efforts and company profits.

_____

_____

_____

_____

_____

4. Explain the difference between the change in cash versus the change to equity.

_____

_____

_____

_____

_____

_____

_____

_____

_____

_____

_____

_____

_____

_____

_____

_____

_____

_____

_____

Notes

AME | Learning

Chapter 6

Revenue Recognition and Cost of Goods Sold

Revenue Recognition and COGS

- ▶ Revenue Recognition
- ▶ Expense Recognition
- ▶ Accounts Receivable
- ▶ Cost of Goods Sold

- ▶ Operating Expenses
- ▶ The Rule of Materiality
- ▶ Owner's Drawings

Revenue Recognition

You will recall when working with personal financial statements that you recorded deposits relating to your salary. The cash deposit increased Net Worth and was called revenue. This principle of increasing Net Worth is exactly the same in business.

There are three ways in which the Net Worth of the business can increase through day-to-day operations. A customer can:

Scenario #1: Customer pays *when* the service is provided.

Scenario #2: Customer pays *after* the service is provided.

Scenario #3: Customer *prepays* before the service is provided.

In all of these scenarios the financial statements need to *recognize* the increase to Net Worth (Owner's Equity). When the service has been provided this is called *revenue*.

The document that is used to record the sale is called an invoice. The moment this document is produced, the double entry is:

1. Increase cash and increase revenue - *if you were paid immediately*

2. Increase accounts receivable and increase revenue - *if you are to be paid in the future*

3. Decrease unearned revenue and increase revenue - *if you had received a prepayment*

Scenario #1: Cash

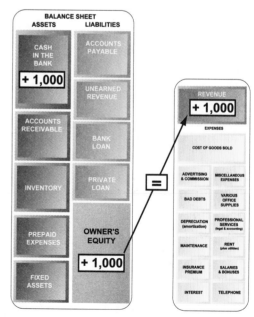

Scenario #2: Accounts Receivable

Sales (revenue) are made by customers, either in cash or billed **on account**. If you allow payment terms to your customer (payment on account) we refer to this as **Accounts Receivable**. Instead of you owing money to your vendor (Accounts Payable or "I Owe You"), the vendor *owes you* money (Accounts Receivable or "You Owe Me").

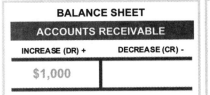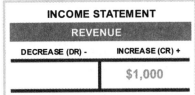

BALANCE SHEET		INCOME STATEMENT	
ACCOUNTS RECEIVABLE		**REVENUE**	
INCREASE (DR) +	DECREASE (CR) -	DECREASE (DR) -	INCREASE (CR) +
$1,000			$1,000

According to the principle of accrual accounting, the revenue must be recorded at the time the product or service was delivered to the customer regardless of whether it has been paid for or not.

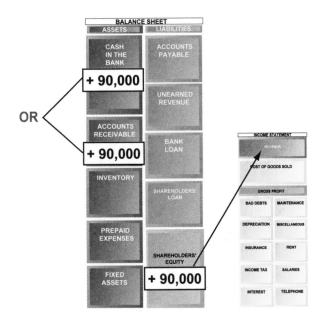

1. Customer paid in cash

2. Customer owes you the cash (*You Owe Me*)

The revenue is **recognized** whether you have been paid or not.

I.O.U. from your customer:

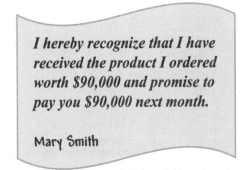

I hereby recognize that I have received the product I ordered worth $90,000 and promise to pay you $90,000 next month.

Mary Smith

An invoice has value even though it's only a piece of paper. An invoice can actually be sold to a finance business that specializes in buying invoices in exchange for a commission. This process is called **factoring**. It proves that the service provided has value, which according to the rule of accruals increases the Net Worth of the business (revenue).

Scenario #3: Unearned Revenue

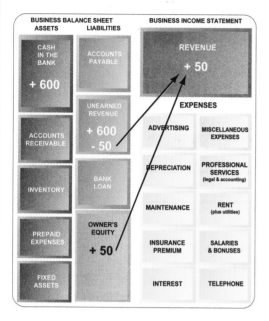

As discussed in Chapter 4, cash (revenue) received in the form of a deposit by a customer for services you have not yet provided, is regarded as **unearned revenue** (a liability). This cash does not belong to you until you provide the service to the customer. In fact, if you fail to provide the service, the cash must be returned to the customer, so the deposit has to be recorded as a liability (it's like an interest-free loan).

Once the service is provided, your *debt* to the customer will decrease by the value of the service provided (i.e. one month's worth).

A reduction in debt, with no change to cash, increases Owner's Equity (revenue). In other words, you are *recognizing* that you are richer (or recognizing the revenue earned).

Unearned revenue is the opposite of prepaid expenses. Here is an example of paying for one year's insurance coverage in advance:

Customer's Balance Sheet:
Prepaid insurance for 1 year

Insurance Company's Balance Sheet:
Received unearned revenue from customer

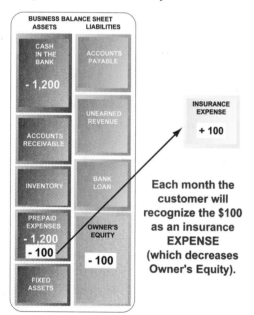

Each month the customer will recognize the $100 as an insurance **EXPENSE** (which decreases Owner's Equity).

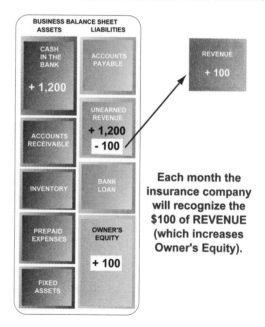

Each month the insurance company will recognize the $100 of REVENUE (which increases Owner's Equity).

Some other examples of prepayments include deposits for web hosting services, deposits received in the magazine subscription business, advance payments in the travel business and trust account monies received by lawyers.

Summary of Revenue Recognition

Consistent with the principle of expense recognition (there are 3 ways to recognize an expense - *see Chapter 4*), there are also 3 ways to recognize revenue (increase Owner's Equity):

❶ You are paid in cash when the product or service is delivered/provided.

❷ The revenue is recognized as earned when the product or service is delivered/provided (unearned revenue is now earned).

❸ The product or service is delivered/provided in another period, after the fact (Accounts Receivable).

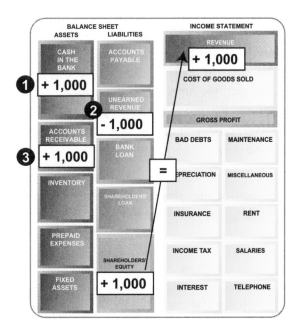

The **matching principle** requires that revenue be **matched** to expenses in the same period, regardless when the cash is paid or received. This rule is part of **GAAP** (Generally Accepted Accounting Principles) and the *Sarbanes-Oxley Law* for publicly traded companies.

Logic: Imagine paying cash for all your expenses in January, but only receiving payment for your services in February. It would appear that you had a loss in January (expenses with no revenue), but made a great profit in February (revenue with no expenses). Of course this would not be true. The **value** of the sale in January must be matched to the **value** of the expenses in January to assess a profit (loss).

Invoices

An invoice is a document (also called a *source document*) that must include the name of the supplier, the date of purchase, the price that was paid and an item description or number.

Some invoices are more detailed than others. Here are some examples:

1. If you buy something at a kiosk in the mall you will receive either a hand-printed invoice (see sample "A" below) or a narrow slip of paper printed from the cash register. It will have the name of the store (company name), the date, an invoice number, the cost of the purchase and any taxes paid. It may even list each item separately, identifying the price of each and the terms of payment (cash, cheque or credit).

2. An invoice received from a vendor (supplier) would identify the vendor's name and address, an invoice number, your account number with them, a description of the goods or service and the total owing including taxes (see sample "B" below). It will also include the terms of the sale (i.e. due in 14 days) and the vendor's tax registration numbers.

3. When purchasing goods from a factory the invoice would include even more details such as the manner in which it should be shipped (rail, courier, truck, etc.), the quantity and cost of each item, confirmation of the quantities shipped and payment terms. Here is an example of payment terms that may be included on the invoice: you may have agreed to pay the bill within 30 days of receiving the goods, or if you pay in less than 30 days you may deduct 2% off the price, etc. (see sample "C" below).

The design of an invoice could differ from business to business. Some invoices are custom-designed, which may include the business logo, while others are simple designs that can be bought at your local stationery store. It is all a matter of preference.

A

B

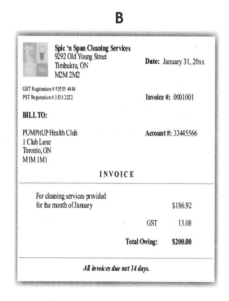

C

Expense Recognition

There are three ways to recognize an expense:

Scenario #1: Cash

Typical examples of expenses that are paid in the same month in which the expense occurs are payroll and rent.

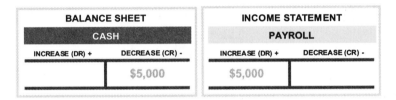

BALANCE SHEET		INCOME STATEMENT	
CASH		**PAYROLL**	
INCREASE (DR) +	DECREASE (CR) -	INCREASE (DR) +	DECREASE (CR) -
	$5,000	$5,000	

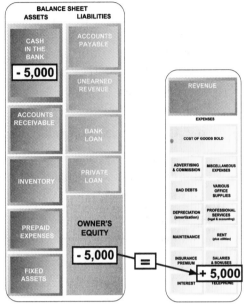

Scenario #2: Accounts Payable

When an expense is not paid in the same month in which it occurs then the amount is owing to the supplier. Some examples are amounts owing on credit cards, telephone bills and professional fees.

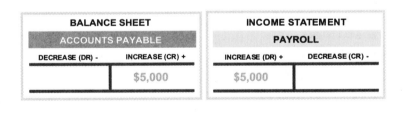

BALANCE SHEET		INCOME STATEMENT	
ACCOUNTS PAYABLE		**PAYROLL**	
DECREASE (DR) -	INCREASE (CR) +	INCREASE (DR) +	DECREASE (CR) -
	$5,000	$5,000	

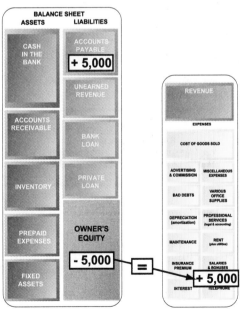

Scenario #3: Decreasing Assets

Assets can decrease in value due to an expense, without involving cash, for example:

a) Accounts Receivable decreases due to bad debts.

b) Inventory is used (decreases) affecting the Cost of Goods Sold.

c) Prepaid Expenses are recognized (decrease) affecting the expense that the prepayment relates to (insurance, internet, web hosting, etc.).

d) Fixed Assets decrease in value due to depreciation.

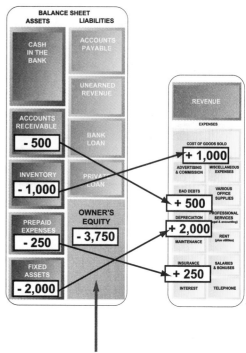

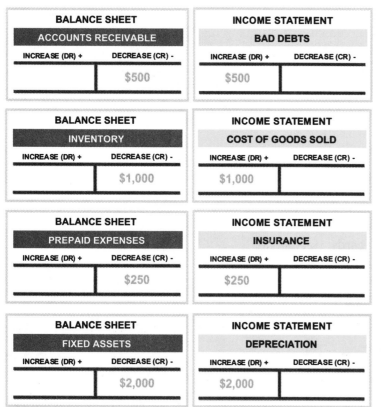

All of these transactions result in a decrease to the Net Worth of the business and must be matched to the related revenue for the same period.

Scenarios #1 and #2: You have learned that expenses must be recognized when the expense occurs, which may not be the same time the expense is paid. In other words, either cash decreases or debt increases, decreasing Net Worth (Owner's Equity). In accounting terms this means that the expense must be recognized in the time period in which it occurs and matched to the related revenue.

Scenario #3: Any other asset that decreases in value also decreases Net Worth (a decrease in Net Worth is called an expense).

Cost of Goods Sold (COGS)

When you sell merchandise there are two distinct pairs of transactions:

One is visible - because we tend to focus on revenue and cash

One is invisible - because we do not actually see it

1. First the **visible** - imagine a customer walking into your store and buying $1,000 worth of clothing. You will record this *visible* pair of transactions just like before. When the customer gives you cash you will **increase** cash and ring up the cash register, thereby increasing sales (writing an invoice).

2. Now for the **invisible** - one does not tend to see this expense. Visualize the customer walking out of the store with the goods. Your inventory will **decrease** in the amount that you *paid for it*. In other words, you will decrease inventory by $500 and increase the cost of the goods that you sold (Cost of Goods Sold) by $500.

Here is the logic: When you sold the goods for $1,000 you did not make $1,000 in profit. You made a profit of $500 ($1,000 minus what you paid for the goods). In other words, your asset was converted to an expense the moment you used it.

Step 1: VISIBLE transaction
Record the sale of the product:

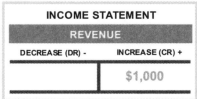

Logical sequence:

1. The visible = increase cash (or accounts receivable) and increase revenue.

2. The invisible = decrease inventory (which decreases Net Worth) and increase COGS.

If you did it the other way around it would be called theft! (It is unlikely the customer would leave with the goods and then come back and pay for them later.)

Step 1: VISIBLE transaction
Decrease inventory and increase COGS in the amount you paid for the product:

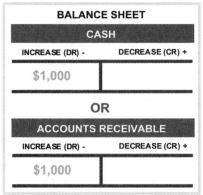

When you examine the balance sheet, the transactions can be seen from another point of view. Here is an example:

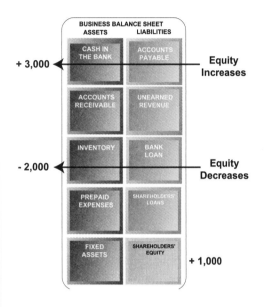

You manufacture widgets and are currently holding a number of them in inventory, at a cost of $2,000.

Step 1: The customer pays you $3,000 in cash for the widgets.

Step 2: The inventory leaves the warehouse, decreasing equity in the amount the widgets cost you.

Summary: The net result to equity is the difference between the value of the sale and what the widgets cost.

Here is a summary of the change to Net Worth (Shareholders' Equity) on the income statement:

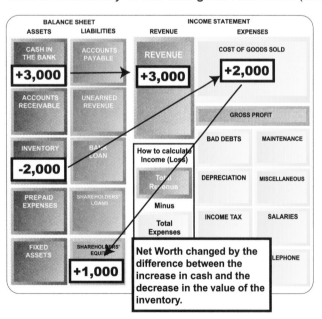

Cash Revenue

- Cost of Goods Sold

= Gross Profit (which contributes toward operating expenses and ultimately to net profit)

When the goods leave the warehouse, the value of the asset decreases in the amount that **it cost,** which of course decreases equity. The value of the sale is **matched** to the cost of the goods, resulting in the Gross Profit contribution. You will notice that there is no cash transaction when the cost of the goods is recognized.

Note: Gross Profit relates to the difference between the value of the goods sold and what it costs. Gross Margin represents the percentage of Gross Profit divided by the sales value. In other words, the gross margin represents what percentage of the sales value is left to pay for all the other operating expenses.

Recap: When merchandise is sold the revenue from the sale does not represent profit. To assess how much profit was actually made, the cost of the goods must be deducted from the selling price. In other words, the COGS is **matched** against the related revenue in the same period *or* we are **recognizing** the expense in the period in which it occurred.

Example:

Operating expenses of the business

1. Travel	$100
2. Business cards	100
3. Flyers for advertising	300
4. Temporary rental space	200
Total Operating Expenses	**$ 700**

Every business has various monthly operating expenses that will occur regardless of services or products being sold. The sale of merchandise (less what it cost) must contribute towards these expenses (Gross Profit).

Let's say you sell 200 shirts

Total sales (200 x $7.00)	$1,400
Less cost of the shirts (200 x $5.00)	1,000
= Gross Profit	**400**
Less Operating Expenses	700
= Profit (Loss)	**($300)**

There is insufficient **Gross Profit** to pay for the operating expenses

Remember that these t-shirts may have been purchased and paid for months before. We are now *recognizing* (matching) the cost of the shirts against the value of the sale.

We have to sell more shirts to make more Gross Profit in order to cover expenses.

Let's say you sell 350 shirts

Total sales (350 x $7.00)	$2,450
Less cost of the shirts (350 x $5.00)	1,750
= Gross Profit	**700**
Less Operating Expenses	700
= Profit (Loss)	**$ 0**

Therefore, you have to sell 350 t-shirts to break even (revenue = expenses)

Let's say you sell 500 shirts

Total sales (500 x $7.00)	$3,500
Less cost of the shirts (500 x $5.00)	2,500
= Gross Profit	**1,000**
Less Operating Expenses	700
= Profit (Loss)	**$ 300**

You have now made sufficient GROSS PROFIT to cover expenses resulting in an operating profit of $300

In other words: the Cost of Goods Sold is calculated by recognizing the cost of the goods deducted from the selling price of the goods at the time the goods are sold.

You already know that revenue less expenses equals a profit or loss. It is therefore crucial to record revenue in the period in which the product is delivered, which must then be **matched** to the related expenses in the same period.

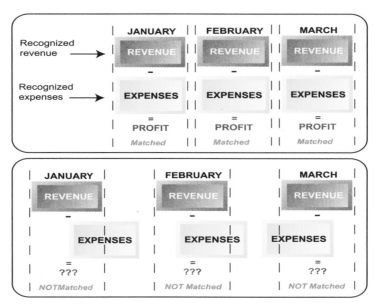

This is called the **Matching Principle.**

Unless revenue is matched to the related expenses in the same time period, it is impossible to assess accurate profitability, which may result in inappropriate business decisions.

If you cannot measure it, you cannot manage it!

Gross Profit

You have already learned that cash in the bank has little to do with a profit or loss, so in the absence of an accurate Profit & Loss statement (income statement) it would be almost impossible to manage your business affairs responsibly. There is nothing stopping you from recording all expenses in one big expense section of your income statement. The problem is that it will be difficult to identify exactly which elements of your business are creating profits or causing losses.

It is therefore prudent to separate the **direct** cost of sales (also called *variable expenses*) from all other expenses to enable the manager to evaluate the amount of profit made each month through the direct sale of the product or service. The **gross profit** generated from the sale is used to pay for all other **fixed** expenses.

Later on in this course we will talk about the impact of discounting, product mix and other factors that can influence gross profit.

Variable versus Fixed Expenses

Variable costs are those that *vary* with the volume of production or sales.

Example #1:

You have a clothing store. Your fixed monthly expenses are $5,000 (including rent, electricity, insurance, etc.). If you do not have any sales for the month then you will not have variable expenses (i.e. cost of the clothes). You will, however, still need to pay the $5,000 in fixed expenses.

Selling $15,000 worth of clothing, that cost you $8,000 (variable), would leave a gross profit of $7,000. This gross profit amount would then be used to pay for the fixed costs of $5,000.

Example #2:

You own a small printing business. Your variable expenses include paper, ink and other consumable products required to complete jobs. During the holiday season you close down your business, which of course means that you will have no sales. You will not have any variable expenses during this time, but you will still need to pay all the fixed monthly costs such as rent and electricity.

In other words, no production or sale = no variable expenses.

Operating Expenses

To support your basic needs in your personal life you need to spend a certain amount of money each month (for rent, car payments, food, insurance, etc.). These expenses should be measured against your monthly income to ensure that your revenue exceeds your expenses, failing which you will need to *get a grip* on your spending habits, or make sure that you can increase your revenue so that you can afford to support your expenses. **If your expenses exceed your revenue for any length of time you will eventually find yourself in financial trouble.**

A business is no different. For a business to survive, it is crucial to ensure that revenue exceeds expenses and that the business maintains accurate financial statements that match revenue to expenses in the same period. If it has been established during the course of the year that the business is not making a profit, the manager can be proactive and do something about it. (There are lots of solutions, such as cutting unnecessary costs, increasing prices, changing product mix, etc.) **In short, the financial statements act as a scoreboard to help management make appropriate business decisions.**

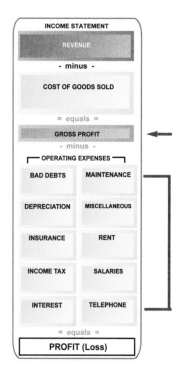

In a merchandise business, various operating expenses are separated from the cost of the merchandise. These expenses include items such as rent, utilities, payroll, printing and commissions. The higher the expenses, the lower the profit, **meaning that the business needs to generate more gross profit to cover the additional expenses.**

An increase in operating expenses requires an increase in gross profit.

It is also important to understand that there are lots of ways that a business configures the income statement (Profit & Loss). Here are some examples of typical layouts:

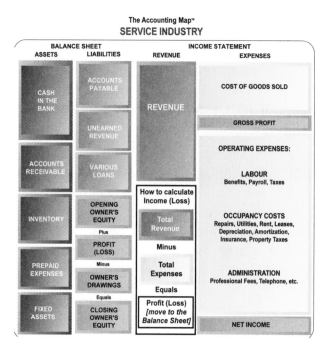

The Accounting Map™
MANUFACTURING INDUSTRY

The Accounting Map™
MANUFACTURING INDUSTRY - with EBITDA

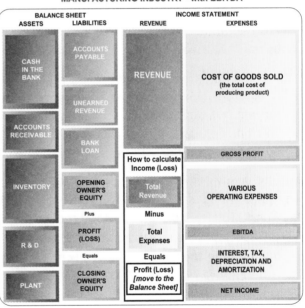

The Accounting Map™
RESTAURANT INDUSTRY

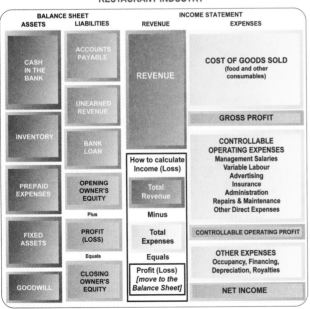

Corporate Fraud - GAAP Rules

What is the Net Worth of your business and are your financial statements reporting the truth?

Matching revenue to expenses in the same period is one of the most important GAAP rules and is often the cause of either business failure or business fraud.

Corporate fraud has repeatedly made the headlines in past years. The *Sarbanes-Oxley Act* was enacted in response to a wave of corporate scandals. It aims to prevent future fraud by holding management more responsible for the accuracy of financial statements and corporate financial reporting.

Fraud costs U.S. businesses more than $600 billion annually, based on estimates from *The Association of Certified Fraud Examiners* (ACFE) in its *Report to the Nation*. Fraud probably occurs in any organization, and one may not be able to totally eliminate it except to minimize the risk. Action is necessary because the ACFE figures that U.S. organizations lose more than $9 per day, per employee, to fraud. This represents about 6% of their total annual revenue. More than half the fraud incidents involve losses of at least $100,000 and one in six cause losses exceeding $1 million.

Here are some examples of typical situations which challenge GAAP and ethical issues:

Sherron Watkins was Enrons Vice President for Corporate Development - this is a copy of her memo to Enron's chairman Ken Lay in August 2001:

I am incredibly nervous that we will implode in a wave of accounting scandals. My eight years of Enron work history will be worth nothing on my résumé, the business world will consider the past successes as nothing but an elaborate accounting hoax. **Skilling** *is resigning now for 'personal reasons' but I would think he wasn't having fun, looked down the road and knew this stuff was unfixable and would rather abandon ship now than resign in shame in two years.*

Is there a way our accounting guru's can unwind these deals now? I have thought and thought about a way to do this, but I keep bumping into one big problem - we booked the **Condor** *and* **Raptor** *deals in 1999 and 2000* [this means that they recognized the revenue as earned]*, we enjoyed wonderfully high stock prices, many executives sold stock, we then try and reverse or fix the deals in 2001, and it's a bit like robbing the bank in one year and trying to pay it back two years later. Nice try, but investors were hurt, they bought at $70 and $80 a share looking for $120 a share and now they're at $38 or worse. We are under too much scrutiny and there are probably one or two disgruntled 'redeployed' employees who know enough about the 'funny' accounting to get us in trouble.*

[Source: "Text of Letter to Enron Chairman After Departure of Chief Executive." The New York Times. January 16, 2002.]

Extract of an article by *Price Waterhouse Cooper* accountants:

*What do **Enron**, **Woldcom**, **Adelphia**, **Ahold** and **Parmalat** have in common? These are all scandals, where senior executives intentionally presented inaccurate financial information and made incorrect statements to the capital markets. Accounting fraud and accounting errors differ based on the intent of those producing financial information. For example, if revenues are unintentionally misstated and misrepresented to the market, this is considered an accounting error and not accounting fraud. On the other hand, if there is intent to mislead, involving the use of deception to obtain an unjust or illegal advantage, then this qualifies as accounting fraud.*

The most common methods of fraudulent financial reporting are:

- Overstating revenues and assets;
- Understating costs, expenses and liabilities;
- Manipulating the timing of when transactions are recorded or events are recognized;
- Incorrectly measuring or estimating the effects of transactions or events;
- Misapplying Generally Accepted Accounting Principles ("GAAP"); and
- Misrepresenting or omitting information material to users of financial information.

Why fraud matters:

Financial reporting fraud generally causes large losses in shareholder value and erodes trust in capital markets. Various U.S. regulatory agencies pursue financial frauds. The U.S. *Securities and Exchange Commission* (SEC), *Department of Justice* (DOJ), state attorneys and class-action lawyers all have a vested interest in pursuing cases of fraud and ensuring that it does not recur. Local European regulators are closely following the U.S. model. A review of regulatory actions over the past five years shows that there is a significant correlation between SEC, DOJ and class actions. The SEC conducts investigations and brings civil enforcement actions in connection with possible violations of securities laws and SEC rules and regulations (Rule 10b-5). The DOJ and U.S. state attorneys investigate and prosecute persons and corporations for acts that are considered a crime under U.S. federal and state laws. Class-action lawyers look at decreases in shareholder value or private litigant losses and attempt to recover these monies from corporations and individuals. As shareholder losses tend to be very large in accounting fraud cases, this triggers large settlements: the class-action settlements for *Ahold*, *WorldCom*, *Enron* and *Cendant* all exceeded $1 billion.

Ethics with GAAP in relation to small business:

Example:

You have a rennovation business and specialize in kitchens. You financed the business with some friends and family to whom you should report your financial results from time to time.

It takes about three months on an average to complete larger jobs, during which time you have to pay for workers, materials, etc. You receive prepayments from your customers at various stages of the work.

It would be fairly easy to report the prepayments as profits without matching the costs to the "revenue", which would indicate to your stakeholders that you were making a great profit. This might entice them to invest more money into your business without realizing that you could, in fact, be losing money. Of course this reported result cannot be sustained and it would only be a matter of time before the company went out of business, causing you to lose your investment together with the investments made by your friends and family.

Good business sense:

Notwithstanding the ethical issue relating to accurate financial reporting, managers need to know if they are selling their product and service for more than it costs them. To assess this properly accurate financial records must be maintained by bookkeepers. These accurate records can be used to help managers make appropriate decisions.

The Rule of Materiality

When should you regard a payment (or debt) as an asset versus an expense? Remember that when an item is regarded as an asset, it does not change the value of equity at that time. Conversely, when it is regarded as an expense it results in a decrease to equity. **The rule of materiality is largely dependent on judgment.**

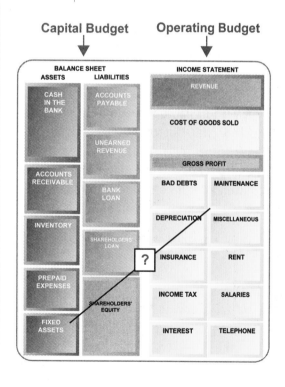

If the item purchased provides value for more than a year, it might be regarded as an asset. However, if the item is only worth say $50, then the value is immaterial and it should be regarded as an expense. Is $2,000 a lot of money? It depends on who you talk to and what was purchased. To a small business a $2,000 computer is regarded as a lot of money and would most likely be regarded as a capital asset. The same computer purchased by a large corporation, with assets totaling $50 million, would probably be considered an expense.

Owner's Drawings

In a proprietary business, when an owner draws cash for personal use there is a decrease in the Owner's Equity account.

A business can often make a profit but have insufficient cash for the owner to draw (remember that a profit does not guarantee cash in the bank). There are various reasons for this lack of cash such as the owner spending too much cash on purchasing new equipment, or the business not collecting Accounts Receivable.

Instead of drawing cash an owner may use various services or products of the business for personal use. Either way, this is regarded as a personal drawing against the Owner's Equity account. The reason drawings are not regarded as a business expense is twofold:

1. **Taxes:** Higher expenses result in a lower profit and lower taxes. If a business owner allocates personal drawings to a business expense the tax obligation of the business is decreased. This also provides tax-free benefits to the owner, which is not allowed by the tax authority.

2. **Responsible bookkeeping:** Allocating various personal expenses to a business would indicate that the expenses are higher than they actually are, resulting in numerous problems (including incorrect decisions by the owner, based on incorrect information).

In a corporation, however, Owners' Drawings do not come from Owners' Equity, but can be taken in two ways: draw as salary like any employee; or draw cash from the Shareholders' Loans, like any lender.

Scenario #1:

Scenario #2:

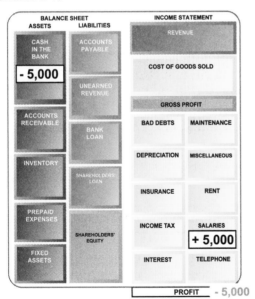

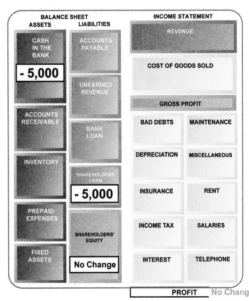

In Scenario #1 the owner will pay tax on the salary, but in Scenario #2 the money withdrawn is not subject to income tax because the owner is simply being paid back for a loan originally provided to the company. Sometimes a bank can insist on certain conditions that may not allow the owner to withdraw from Shareholders' Loans. (We will discuss this further in the Financial Analysis chapter.)

Notes

AME | Learning

Exercises: Chapter 6

Exercise #1

FIXED VS. VARIABLE EXPENSES

Place an 'x' under the *fixed* or *variable* column to describe what type of expenses these are:

	Description of Expense	Fixed	Variable
1	Rent		
2	Depreciation		
3	Manager's salary		
4	Paper used in printing		
5	Direct labour in manufacturing		
6	Cost of sand when building roads		
7	Overtime when manufacturing product		
8	Electricity		
9	Legal and accounting fees		
10	Cost of carton to ship product to customers		

Exercise #2

GROSS PROFIT VS. GROSS MARGIN

Gross Profit is an actual dollar amount:

Revenue - COGS

Gross Margin is the % of revenue remaining after deducting COGS:

$$\frac{\text{Gross Profit}}{\text{Revenue}} \times 100$$

For example:

Revenue	$ 80.00
COGS	60.00
Gross Profit	20.00
Gross Margin	25% (20 ÷ 80 x 100)

Calculate the Gross Profit and Gross Margin for the list below. *We have completed an example for you.*

	Cost Price	Selling Price	Gross Profit $	Gross Margin %
	4.00	**10.00**	**$6.00**	**60.00%**
1	12.55	15.00		
2	35.00	45.00		
3	155.00	187.00		
4	0.86	1.00		
5	1,350.00	1,520.00		
6	93.00	101.00		
7	576.00	627.00		
8	9.95	10.50		
9	6.00	9.00		
10	15.25	18.95		

Exercise #3

REVENUE RECOGNITION

Complete the following transactions on the worksheets provided below.

Transactions:

1.	Deposit an advance payment from a customer	$5,000
2.	Sell your services for cash	3,000
3.	Bill customer for services rendered - they will pay next month	5,000
4.	Recognize unearned revenue as earned (this was paid in advance)	2,000
5.	Pay various cash expenses	6,000

T-Account Worksheets:

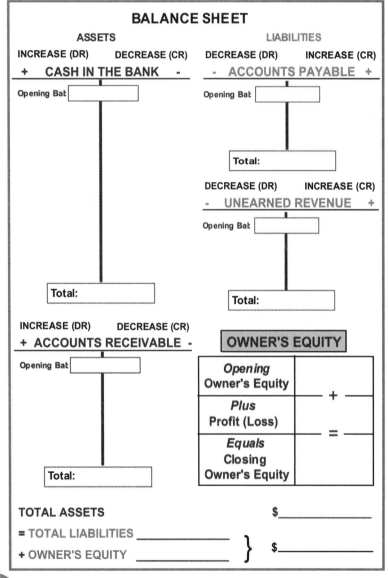

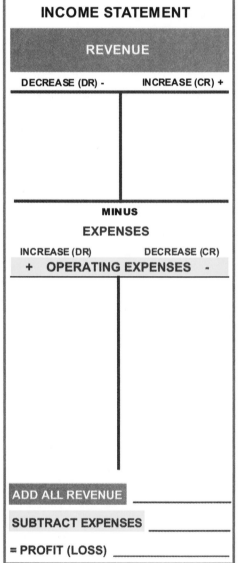

Exercise #4

EXPENSE RECOGNITION

Complete the following transactions on the worksheets provided below.

Transactions:

1.	Sell your services for cash	$10,000
2.	Prepay insurance for the year in advance	6,000
3.	Pay cash for miscellaneous expenses	1,500
4.	Bill advertising charges to the company credit card	2,000
5.	Recognize prepaid insurance for the month	500

T-Account Worksheets:

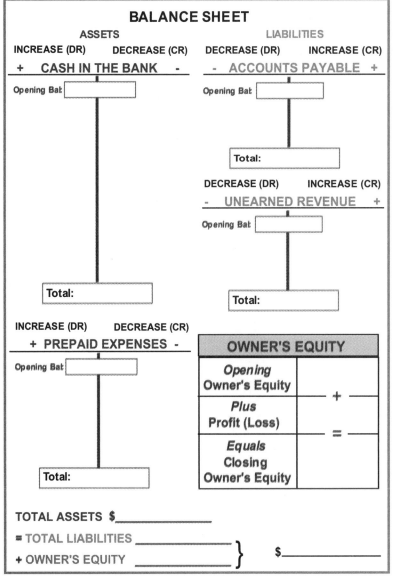

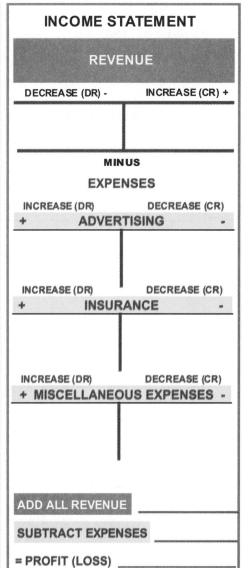

Exercise #5

COST OF GOODS SOLD

Complete the following transactions on the worksheets provided on the next page. *Note the opening balances on some accounts.*

Transactions:

1.	Buy inventory - record the bill to be paid next month	$35,000
2.	Sell product - customer will pay you next month	30,000
3.	Recognize the COGS for the $30,000 in product sold	18,000
4.	Pay wages and benefits	5,000
5.	Bill advertising expenses to the company credit card	3,000
6.	Pay rent for the month	2,000
7.	Record a bill received for maintenance - to be paid next month	1,000
8.	Collect accounts receivable and deposit the cash	2,000

Once you have completed the worksheet, explain why the bank balance is different to the profit.

_____

_____

_____

_____

_____

_____

_____

_____

_____

_____

_____

_____

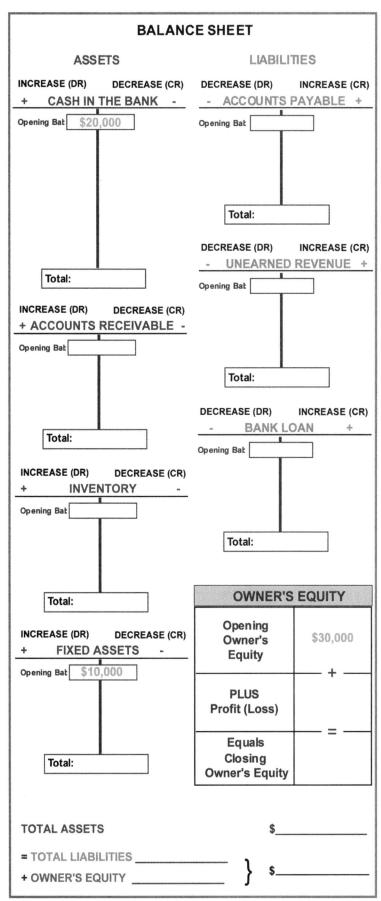

BALANCE SHEET

ASSETS

INCREASE (DR) +   **DECREASE (CR)** -
CASH IN THE BANK

Opening Bal: $20,000

Total:

INCREASE (DR) + **ACCOUNTS RECEIVABLE** -

Opening Bal:

Total:

INCREASE (DR) +   **DECREASE (CR)** -
INVENTORY

Opening Bal:

Total:

INCREASE (DR) +   **DECREASE (CR)** -
FIXED ASSETS

Opening Bal: $10,000

Total:

LIABILITIES

DECREASE (DR) -   **INCREASE (CR)** +
ACCOUNTS PAYABLE

Opening Bal:

Total:

DECREASE (DR) -   **INCREASE (CR)** +
UNEARNED REVENUE

Opening Bal:

Total:

DECREASE (DR) -   **INCREASE (CR)** +
BANK LOAN

Opening Bal:

Total:

OWNER'S EQUITY

Opening Owner's Equity	$30,000
PLUS Profit (Loss)	+
Equals Closing Owner's Equity	=

TOTAL ASSETS $_____

= TOTAL LIABILITIES _____

+ OWNER'S EQUITY _____ } $_____

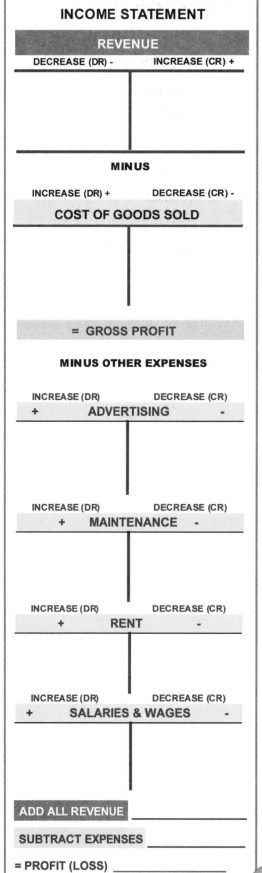

INCOME STATEMENT

REVENUE
DECREASE (DR) -   **INCREASE (CR)** +

MINUS

INCREASE (DR) +   **DECREASE (CR)** -
COST OF GOODS SOLD

= GROSS PROFIT

MINUS OTHER EXPENSES

INCREASE (DR)   **DECREASE (CR)**
+ **ADVERTISING** -

INCREASE (DR)   **DECREASE (CR)**
+ **MAINTENANCE** -

INCREASE (DR)   **DECREASE (CR)**
+ **RENT** -

INCREASE (DR)   **DECREASE (CR)**
+ **SALARIES & WAGES** -

ADD ALL REVENUE _____

SUBTRACT EXPENSES _____

= PROFIT (LOSS) _____

179

Exercise #6

COGS AND REVENUE RECOGNITION

Enter the new cash balance and Owner's Equity value for each transaction. Write either the "+" or "_" amount or "no change". *We have completed an example for you.*

	TRANSACTION	Change to Cash Balance	Change to Owner's Equity
	Record cash sales of $3,000 (COGS is $2,000)	+ 3,000	+ 1,000
1	Sell product for $10,000 (cost is $8,000) - customer will pay next month		
2	Sell services for $600 cash		
3	Give away $400 worth of product for free		
4	Deposit unearned revenue of $1,000 from a customer		
5	Recognize $500 of unearned revenue as earned		
6	Refund a deposit of $600 from a customer because you were not able to deliver the product as promised		
7	Sell product for $6,000 (cost is $4,000) - the customer pays $1,000 now and promises to pay the balance next month		
8	Collect $500 in Accounts Receivable owing from a customer		
9	Sell services for $1,000 - the customer prepaid this amount to you last month		
10	Sell product for $800 that cost you $600 - the customer pays cash		

Exercise #7

MATERIALITY

Would you regard the following items as material (asset) or not material (expense)? Check the correct answer.

	TRANSACTION	Material	NOT Material
1	Your business has assets worth $20,000. You purchase a new hard drive for $200.		
2	Your business records expenses in the amount of $100,000 each year. Prepay $1,000 for a trade show, which is taking place next year.		
3	Buy a new high definition T.V. for your home. How would you record this on your *personal* financial statements?		
4	Your company owns 4 trucks and you need to repair one of them for $3,000.		
5	Add 4 new tires to all your trucks.		
6	Enhance all 6 of your computers in the office with new monitors for $500 each.		
7	Buy new software for your computers at the office and charge $1,200 to your credit card.		
8	Pay $6,000 in leasehold improvements for the office - these improvements are expected to last for the next 3 years.		
9	Prepay insurance for 12 months in the amount of $3,000.		
10	Buy a large supply of CD's to do back-ups - the purchase amounts to $800.		

Exercise #8

CHANGES IN CASH VS. EQUITY

Place 'x' under the correct column to show whether the following transactions cause an increase, decrease, or no change to the bank balance and equity. Also enter the new cash balance and Owner's Equity value after each transaction. We have completed an example *for you*.

Transaction	Amount	Bank Balance				Equity			
		Increase	Decrease	No Change	Cash Balance	Increase	Decrease	No Change	Equity Balance
Opening balances					$0				$0
Deposit share capital	$1,000	x			1,000	x			1,000
1 Transfer personal funds (Shareholders' Loans)	120,000								
2 Deposit bank loan	60,000								
3 Purchase fixed assets	140,000								
4 Prepay insurance for 12 months	6,000								
5 Deposit unearned revenue	15,000								
6 Buy raw materials - pay next month	60,000								
7 Pay direct labour to assemble product	12,000								
8 Pay indirect labour costs	2,000								
9 Pay cash for manufacturing portion of rent	3,000								
10 Record depreciation of machinery	2,000								
11 Pay for other manufacturing expenses	4,000								
12 Recognize unearned revenue as earned	10,000								
13 Record maintenance fees (pay next month)	7,000								
14 Sales on account (will collect next month)	90,000								
15 Record the Cost of Goods Sold	72,000								

AME Learning

Practical Insights

Practical Insights

The This section covers the topics of sub-ledgers and sales taxes. We start off with sub-ledgers, and how they are used to control receivable, payables, and other accounts. Sales taxes are covered on page 188.

CONTROLLING RECEIVABLES & PAYABLES

Subsidiary ledgers are designed to ensure that assets are protected and records are accurate. Before the advent of computers, financial statements were referred to as "the books" of a business. This term arose as the financial records of a business were comprised of a number of recordkeeping books such as:

1. General journal for special period end adjustments
2. Sales journal to record all sales
3. Purchase journal to record all purchases
4. General ledger to record the balances of all income statement and balance sheet accounts
5. Accounts Receivable ledger to record the balances owed by each customer
6. Accounts Payable ledger to record how much is owed to each separate vendor
7. Cash book to record all cash transactions

The above-mentioned "books" are typically the minimum requirements in a small business. Larger businesses would traditionally use many more types of books such as payroll journals, etc.

In today's modern environment of computers and the availability of off-the-shelf accounting software, many of these traditional books have been eliminated as most functions are automatic in standard accounting packages. Here are some examples of automation:

1. **Entering a sale:** Select the sales section of the program. When the value of the sale is entered, the system will usually request what type of sale (consulting, product type, etc). Once entered, the system will automatically debit Accounts Receivable while crediting sales, resulting in a balanced entry.

2. **Purchasing a machine:**
   a. Select the section under "purchases".
   b. Enter the name of the vendor.
   c. Enter the amount.
   d. When selecting the item that you purchased (the machine), the system will debit (increase) machines (assets) and automatically credit (increase) Accounts Payable.
   e. When paying the account, select the account that needs to be paid. As you are processing cheques, the system will credit cash and automatically update Accounts Payable.

Subsidiary ledgers must be balanced with control accounts. If the sum of the individual ledger accounts is not equal to the control account, an error has occurred and must be corrected. Subsidiary ledgers are a form of detective control. Detective controls are designed to find errors or irregularities after they have occurred.

Subsidiary ledgers protect assets by confirming that Accounts Receivable are properly accounted for and can similarly be used to confirm that Accounts Payable (liabilities) are correctly recorded.

For example, a manager may want to know how much product was purchased from a particular supplier, over what time period, when it was paid for, what discounts were allowed for early payment, etc. To access this information, an individual account should be maintained for each supplier, handled in the same way as a general ledger account. The ledger, which records the individual activities for each account payable, is called the **Accounts Payable Subsidiary Ledger**. The total of all the closing balances for each account in the Accounts Payable Subsidiary Ledger is copied into the Accounts Payable **General Ledger**.

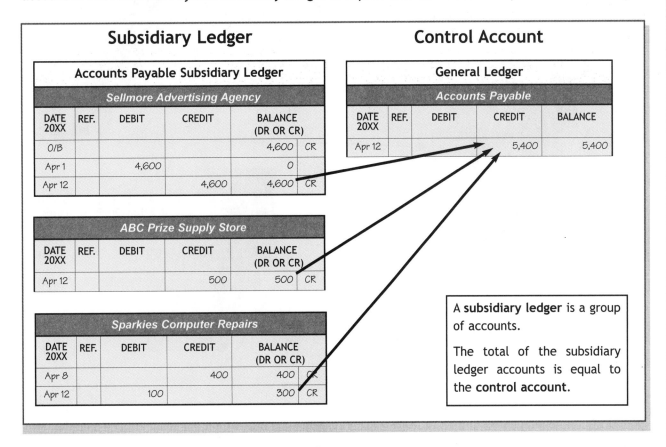

Subsidiary Ledger

Accounts Payable Subsidiary Ledger

Sellmore Advertising Agency

DATE 20XX	REF.	DEBIT	CREDIT	BALANCE (DR OR CR)	
O/B				4,600	CR
Apr 1		4,600		0	
Apr 12			4,600	4,600	CR

ABC Prize Supply Store

DATE 20XX	REF.	DEBIT	CREDIT	BALANCE (DR OR CR)	
Apr 12			500	500	CR

Sparkies Computer Repairs

DATE 20XX	REF.	DEBIT	CREDIT	BALANCE (DR OR CR)	
Apr 8			400	400	CR
Apr 12		100		300	CR

Control Account

General Ledger

Accounts Payable

DATE 20XX	REF.	DEBIT	CREDIT	BALANCE
Apr 12			5,400	5,400

A **subsidiary ledger** is a group of accounts.

The total of the subsidiary ledger accounts is equal to the **control account**.

There are different subsidiary ledgers and journals to control the various activities, e.g. inventory, cash, sales, etc. We are only addressing the Accounts Payable and Accounts Receivable ledgers.

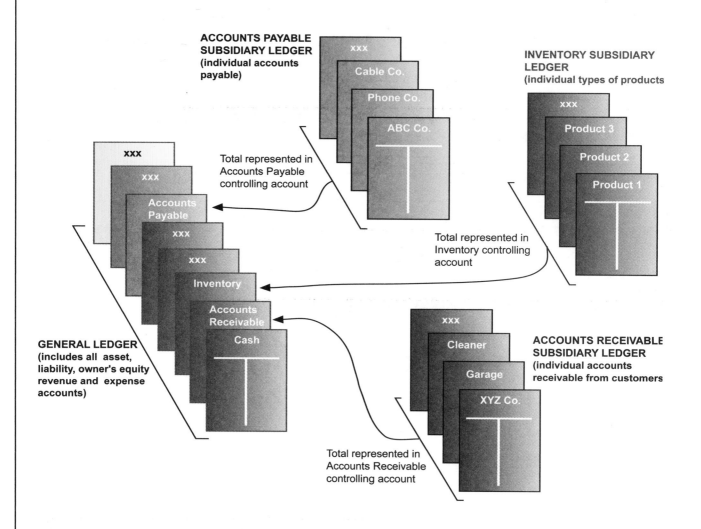

ACCOUNTS PAYABLE
SUBSIDIARY LEDGER
(individual accounts
payable)

INVENTORY SUBSIDIARY
LEDGER
(individual types of products

xxx
Cable Co.
Phone Co.
ABC Co.

xxx
Product 3
Product 2
Product 1

Total represented in
Accounts Payable
controlling account

Total represented in
Inventory controlling
account

xxx
xxx
Accounts
Payable
xxx
xxx
Inventory
Accounts
Receivable
Cash

xxx
Cleaner
Garage
XYZ Co.

GENERAL LEDGER
(includes all asset,
liability, owner's equity
revenue and expense
accounts)

ACCOUNTS RECEIVABLE
SUBSIDIARY LEDGER
(individual accounts
receivable from customers

Total represented in
Accounts Receivable
controlling account

An example of an Accounts Receivable ledger and an Accounts Payable ledger are as follows:

ANALYZE RECEIVABLES   X

Customer Report - all customers

	Customer	Total	0-30	31-60	60-90	90+
⇨	Slo-Pay Joe	5,950.00	5,350.00	600.00		
⇨	On The Ball Inc.	50.00		50.00		
⇨	Better Late Ltd.	1,720.00			1,720.00	
⇨	Way Past Due Corp.	570.00				570.00
	Total	8,290.00	5,350.00	650.00	1,720.00	570.00
	Aging percent	100%	65%	8%	21%	7%

This drills down to detailed analysis per customer below.

Detailed Customer Report - by customer: **Slo-Pay Joe**

	Invoice #	Amount	0-30	31-60	60-90	90+
⇨	122222	4,470.00			3,900.00	570.00
⇨	122255	900.00		900.00		
⇨	122280	300.00	300.00			
⇨	122262	280.00	280.00			
	Total	5,950.00	580.00	900.00	3,900.00	570.00
	Aging percent	100%	10%	15%	66%	10%

This drills down to each invoice.

ANALYZE PAYABLES   X

Supplier Report - all vendors

		Total	0-30	31-60	60-90	90+
⇨	Ironman Weekly	1,400.00	800.00	600.00		
⇨	Bell Canada	200.00	100.00	100.00		
⇨	Jean the Cleaning Machine	160.00	80.00	80.00		
⇨	Visa	1,120.00	860.00			260.00
	Total	2,880.00	1,840.00	780.00	0.00	260.00
	Aging percent	100%	64%	27%	0%	9%

This drills down to detailed analysis per customer below

Detailed supplier report by vendor: **Ironman Weekly**

	Invoice #	Date	Amount	0-30	31-60	60-90	90+
⇨	00465	October 11 2006	400.00	400.00			
⇨	00493	October 18 2006	400.00	400.00			
⇨	00494	September 25 2006	600.00		600.00		
⇨	00495		0.00				
	Total		1,400.00	800.00	600.00	0.00	0.00
	Aging percent		100%	57%	43%	0%	0%

SALES TAXES

Sales taxes are the means by which governments raise money to pay for the amenities we all enjoy, for example: roads, firehalls, garbage pickup, military protection, etc. Various levels of government may charge sales taxes. In Canada, sales taxes are charged by the federal government, and most provincial governments. In the United States, some cities also charge a local sales tax.

The various governments require vendors to charge sales taxes on items sold or services provided. The vendors subsequently remit (send) the sales taxes collected to the appropriate government body. The government pays the vendor a minimal commission for collecting the sales tax.

Not all sales are subject to sales tax. The seller must be familiar with the various rules and regulations, and charge the appropriate tax as stipulated in the laws that govern the collection of sales taxes.

The sales taxes collected are a liability owing to the government, and must be accounted for when recording each sale.

Provincial sales taxes (PST) are a tax on consumers. When the product is sold to the final customer, the tax is charged, collected from the customer, and remitted to the government. Transactions at the wholesale and manufacturing level are exempt from tax. To avoid paying taxes at this level, retailers must have a sales tax number. A retailer purchasing goods from a wholesaler would provide the sales tax number to the wholesaler to notify the wholesaler that tax should not be charged on the transaction. When the retailer subsequently sells the goods, the retailer charges the tax to the ultimate customer. Each Canadian province has its own rate of tax. The administration of PST requires a PST payable account.

The federal sales tax is called the Goods and Services Tax (GST). GST is a value-added tax, and is charged at each level of a transaction. For example, when a manufacturer buys raw materials from a supplier, the supplier charges the manufacturer GST. When the manufacturer sells the finished goods, the manufacturer charges the wholesaler GST. When the wholesaler sells goods to a retailer, the wholesaler charges the retailer GST. And when the retailer finally sells the product to the customer, the retailer charges the customer GST. It would appear that GST is charged at ever-increasing amounts, however, the GST system allows those further down the line (manufacturer, wholesaler, retailer) to recover the GST paid. The method by which this is done will become clear by following the example that follows. The administration of GST requires both a GST Paid, and a GST Collected account.

In the provinces of New Brunswick, Nova Scotia, and Newfoundland and Labrador, GST is combined with the provincial sales taxes. The resulting tax is called Harmonized Sales Tax (HST).

Example:

For this example, assume that the vendor is located in British Columbia, where the provincial sales tax rate is 7%. The current GST rate is 6%. GST is not charged on GST.

The vendor buys a product for resale, for cash, from a wholesaler for $100 on November 16, 2007.

The required Journal Entry is as follows:

GENERAL JOURNAL

DATE: 20XX	ACCOUNT TITLE AND EXPLANATION	GL NO.	DEBIT	CREDIT
November 16	Inventory		$100	
	GST Paid		$ 6	
	Cash			$106
	Purchase of item for resale			

Note that there is no PST charged on this transaction. That is because the transaction is at the wholesale level. The purchaser, a retailer, will have to state the PST number (and show the PST license) to the wholesaler in order to avoid paying the PST.

On November 23, the purchaser sells the inventory item (the product) at retail to a customer for $200 cash.

GENERAL JOURNAL

DATE: 20XX	ACCOUNT TITLE AND EXPLANATION	GL NO.	DEBIT	CREDIT
November 23	Cash		$226	
	Cost of Goods Sold		$100	
	GST Collected			$ 12
	PST Payable			$ 14
	Inventory			$100
	Sales			$200
	Item sold for $200 (cost $100)			

This time, both GST and PST are collected. PST is collected, because the retailer customer does not have a Sales Tax License, and the sale is to the final customer. GST is charged on sales at all levels.

At a later date, usually the following month for large companies, and quarterly for the smallest companies, the seller must send the tax collected to the government. First, let's look at how PST is handled. The PST owing is paid on the 15th of the month following collection.

GENERAL JOURNAL

DATE: 20XX	ACCOUNT TITLE AND EXPLANATION	GL NO.	DEBIT	CREDIT
December 15	PST Payable		$ 14	
	Cash			$ 14
	Payment of PST collected in November			

After the PST is paid, the balance in the PST Payable account is zero.

For the GST, the seller pays the government the difference between the GST Collected, and the GST Paid.

GENERAL JOURNAL

DATE: 20XX	ACCOUNT TITLE AND EXPLANATION	GL NO.	DEBIT	CREDIT
December 15	GST Collected		$ 12	
	GST Paid			$ 6
	Cash			$ 6
	Payment of GST owing for November			

After the GST is paid, the balances in both the GST Collected, and the GST Paid accounts are zero. If it occurs that more GST was paid than collected, the federal government would owe the seller.

As an interesting side note, some dishonest persons have taken advantage of the fact that sometimes the federal government will have to pay a seller. These people reported phoney purchases and sales to the federal government, showing a balance due to the seller. The government then issued a cheque to the fraudsters. The fraud amounted to millions of dollars!

Chapter 7

Adjustments, Depreciation and AFDA

ADJUSTMENTS, DEPRECIATION & AFDA

▶ Adjustments
▶ Bad Debts - Allowance for Doubtful Accounts (AFDA)
▶ Methods of Depreciation

Adjustments

Remember the **GAAP** rule? *How much is the net worth of the business and does it reflect the truth?*

Financial statements need to be adjusted to reflect the true Net Worth of a business. There are several types of adjustments, however, for operational purposes (the *big picture*) there are 2 types of adjustments to care about:

1. **Adjusting assets (eg. recognized as expenses) and liabilities (eg. recognized as revenue)** according to the *matching principle*. This relates in part to GAAP, which requires that revenue be matched to the related expenses in the same period. These adjustments impact Owner's Equity.

2. **Adjusting accounts.** This relates to re-allocating to the correct account - correct account coding for management purposes. These adjustments *do not* impact Owner's Equity.

Month-end adjustments

The accrual accounting system requires that revenue should be matched against the related expenses in the same accounting period. These include all cash and non-cash transactions. However, there are certain transactions that are not recorded on a day-to-day basis. For example, various fixed assets such as furniture, computers, motor vehicles, etc. will depreciate in value over a period of time. To assess the true financial position of the business at the end of a period it is necessary to record the depreciation expense for that period. This is a typical non-cash expense (decrease fixed assets and increase expense). The completion of this transaction is called a *journal entry*, which is typically recorded prior to the closure of the income statement at the period end.

Here are some examples of adjustments:

Adjusting assets to match revenue to expenses.

Recognizing a prepaid expense as an expense:

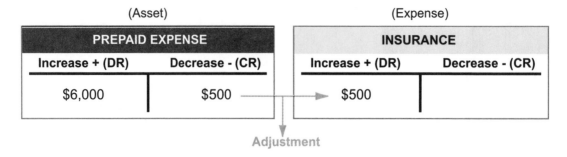

	(Asset)			(Expense)	
	PREPAID EXPENSE			**INSURANCE**	
Increase + (DR)		Decrease - (CR)	Increase + (DR)		Decrease - (CR)
$6,000		$500	$500		

Adjustment

Typical expense recognition adjustments:

Balance Sheet Account	Income Statement Account
Accounts Receivable →	Bad Debts
Fixed Assets →	Depreciation
Inventory →	COGS
Goodwill →	Amortization

Recognizing unearned revenue as earned:

(Liability)

UNEARNED REVENUE	
Decrease - (DR)	Increase + (CR)
$6,000	$10,000

(Revenue)

REVENUE	
Decrease - (DR)	Increase + (CR)
	$6,000

Typical revenue recognition adjustments (such as those that concern accounts receivable and cash) are not adjustments in the traditional sense, because they may not have been entered prior to the month or year end in the first place. These events might occur when the billing is not matched exactly in the time in which the work was done, resulting in the entry being completed at the end of a period to match the related expenses.

Typical expense recognition adjustments:

Balance Sheet Account	Income Statement Account
Unearned Revenue →	Revenue
Accounts Receivable →	Revenue
Cash →	Revenue

Adjusting accounts with no impact on Owner's Equity.

(Expense)

BASE PAYROLL	
Increase + (DR)	Decrease - (CR)
	$500

(Expense)

PAYROLL BENEFITS	
Increase + (DR)	Decrease - (CR)
$500	

In this example a payment was made to an employee and recorded as part of their regular pay instead of a benefit.

Bad Debts

From time to time it will become apparent that an account will not be collected:

· A newspaper notice states that the company is bankrupt.

· A longtime customer disputes an item and, as a goodwill gesture, you decide to ignore the amount.

· It will cost more in legal fees to collect the amount than the total amount receivable.

In such circumstances you must record the bad debt. The GAAP principle states that expenses are recognized as soon as possible. This in effect decreases equity, which of course is an expense (bad debt).

There are four possible scenarios relating to overdue accounts:

1. The money will definitely never be collected (eg. the company went bankrupt).

2. It is possible to be collected but unlikely (eg. the customer has serious financial issues and is waiting to see if they can raise finance to pay you and other suppliers).

3. You will likely not get paid because there is a dispute, in which case the sales should never have happened in the first place.

4. You will definitely get the money, but it's going to take time.

We will address each of these separately.

Scenario #1: The money will definitely never be collected

If, during the fiscal year, you know that you will not be able to collect monies owing to you, it is appropriate to *write off* the amount owing from the Accounts Receivable account. You will recall that when the account was created in the first place it increased Accounts Receivable, which is an asset account that subsequently increases the Net Worth of the business (the amount was recognized as revenue at the time). This amount owing has to be taken off Accounts Receivable, reducing Net Worth, which is called a **bad debt expense**.

This is the **Direct Method**

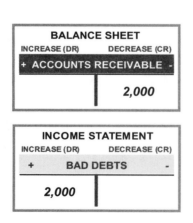

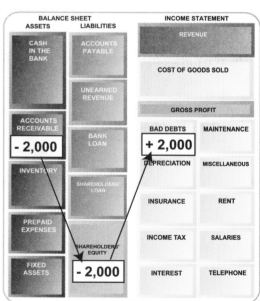

Scenario # 2: It's possible to be collected but unlikely.

Bad debts typically only surface months after a sale has occurred. Therefore, an *Allowance for Doubtful Accounts* account is used to estimate the bad debts in the same time period (the fiscal year) when the sale is recorded. This ensures that the bad debt expense is matched with revenue for the same period.

If a sale from, say, January turned bad and you had already completed the books for May, it would be impractical to go back and adjust the statements for January. This would also be an issue once you have completed the financial year-end. Sometimes, the sales that went bad could apply to several months of activities. In this event, how would you know in which month you should match the bad debt? To resolve this dilemma and to ensure that the Matching Principle is adhered to, the bad debts expense for the entire period is matched to the sales for the entire period.

The Allowance for Doubtful Accounts is a contra-asset account (for the technically inclined this is called a credit) and is deducted from Accounts Receivable on the balance sheet. This is the Indirect Method.

For example: Several customers owe a total of $100,000. Four of the customers may not pay you (they owe $5,000 in total), however, there is a small chance that you may get the money so you want to ensure that they remain on the Accounts Receivable list. The Accounts Recievable account therefore must remain with an increase (debit) balance. The separate asset account, the Allowance for Doubtful Accounts, always has a decrease (credit) balance thus the total asset value is decreased. When the asset account decreases (also decreasing Net Worth), the opposite entry will be to bad debt expense.

Write-off:

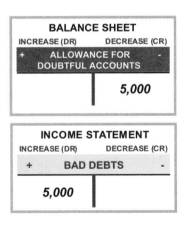

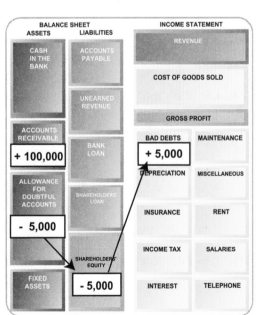

Subsequent collection of an amount previously written off:

Occasionally, after an amount has been written off, part or all of the amount will be collected (eg. when you turn the account over to a collection agency). Most collection agencies charge a large fee (sometimes more than 50%!) to collect an account. However, business owners take this in their stride on the basis that since they already wrote the amount off, and they didn't expect anything, any amount received is a bonus.

Under these circumstances, you remove the amount from the Allowance, **reinstate it in Accounts Receivable** and then record the amount received.

Assume that you receive $250 from the collection agency on the account of ABC company, which was previously written off (for simplicity we will ignore the collection fee).

First, reinstate the amount in Accounts Receivable:

Then record the cash receipt:

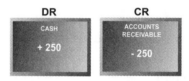

According to GAAP, it is important that the amount of Accounts Receivable reduction through the AFDA is supported with reasonable backup that these accounts may actually be uncollectable. Keep in mind that a bad debt expense decreases profits, which decreases tax.

  At some future date, once it is decided that the account wil never be collected, it must be taken off the Accounts Receivable sub-ledger. When this happens, Accounts Receivable is decreased and the AFDA contra account is increased (this will clear out the accounts).

The account is neutralized with no impact on Net Worth as it was already accounted for.

Scenario #3: You will likely not get paid due to a dispute.

In this case there is no bad debt, because the sale should not have occurred in the first place. The sale is simply reversed by decreasing Accounts Receivable and decreasing Revenue.

This is important because in many states and provinces various taxes are collected on behalf of the government. These will be given back to you if the sale is reversed, but will not be refundable if it is regarded as an expense.

Scenario #4: You will definitely get the money, but it's going to take time.

In this case there is no accounting entry ... you just wait it out.

Methods of Depreciation

In your personal life an asset can depreciate or appreciate according to market value. However, in a business there are rules that dictate how assets are depreciated.

The process of accounting (in both our personal lives and in business) helps us record the value of our assets as *accurately as possible*. Depreciation works the same way in business. Assets that you buy will lose their value over time. Different assets will last longer than others. For example: A computer might only last 3 years, whereas furniture may last 5 years. The reduction in value of these assets is called depreciation.

The cost of an asset less depreciation is called the *book value* of the asset. The market value of an asset represents the selling price of the asset. **Market value is not recorded on a balance sheet.**

According to GAAP the Net Worth of a business should always be presented in a conservative manner. A good example of this concept relates to the value of assets, which must always be recorded at the original price paid, less the accumulated depreciation. Assets are never recorded for more than they originally cost.

For example: A business buys a building for $100,000 and depreciates the property to a value of $60,000 after a number of years (only the building can depreciate and not the land itself). However, the true current market value of the property may be $300,000. The balance sheet can only record the value at $60,000. If the owner wishes to sell the property, the profit made (a gain) is considered income.

The market value of a business is usually different from the net *book value* of the business (assets less liabilities).

There are three methods for depreciation:

Straight-line - An accounting method in which a depreciable asset is depreciated by the same amount each year over a specified period of time.

Declining balance - This method allows for a depreciation rate to be applied against the non-depreciated balance remaining. Instead of spreading the cost of the asset evenly over its life, the asset is expensed at a constant rate, which results in declining depreciation charges in each consecutive period.

Units of activity - The cost of the asset is amortized over the expected number of units produced from the asset.

An example - using the straight-line method:

A cab driver owns a cab that he bought for $24,000, which records as an asset at the time of purchase. At the moment of purchase his Net Worth did not decrease. The expected useful life of the cab is about 5 years (60 months) - therefore he will use 1/60th of its value each month ($400 per month). He records an expense of $400 per month matched against the cab fare sales for the same month.

The transaction is as follows:

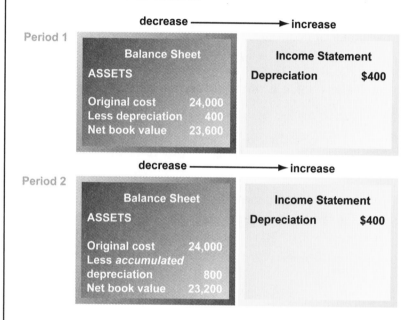

❶ Buy a taxi cab - no change to Net Worth this period.

❷ Expense some of the cab's value - poorer by $400 - no change to your bank balance this period.

The remaining $23,600 represents the remaining undepreciated value of the cab. This amount will be written off over future periods. (The undepreciated value does not represent the current market value of the cab.)

An example - using the declining balance method:

Under the declining balance method the cab driver will determine a consistent percentage rate of depreciation that will be applied each year to the non-depreciated portion of the cab. Let's say that the driver decides to use a rate of 25%. This means that in the first year the monthly depreciation expense will be $24,000 x .25 = $6,000 ÷ 12 months = $500. In the second year the driver will use the rate of 25% on the non-depreciated portion, which is $18,000 ($24,000 - $6,000 already expensed), making the monthly depreciation amount $375. In the third year the remaining non-depreciated value will be $13,500, making the monthly depreciation amount $281.25 ... and so on ...

An example - using the units of activity method:

In the case of the taxicab example, this method could relate to the cost of the taxi divided by the number of kilometers driven. In other words, when the asset is purchased, the driver estimates its life in terms of the level of activity. The driver assumes the cab is estimated to go 60,000 kilometers in its lifetime. He calculates a per-km depreciation rate: ($24,000 cost ÷ 60,000 kms = $0.40 per km. Each year, the driver will calculate the depreciation expense by multiplying the per-km rate by the actual activity level (the amount of kilometers driven).

Accumulated Depreciation

Of course you know that depreciation is an expense that decreases Owner's Equity (Net Worth). Your Accountant will advise you that you are obliged to reflect the assets according to the true value even though it makes your profits decrease. By how much must you depreciate your assets?

Accumulated depreciation is an example of a contra-asset account.

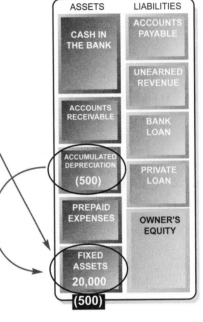

It has a credit balance (decrease) and is used to offset an asset account, to produce the proper balance sheet value for the asset. Depreciation is the expense that decreases the value of the related asset. Therefore, accumulated depreciation has a CREDIT balance (decrease), even though it is recorded as an asset.

Although the credit side of a depreciation entry could be recorded directly to the asset account, it is more efficient to record such credits in a separate company account. This way, the original cost and the total amount of depreciation can more easily be determined.

Accountants always like to know the original cost.

Each month the depreciation will accumulate, resulting in an increase to the accumulated depreciation contra-asset account. The balance sheet would look like this:

January

Fixed Asset (original value)	$20,000 (increase (DR))
LESS Depreciation	-500 (decrease (CR))
Asset value, net	$19,500

February

Fixed Asset (original value)	$20,000
LESS Accumulated Depreciation	-1,000 (last month + $500 for this month)
Asset value, net	$19,000

March

Fixed Asset (original value)	$20,000
LESS Accumulated Depreciation	-1,500 (previous months + $500 for this month)
Asset value, net	$18,500

It is traditional to report the original price paid for a fixed asset separate from the depreciation of the asset. The only time the fixed asset account will decrease is in the event of selling fixed assets. The accumulated depreciation account is an asset on the balance sheet, but is called a contra account because it is recorded in reverse to the fixed asset. Here is an example:

	Increase (DR)	Decrease (CR)
Buy machine on account		
Fixed assets	1,000	
Accounts Payable		1,000
Depreciate machines - year 1		
Depreciation expense	200	
Accumulated depreciation		200

The original debit balance of fixed assets always remains unchanged. The accumulated depreciation account is a contra balance sheet account, which in effect decreases assets resulting in a decrease to equity (called a depreciation expense).

Depreciate machines - year 2		
Depreciation expense	200	
Accumulated depreciation		200

The accumulated depreciation account is now $400 with no change to the original purchase value of $1,000 on the fixed asset account.

Depreciate machines - year 3		
Depreciation expense	200	
Accumulated depreciation		200

The accumulated depreciation account is now $600 with no change to the original purchase value of $1,000 on the fixed asset account.

Goodwill

This asset account will always remain at the value that was paid for the Goodwill, unless it is deemed to have been impaired, in which case the entry will be:

Goodwill impairment expense	500	
Goodwill (asset)		500

Unlike accumulated depreciation, the impairment is not accumulated. The goodwill account will simply say "net goodwill" and is explained in the notes to the financial statements.

Amortization of Loans

Amortization and depreciation are terms often heard in accounting discussions. Generally speaking, tangible assets are depreciated, and intangible assets are amortized. Recently the term amortization has become synonymous with depreciation and both terms are used interchangeably, however, the preferred usage is as explained above.

With reference to assets, depreciation/amortization is the process of allocating the cost of the asset over its useful life. Thus, each income statement reflects an expense equal to management's estimate of the portion of the asset that is used up in the year.

With reference to loans, amortization means reducing the amount of the loan. Normally, a payment is made each month to the loan company. The payment is enough to pay the interest on the loan, plus pay a portion of the loan principal (called a blended payment). Because each payment reduces the principal by a small amount, the interest paid gets smaller each month, and the principal portion becomes larger.

Ethical Issues

Accountant's responsibility: Many rules of accounting ethics are involved in the accountant's advice and warning. The accountant must be diligent in his practice. The accountant would obviously know the GAAP that must be applied. Also, the accountant must maintain integrity, both for himself and the profession. He could not advise his client to break the rules of GAAP. The accountant could even be liable to a lending bank under certain circumstances, if a loan was granted on the basis of misleading statements. Finally, accountants must not associate with clients they know or believe to be dishonest.

If the business owner were to ignore this advise from his accountant, the accountant would be obliged to drop him as a client. The owner would then have difficulty finding a new professional accountant for advice because of his lack of integrity.

Accounts Receivable:

Ethical Issue: Banks and other finance companies will often lend a business money based on the value of various assets, which include accounts receivable (the monies owed by customers). The accounts receivable are used as security in the event that the business does not pay loans back to the lender, in which case the lender will take possession of the accounts receivable and collect the money for themselves. An ethical issue arises when the accounts receivable are not collectable. In other words, you provided payment terms to the customer who has a poor credit history. What is the potential issue?

If you borrow money against the receivables, knowing that much of it is uncollectable, the value of the collateral will leave your lender with poor security causing them to lose what they loaned you. It is therefore important to record the accounts receivable debts that are unlikely to be collected.

Management Issue: You cannot manage your business properly if you do not know what it costs to operate. It is therefore important to record the potential non-collectable debts owing to you, which are regarded as an expense in the correct period to help you manage your customer credit risk responsibly and to assess the period's profitability.

Fixed Assets:

Ethical Issue: Consistent with borrowing money by using accounts receivables as collateral, banks and other finance companies will often lend money to a business based on the value of fixed assets (machines, furniture, computers, etc.). In other words, they may agree to lend you $10,000 based on the book value of assets of $30,000 [the book value is the cost less the depreciation]. However, if the asset has not been depreciated appropriately, or perhaps the asset is no longer even functional, then the asset might be worthless to the bank should they need to take your asset to cover your non-payment of the debt. Depreciating assets to reflect their true value is important to lenders using your assets as security. In addition to the value of the asset for lending purposes, lenders also want to know if you are profitable. Slowing down the depreciation process to reflect a higher asset value will lesson the costs and will falsely increase the value of the business.

Management issue: Fixed assets are used to make profits and therefore the cost of the asset must be matched to the revenue that is generated. For example: A cab is a fixed asset and is used to generate sales through its services. The cab will last for approximately 5 years, which means that the cab is being "consumed" over the five-year period. A business operator needs to know how much profit is being made month-to-month and year-to-year, so it is important to ensure that the cost of the asset [such as the cab] is depreciated appropriately.

Exercises: Chapter 7

Exercise #1

METHODS OF DEPRECIATION

Using the **straight-line method** of depreciating assets, complete the following chart:

	Years of Depreciation: 5	Cost of Asset: $20,000
	Depreciation Amount	Book Value of Asset
Depreciation - Year 1		
Depreciation - Year 2		
Depreciation - Year 3		
Depreciation - Year 4		
Depreciation - Year 5		

Exercise #2

METHODS OF DEPRECIATION

Using the **declining balance method** of depreciating assets, complete the following chart:

	% Rate of Depreciation: 20%	Cost of Asset: $20,000
	Depreciation Amount	**Book Value of Asset**
Depreciation - Year 1		
Depreciation - Year 2		
Depreciation - Year 3		
Depreciation - Year 4		
Depreciation - Year 5		
Depreciation - Year 6		
Depreciation - Year 7		
Depreciation - Year 8		
Depreciation - Year 9		
Depreciation - Year 10		

Exercise #3

METHODS OF DEPRECIATION

Using the units of activity method of depreciating assets, complete the following chart:

Cost of the asset	$20,000
Units expected to be produced	100,000
Cost per unit	

Salvage Value

In some cases, assets may not be depreciated to zero because they will always have some value. In this event, the asset will be depreciated by the cost less the salvage value. The salvage value is the estimated value of an asset at the end of its useful life (or its remaining value after depreciation).

For example, if an asset costs $20,000 and the salvage value is deemed to be $2,000, then the asset is only depreciated by $18,000.

According to your judgment, over what period of time should the following assets be depreciated and what do you think the salvage value should be, if any?

Asset	Original Value of Asset	Years of Depreciation	Salvage Value
Computer	$2,000		
Automobile	$35,000		
Photocopier	$12,000		
Mobile Home	$110,000		
Snowmobile	$8,000		
Stereo system	$5,000		
Leather Sofa	$2,000		
Lawnmower	$600		

Exercise #4

BAD DEBTS

Financial figures for *Easy Business Incorporated*:

Results for 2008

Sales for the year	$200,000
COGS	150,000
Operating Expenses	20,000
Accounts Receivable	40,000

It is now March 2009 and your accountants are finalizing your financial statements for the year ended December 2008. It is anticipated that approximately $2,000 of receivables may not be collected.

How much net profit will be reflected for the 2008 financial year once this anticipated loss is recorded?

$_____

Explain your answer:

_____

_____

_____

_____

_____

_____

_____

_____

_____

_____

_____

_____

_____

_____

_____

_____

_____

Notes

AME | Learning

Chapter 8
Inventory Systems and Shrinkage

INVENTORY and SHRINKAGE

▶ Inventory Systems
▶ Shrinkage & COGS Valuation

Inventory Systems

There are several ways to calculate the value of inventory on-hand and the Cost of Goods Sold (COGS). The value of inventory on-hand is determined according to the evaluation method. The preferred method is often determined by the industry. The four methods of valuing inventory are:

WAC — Weighted Average Cost

This is the simplest method of valuing inventory. Using this method, the value of *Finished Goods* is calculated by dividing the **cost** of the units available for sale by the **total number of units** available for sale to get an average per-unit cost. In large factories, with millions of units and with similar unit costs, it may be impractical and unnecessary to value each unit individually. If management decides that a more accurate inventory valuation is immaterial, the company can save time and money by using this crude method. The major disadvantage is that WAC is not as precise as some other valuation methods.

FIFO — First In First Out

Imagine loading a vending machine from the back. The first unit placed in the machine will be the first unit sold to a customer. This **first unit sold** is from the **beginning inventory.** The value of the units remaining at the end of the period will equal the value of the units that the vendor purchased last.

LIFO — Last In First Out

Now imagine loading a vending machine from the front. The first unit placed in the vending machine will be the last unit sold to a customer. Unless the machine runs out of stock, that last unit will sit there forever! The first unit sold will be the most recent purchase (by the vendor), and the value of the goods on hand at the end of the period will be the value of the units that were purchased first (including the beginning inventory). In-transit goods purchased FOB shipping point (you own them even though they haven't arrived) are assumed to be sold under the LIFO method.

LIFO is the least used valuation method. This is because the older the inventory is, the less accurate its true value will be. Despite this inaccurate valuation on the balance sheet, LIFO will give you the most accurate value of COGS on the Income Statement because it assumes that the most recently purchased items were sold.

Specific Identity

Specific Identity is the most accurate valuation method. It requires the use of a perpetual inventory system, in which each unit sold can be tracked by product tag (also called a SKU). Although Specific Identity exactly matches costs and revenue, it is relatively more costly to implement and maintain.

The accounting entry for the purchase of goods is as follows:

Description	Increase	Increase
Inventory	950	
Accounts Payable		950

Purchased inventory on credit (on account)

When an independent trucking company ships the goods and bills you for the service, you need to complete another transaction:

Description	Increase	Increase
Inventory	50	
Accounts Payable		50

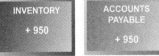

Paid for shipping of inventory

Notice that the inventory has increased by $1,000 in total.

FOB (Free On Board): More often than not, a vendor excludes shipping costs when quoting the price of a product, even though the buyer will have to pay for those shipping costs. The term used for this condition is **FOB Shipping Point**. When the vendor includes the cost of the shipping in the price, the term used is **FOB Destination**.

FOB Shipping Point (Buyer Pays)	Carrier	FOB Destination (Seller Pays)

	Ownership transfers when goods passed to	Transportation costs paid by
FOB Shipping Point	Carrier	Buyer
FOB Destination	Buyer	Seller

Shrinkage & COGS Valuation

Shrinkage is the term used to describe a reduction in inventory due to theft, obsolescence, spoilage, etc. The Cost of Goods Sold (COGS) includes the units sold and the units lost due to shrinkage.

What causes shrinkage, how do you know if it exists, and how is it recorded?

- If inventory is missing, you need to correct your records. The goods that are missing were purchased for the purpose of resale and need to be recorded as the cost of goods (not sold). You will decrease Inventory to reflect the correct value of the merchandise remaining in your warehouse. The transaction is: decrease Inventory and increase Cost of Goods Sold.

- The increase in COGS decreases Gross Profit, which then contributes less towards operating expenses and has a negative impact on operating profit.

- Putting things into perspective: 1% shrinkage relative to revenues does not seem significant, but if you are only making a 5% profit, for example, 1% represents 20% of your profit. Always compare an improvement to the bottom line, not to revenues.

- Some examples of shrinkage are theft, goods signed for and not received, spoiled goods, incorrect inventory count, etc.

How do you know how much inventory was used?

1. Start with opening inventory for the period.
2. Add all purchases for the period (do not forget to include in-bound shipping costs and all other expenses relating to the cost of the goods).
3. Deduct closing inventory for the period.

The result equals the amount of inventory **used** for the period (Cost of Goods Sold).

Example:

		Results of $2,000 Shrinkage
Sales for the period	$200,000	$200,000
Opening Inventory	50,000	50,000
Add: Purchases for the period	100,000 Less	100,000 Less
	= 150,000	= 150,000
Deduct: Closing Inventory	40,000	38,000
Total Inventory used for the period (COGS)	= 110,000	= 112,000
Gross Profit for the period (revenue less COGS)	$ 90,000	$ 88,000
Gross Margin	$90,000 ÷ $200,000 (45%)	$88,000 ÷ $200,000 (44%)

Shrinkage cannot be identified without counting inventory and since shrinkage impacts Gross Margin, you really must count inventory. In the example on the previous page Gross Margin reduced from 45% to 44%, indicating that $2,000 worth of inventory was unaccounted for. This is due to shrinkage. **Changes in Gross Margin can only be discovered through the process of counting inventory.**

Inventory under/over statement

An overstatement or understatement of inventory can affect two years' of financial statements. Here is a simple example - assume that there is no opening inventory. The Cost of Goods Sold is calculated as follows:

Opening Inventory	$0
Purchases	500,000
Cost of Goods available for sale	500,000
Closing inventory	100,000
Cost of Goods Sold **1**	$400,000

Consider the following:

· If the closing inventory is overstated, is the cost of goods overstated, or understated?

· If the closing inventory is understated, is the cost of goods overstated, or understated?

You can figure out the answers by changing the closing inventory numbers. If closing inventory is overstated, you are deducting too much, and the COGS is understated. If the closing inventory is understated, you are not deducting enough, and the cost of goods sold is overstated.

The Cost of Goods Sold has an effect on Gross Profit and net income for the year. Let's see how:

Sales	$1,000,000
Cost of Goods Sold **1**	400,000
Gross Profit	600,000
Operating Expenses	300,000
Net Income	$300,000

If COGS is overstated, are Gross Profit and Net Income overstated or understated? You can determine this, as above, by changing the numbers. If COGS is overstated, you are deducting too much and the Gross Profit and Net Income will be too low (understated).

Since Net Income is carried forward to Owner's Equity, a mis-statement of inventory also has an effect on Owners' Equity. If Net Income is overstated, so is Owner's Equity. If Net Income is understated, Owner's Equity is understated.

Here is a table summarizing the preceding discussion:

Closing Inventory	Cost of Goods Sold	Gross Profit	Net Income	Owner's Equity
Overstated	Understated	Overstated	Overstated	Overstated
Understated	Overstated	Understated	Understated	Understated

Using the first row in the table above, let's examine the scenario: if the total inventory was $10,000 but was accidentally recorded as $12,000, it would indicate that the amount of goods that were sold was understated (second column). As a result, you would believe that less inventory was used for sales, resulting in an overstatement of Gross Profit, leading to an overstatement in Net Income, resulting in an overstatement of Owner's Equity. All because of one "minor" error.

The closing inventory for the current year is the opening inventory for the next year. The effects of the error would be reversed as follows:

Opening Inventory	Cost of Goods Sold	Gross Profit	Net Income	Owner's Equity
Overstated	Overstated	Understated	Understated	Understated
Understated	Understated	Overstated	Overstated	Overstated

If the inventory error is material, it should be corrected. If the error is small, you can ignore it. It will correct itself in the next year.

Periodic & Perpetual Inventory Systems

In a perfect world, inventory is recorded and matched against the related sales after each transaction. The inventory that remains after the sale represents inventory that is available for future sales. In other words, if you were to deduct the cost of the inventory sold from the opening inventory value, the remaining inventory value should equal what is actually available to sell.

Example:

Opening inventory	$10,000
Less inventory sold	6,000
= Closing inventory available to sell	**$ 4,000**

This represents the value that is recorded on the balance sheet.

Some businesses do not record the cost of the merchandise with each sale. So how would you know how much inventory was used for the related sales for the period? You will only know this by counting the inventory at the end of the period and calculating the cost of that merchandise. This is called a **periodic** inventory system. You would **periodically** count how much inventory is in stock.

Recording the cost of the inventory with each sale is called a **perpetual** inventory system. A perpetual inventory system requires a sophisticated computer system that can track the cost of the merchandise *each time it is sold*. This system is typically used in supermarkets, grocery stores or large department stores. Each item is bar-coded to enable the computer to record the value of the sale and the cost of the product at the same time. At the time of the transaction, the computer deducts the product and its cost from inventory, while updating revenues and recording the new inventory balance.

Determining how much inventory is unaccounted for requires a physical count under both the Periodic and Perpetual inventory systems.

Valuing the inventory on hand: If a business sold only one product and paid only one price for the entire period, the valuation of inventory would be easy. Most businesses, however, sell many types of products and may pay different prices for the same product in a single period.

Ethical Issues

Inventory

Ethical Issues: As with accounts receivable and fixed assets, banks will sometimes lend a business money against the value of inventory. The amount that they will lend the business will largely depend on the type of inventory. For example, if the business is a jewellers with valuable gold, diamonds and other precious stones, the bank may lend them 70% of the cost value of the inventory. However, if it is a fashion business, the bank may only lend 20% of the cost value of the inventory. Over-valuing inventory exposes lenders to higher risk.

Valuation of inventory: It is common for the value of inventory to decrease for various reasons. Some examples include:
- Fashion clothing that has gone out of style
- Food that is past its shelf life
- Spare parts being outdated (imagine trying to sell a *Pentium* 2 computer chip today!)
- Cell phones that are outdated

Valuing the original cost of inventory in the retail or distribution industries is quite easy because the cost is simply the invoice value (how much was paid for the items) plus the cost of shipping. In the manufacturing industry, however, it can be much more complicated and open for abuse.

If a manufacturer, for example, wishes to increase the cost of inventory, it is easy to increase the amount of expenses allocated to that cost. Management salaries could be included and *justified* as part of manufacturing. Or perhaps, various operating expenses could be included into the cost of the product, such as allocating more rent to manufacturing instead of to administration. Of course it is only a matter of time before this type of behaviour would catch up.

Recording inventory at its true value is a GAAP rule and ethically correct, especially when reporting financial statements to external stakeholders.

Management Issue: You cannot manage your business properly if you do not know what it costs to operate. It is therefore important to match the *true* cost of inventory against sales to assess gross profit, otherwise it would be impossible to know how much to charge for the product.

Notes

AME | Learning

Exercises: Chapter 8

Exercise #1

INVENTORY SYSTEMS

Complete the following charts to determine the total inventory used, the gross profit and gross margin.

1.

Item	Amount
Sales	$250,000
Opening inventory	120,000
Purchases for the period	30,000
Closing inventory	40,000
Total inventory used	
Gross Profit	
Gross Margin	

2.

Item	Amount
Sales	$150,000
Opening inventory	110,000
Purchases for the period	25,000
Closing inventory	42,000
Shrinkage	2,000
Total inventory used	
Gross Profit	
Gross Margin	

3. Explain the logic behind having to count inventory on a regular basis.

_____

_____

_____

_____

_____

_____

_____

_____

_____

_____

_____

_____

AME Learning

4. Explain the difference between a perpetual and a periodic inventory sytem.

_____

_____

_____

_____

_____

_____

_____

_____

_____

_____

_____

_____

_____

_____

_____

_____

_____

_____

_____

_____

_____

_____

_____

Notes

AME | Learning

Chapter 9

Statement of
Cash Flow

STATEMENT OF CASH FLOW

Statement of Cash Flow

The Statement of Cash Flow indicates the SOURCES of cash (where the cash came from) and USES of cash (what the cash was used for). **This document assumes that all transactions are cash instead of accruals (accruals are ignored).**

Why is a Statement of Cash Flow so important? In a perfect world all the profit on the Income Statement would result in an equivalent increase in cash. In reality, there are various activities that impact cash in the bank that are not related to profits.

A balance sheet and income statement are very useful documents, but they do not help the reader understand how cash was used or where it came from.

The cash flow statement commences with the opening balance of cash at the beginning of the period and assumes that all transactions are recorded on a **cash basis**. In other words, it ignores the accrual principle for this purpose.

You have already learned that there are three ways to generate cash in your personal life:

1. Ensure that revenue exceeds expenses (increases Net Worth)

2. Sell assets (no impact on Net Worth)

3. Borrow money (no impact on Net Worth)

Clearly number 1 is the only sustainable method of ensuring a positive cash flow. Remember that you will eventually run out of assets to sell and there is a limit to how much cash you can borrow.

A business works in exactly the same manner. There are three ways of generating cash into a business:

1. Ensure that revenue exceeds expenses (increasing Owner's Equity) - this is called **Cash Flow from Operations**

2. Buy or sell assets (no impact on Owner's Equity) - this is called **Cash Flow from Investments**

3. Borrow or repay loans (no impact on Owner's Equity) - this is called **Cash Flow from Financing**

Part 1 - Cash Flow from Operations

The calculation of cash flow from operations is as follows: commence with the opening cash balance and add profits. The profits include depreciation, which is a non-cash expense (meaning that it must be added back to the profits).

Example:		
	Opening Cash	**$10,000**
	Add Profits	2,000
	New Cash Balance	12,000
	Add Depreciation	500
	New Cash Balance	**$12,500**

The next step deals with the difference between current assets such as inventory, accounts receivable and prepaid expenses.

A *decrease* in accounts receivable means that customers have paid their outstanding accounts. This will cause an *increase* to cash.

An *increase* in inventory means that cash must have *decreased* because cash had to be used to pay for the inventory.

We then calculate the difference between the current liabilities (except loans, which fall into the finance section) such as accounts payable.

A *decrease* in accounts payable is due to a reduction in debt, which means that cash will also *decrease*.

Part 2 - Cash from Investments

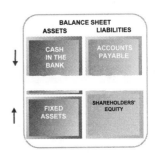

If fixed assets *increase* it means that cash *decreases* because cash had to be used to purchase the fixed assets. ⟶

Part 3 - Cash Flow from Financing

If bank loans *increase* it means that cash must also *increase*. ⟵

A word of caution regarding cash flow statements:

A Statement of Cash Flow can be quite misleading. For example: If you hold back payments to suppliers the cash flow statement will reflect that cash from operations has increased (an increase to debt results in an increase to cash). In reality, you did not generate more cash flow from operations, but instead you simply withheld payments to creditors. It is important to compare payments and accounts receivable collection trends with historical data to ensure that the timing is consistent.

Statement of Cash Flow - *Example*

Income Statement	Period 1	Period 2
Sales	$1,150,000	$1,270,000
Cost of Goods Sold	362,000	450,000
Gross Profit	788,000	820,000
Operating Expenses		
Administration charges	23,000	37,000
Advertising & marketing	62,000	68,000
Depreciation - fixed assets	36,000	30,000
Financing costs (interest)	6,000	5,200
Insurance	12,000	12,000
Labour and benefits	196,000	246,000
Management salaries	83,000	92,000
Occupancy (rent, cleaning, etc.)	120,000	120,000
Other operating expenses	72,000	73,000
Owner's drawings	100,000	70,000
Repairs & maintenance	32,000	23,000
Total Expenses	742,000	776,200
Net Operating Profit Before Tax	46,000	43,800
Tax	6,000	3,000
Net Profit (Loss) *added to Retained Earnings*	$40,000	$40,800

(2) Increased = more cash

(1)

Balance Sheet	Period 1	Period 2
Assets		
Current Assets		
Cash	$53,000	$12,800
Accounts receivable	30,000	10,000
Prepaid Expenses	12,000	12,000
Inventory	17,300	13,300
Total Current Assets	112,300	43,100
Fixed Assets		
Equipment	210,000	260,000
Less Accumulated Depreciation	-66,000	-96,000
Total Fixed Assets	144,000	164,000
Total Assets	$256,300	$207,100
Liabilities		
Current Liabilities		
Accounts Payable	$49,000	$9,000
Current portion of bank loan	20,000	20,000
Shareholders' Loans	30,000	5,000
Total Current Liabilities	99,000	34,000
Long Term Debt	40,000	20,000
Total Liabilities	$139,000	$54,000
Shareholders' Equity		
Opening Owners' Equity	$77,300	$117,300
Plus Profit for Current Period	40,000	40,800
Closing Shareholder's Equity	$117,300	$158,100
Liabilities + Equity	$256,300	$212,100

(9)

(3) Decreased = more cash

(4) Decreased = more cash

(6) Increased = less cash

(2) Increased = more cash (move to income stmt)

(5) Decreased = less cash

(8) Decreased = less cash

(7) Decreased = less cash

Add or subtract the increases or decreases from the balance sheet accounts

			New Cash Balance
Opening cash balance			$53,000
Cash Flow from OPERATIONS			
Add Net Profit Amount	①	40,800	93,800
Add Depreciation	②	30,000	123,800
Record the **change** in balance for the remainder:			
Change in Assets & Liabilities:			
Accounts Receivable	③	20,000	143,800
Prepaid Expenses		0	143,800
Inventory	④	4,000	147,800
Accounts Payable	⑤	(40,000)	107,800
Change in Cash due to OPERATIONS			**54,800**
Cash Flow from INVESTMENT			
Change in fixed assets	⑥	(50,000)	57,800
Change in Cash due to INVESTMENT			**(50,000)**
Cash Flow from FINANCING			
Owners' Drawings	⑦	(25,000)	32,800
Bank payment	⑧	(20,000)	12,800
Change in Cash due to FINANCING			**(45,000)**

SUMMARY	
Opening cash balance	**53,000**
Add cash from Operations	54,800
Deduct cash from Investments	(50,000)
Deduct cash from Financing	(45,000)
Closing cash balance	**12,800** ⑨
Total Change in Cash	**(40,200)**

① Net Profit amount

② Add back Depreciation: ($66,000) - ($96,000) = $30,000

③ Accounts Receivable: $30,000 - $10,000 = $20,000

④ Inventory: $17,300 - $13,300 = $4,000

⑤ Accounts Payable: $9,000 - $49,000 = ($40,000)

⑥ Change in Fixed Assets (Equipment): $210,000 - $260,000 = ($50,000)

⑦ Owners' Drawings (Shareholders' Loans): $5,000 - $30,000 = ($25,000)

⑧ Bank payment (long term debt): $20,000 - $40,000 = ($20,000)

⑨ Closing bank balance

Notes

AME | Learning

Exercises: Chapter 9

Exercise #1

Using the following income statement and balance sheet complete the Statement of Cash Flow on the next page.

Income Statement	Period 1	Period 2
Sales	$600,000	$650,000
Cost of Goods Sold	320,000	330,000
Gross Profit	280,000	320,000
Operating Expenses		
Administration charges	5,000	5,000
Advertising & marketing	5,000	6,000
Depreciation - fixed assets	10,000	12,000
Financing costs (interest)	6,000	5,000
Insurance	12,000	12,000
Labour and benefits	80,000	90,000
Management salaries	40,000	40,000
Occupancy (rent, cleaning, etc.)	10,000	10,000
Other operating expenses	40,000	50,000
Owner's drawings	20,000	30,000
Repairs & maintenance	12,000	13,000
Total Expenses	240,000	273,000
Net Operating Profit Before Tax	40,000	47,000
Tax	6,000	7,000
Net Profit (Loss) *added to Retained Earnings*	$34,000	$40,000

Balance Sheet	Period 1	Period 2
Assets		
Current Assets		
Cash	$2,000	$25,000
Accounts receivable	80,000	90,000
Prepaid Expenses	12,000	11,000
Inventory	60,000	70,000
Total Current Assets	154,000	196,000
Fixed Assets		
Equipment	150,000	180,000
Less Accumulated Depreciation	-26,000	-28,000
Total Fixed Assets	124,000	152,000
Total Assets	$278,000	$348,000
Liabilities		
Current Liabilities		
Accounts Payable	$40,000	$50,000
Current portion of bank loan	30,000	30,000
Shareholders' Loans	20,000	50,000
Total Current Liabilities	90,000	130,000
Long Term Debt	30,000	20,000
Total Liabilities	$120,000	$150,000
Shareholders' Equity		
Opening Owners' Equity	$124,000	$158,000
Plus Profit for Current Period	34,000	40,000
Closing Shareholder's Equity	$158,000	$198,000
Liabilities + Equity	$278,000	$348,000

Add or subtract the increases or decreases from the balance sheet accounts

	Add or subtract the increases or decreases from the balance sheet accounts	New Cash Balance
Opening cash balance	↓	$2,000
Cash Flow from OPERATIONS		
Add Net Profit Amount		
Add Depreciation		
Record the **change** in balance for the remainder:		
Change in Assets & Liabilities:		
Accounts Receivable		
Prepaid Expenses		
Inventory		
Accounts Payable		
Change in Cash due to OPERATIONS		
Cash Flow from INVESTMENT		
Change in fixed assets		
Change in Cash due to INVESTMENT		
Cash Flow from FINANCING		
Owners' Drawings		
Bank payment		
Change in Cash due to FINANCING		

SUMMARY	
Opening cash balance	
Add cash from Operations	
Deduct cash from Investments	
Deduct cash from Financing	
Closing cash balance	
Total Change in Cash	

Detailed Summary	Change in cash
Add net profit	
Add back depreciation (non-cash expense)	
Accounts Receivable	
Inventory	
Prepaid Expenses	
Accounts Payable	
Fixed assets	
Owner's Drawings	
Bank Loan	
Change in cash	

Exercise #2

STATEMENT OF CASH FLOW

For the following transactions, determine whether cash increases, decreases or stays the same.

	Transactions	Cash Increase	Cash Decrease	No Change to Cash
1	Profits increase			
2	Fixed assets decrease			
3	Prepaid expenses increase			
4	Bank debt increases			
5	Shareholders' Loans decrease			
6	Accounts Payable decreases			
7	Long term debt decreases			
8	Inventory decreases			
9	Prepaid expenses decrease			
10	Investment in shares increases			

Exercise #3

1. Name 3 ways to increase cash in a business and explain the impact of each on Owner's Equity.

   (1) _____

   _____

   _____

   (2) _____

   _____

   _____

   (3) _____

   _____

   _____

2. Why do you suppose that raising cash from selling investments is not the most desirable manner to increase cash flow?

   _____

   _____

   _____

   _____

   _____

   _____

   _____

   _____

   _____

   _____

   _____

   _____

   _____

   _____

Exercise #4

1.   Borrowing money to improve cash flow is called:

   a.   Cash flow from operations

   b.   Cash flow from financing

   c.   Cash flow from investments

2.   The purchase of assets has been recorded as:

   a.   Cash flow from operations

   b.   Cash flow from financing

   c.   Cash flow from investments

3.   Recording depreciation impacts which of the following:

   a.   Cash flow from operations

   b.   Cash flow from financing

   c.   Cash flow from investments

4.   Making a profit is recorded in which of the following sections of a cash flow statement:

   a.   Cash flow from operations

   b.   Cash flow from financing

   c.   Cash flow from investments

5.   Collecting accounts receivable in a timely manner impacts which of the following:

   a.   Cash flow from operations

   b.   Cash flow from financing

   c.   Cash flow from investments

6.   Reducing bank debt impacts:

   a.   Cash flow from operations

   b.   Cash flow from financing

   c.   Cash flow from investments

7.   Paying suppliers impacts:

   a.   Cash flow from operations

   b.   Cash flow from financing

   c.   Cash flow from investments

Chapter 10
Trade Math

Trade Math

▶ Mark-Up vs. Margin
▶ Discounting
▶ Up-Selling
▶ Performance Indicators

Mark-Up vs. Margin

Imagine if this piece of paper represents 100% revenue:

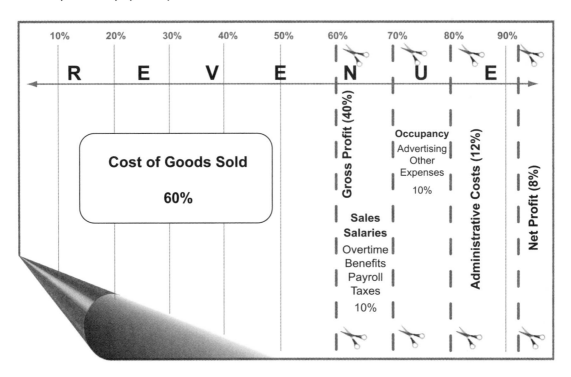

After *cutting away* expenses, the remaining piece represents profit. To increase profit, either revenue must increase, expenses must decrease or a combination of both.

To plan and monitor these improvements, it is necessary to measure both the hard currency amount of change and also the percentage (efficiency) of the change relative to 100% revenue. There are several profitability measurements that can be used, however, the primary profit drivers that should be understood are **mark-up** and **margin**.

A product must be sold for more than it costs to make a profit. There are two ways to calculate the amount of gross profit that is made.

1. *Bottom up:* adding dollars onto the cost of product to determine selling price is called **mark-up.**

2. *Top down:* determining how much profit is made for every dollar sold is called **margin.**

Calculating Mark-up

Example: You are in the business of buying and selling used computers, printers and other electronic equipment. Your business has to pay for various operating expenses such as rent, telephone, advertising and technical labour. Of course if you sell your product for the same amount you pay for it you will not make a profit and will soon be out of business.

So how much profit is required to cover your expenses and make sufficient profit so that you can earn a good living? For simplicity, let's assume that you only sell one type of product.

Facts that you know:

· Monthly operating expenses such as rent, salaries, insurance, etc. amount to $10,000

· You need $5,000 per month for living expenses

· Therefore you need to make at least $15,000 profit (gross profit) on the computers that you sell to support the business and your personal expenses

· The cost of the computers is $20,000

What should the mark-up be on the computers to ensure that you make sufficient profit?

Cost	20,000	the cost of the product
Gross Profit	15,000	the gross profit required
Selling Price	**35,000**	**selling price (add the cost to the required gross profit)**

By what percentage must the cost be marked up?

Cost	20,000	the cost of the product
Gross Profit	15,000	the gross profit required
Mark-up (GP ÷ cost)	**75%**	**% needed to mark-up the cost of the product**

Gross Profit (15,000) ÷ Cost (20,000) = 75%

Gross Margin

Gross margin is different from gross profit:

➲ Gross profit represents the actual profit generated on the sale of products (the hard dollar amount).
➲ Gross margin represents the percentage of gross profit relative to sales.

Example:

Sales	$100	
Cost	60	
Gross Profit	$ 40	
Gross Margin	40%	(GP ÷ Sales)

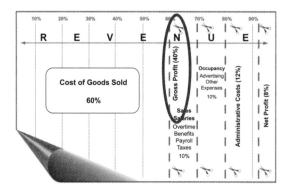

Imagine this piece of paper once again. Sales represent 100% and each expense that is *cut away* leaves a smaller percentage. If sales are, say, $1,000 representing 100% of the piece of paper and the cost of goods sold is $600 then there will be $400 left, which is the gross profit (40% gross margin).

Caution: Gross profit can increase in actual dollars while gross margin decreases and vice versa. Here are some examples:

	January	February	March
Selling Price	10,000	15,000	19,000
Cost	6,000	10,000	13,000
Gross Profit	4,000	5,000	6,000
Gross Margin	40%	33%	32%

Notice that sales and gross profit have increased significantly each month. However, gross margin percentage has decreased each month. While the actual dollars are increasing, a decrease to gross margin percentage can be very dangerous because it decreases the percentage of every dollar earned that must be used to pay general and administrative expenses.

Growth in sales is important, but you also need to generate profit.

	January	February	March	April	May	June
Selling Price	10,000	15,000	16,000	18,000	20,000	16,000
Cost	6,000	10,000	10,000	13,000	16,000	9,000
Gross Profit	4,000	5,000	6,000	5,000	4,000	7,000
Gross Margin	40%	33%	38%	28%	20%	44%
Mark-up	4,000	5,000	6,000	5,000	4,000	7,000
Mark-up %	67%	50%	60%	38%	25%	78%

Notice on this chart that sales have increased significantly from January to May, however, the gross margin has fluctuated with the lowest margin being in May and highest in June. The best performing month is June - both gross profit and gross margin increased. The last two rows indicate by what percentage the product needs to be marked up to achieve the desired margin percentage.

What causes a decrease to gross margin?

· Discounting

· COGS increases without increasing the price

· Shrinkage

· Paying for goods that were never received

· Administration errors such as incorrect inventory counting

In the next section, you will learn to calculate how much volume (e.g. the number of computers) you must sell to compensate for the loss of gross profit when discounting.

Discounting

It is very common for sales people or business owners to discount product or services to generate more sales. However: sales are not profits. Examine this chart:

	January	February
Revenue	30,000	40,000
Cost	18,000	32,000
Gross Profit	12,000	8,000
Operating Costs	6,000	6,000
Net Profit	6,000	2,000

· Sales increased significantly in February

· Gross profit decreased

· Operating expenses remained the same

· Net profit decreased

Business Case

Sheila owns a retail store that specializes in the sale of computers. In January she sold 15 computers for $1,500 each and made a gross profit of $7,500. She decided to discount the selling price by $200 to increase sales.

In February it appeared that Sheila's sales technique paid off because she sold 18 computers with increased gross sales from $22,500 to $23,400. On first impression she was doing well until she examined the gross profit, which decreased from $7,500 to $5,400. This in turn decreased the net profit by the same amount.

How many computers should Sheila have sold at the same discounted price to maintain the same $7,500 gross profit amount before discounting?

Answer: 25 computers - relating to an increase of 66.6%. If you examine the chart (next page), you will see that 25 computers at a sales price of $1,300 (discounted by $200) resulted in the same gross profit contribution ($7,500) as 18 computers sold at the higher price of $1,500.

	January	February Scenario #1	February Scenario #2
Number of computers sold	15	18	25
Cost per computer	1,000	1,000	1,000
Selling price per unit	1,500	1,300	1,300
Revenue	22,500	23,400	32,500
Cost	15,000	18,000	25,000
Gross profit	7,500	5,400	7,500
Operating costs	5,000	5,000	5,000
Profit	2,500	400	2,500

How to calculate the required volume increase

There are a few ways of calculating volume. The most common way of doing this is:

Discount $ amount ÷ New Gross Profit (after the discount)

Example: Your company sells shirts and you decide to discount the regular selling price of $100 by 10% in the hope of selling more volume to make more profit. How many shirts, at the discounted price, must be sold to maintain the same gross profit contribution before you can make more profit than the original $4,000?

100 shirts sold before discount 10% discount	Original	New	
Selling price per shirt	$100.00	$90.00	Discount of $10.00
Cost per shirt	60.00	60.00	
Gross Profit	40.00	30.00	New GP after discounting
% Increase in volume required		33.3%	Discount $ ÷ new GP
New quantity of product to be sold		133	Volume increase required
PROOF - Gross Profit before and after	$4,000	$4,000	Gross profit remained the same
Total sales value for the offering	$10,000	$12,000	Gross sales increased

Summary of the calculation:

Discount dollars	10% of $100 = **$10**
Gross profit after discount	$90 - $60 = **$30**
Discount $ ÷ new gross profit	$10 divided by $30 = **33% increase**
Add 33% to the original amount of 100 sold	= **133**

Up-Selling

Have you ever been to a fast food restaurant and been asked by the server if you would "like fries with that" or if you want to "make that a large drink for only 25¢ more". If so, you have experienced the art of **up-selling.**

Up-selling can have a serious positive impact on profits. We will use a restaurant model for this example.

Business case:

The *gross* profit per sale does not represent the *net* profit per sale, which of course includes all operating expenses. (For example, it would be impractical to allocate a portion of rent, insurance, etc. to each burger sale.) This model assumes that the net profit per sale is calculated by applying the net profit percentage per store to the average sale value. The gross profit of the up-sell is then added to this number, representing pure profit (operating expenses are already paid).

	Assumptions	A	
1	Net profit % for the restaurant	10.00%	
2	Invoice value of original sale	$20.00	
3	Selling price of up-sell (fries)	$1.00	
4	Margin of up-sell	70.00%	**B**
		Original Sales (pre-up-sell)	**Impact of Up Sell relative to original Net Profit**
5	Average invoice value (original sale) from assumptions	$20.00	$1.00
6	Margin of up-sell (from assumptions)		70.00%
7	Net % of profit per sale (from assumptions)	10.00%	
8	Total net profit of original sale in dollars	$2.00	$0.70
9	Total net profit of original sale + up-sell		$2.70
10	Net profit increase % after the up-sell		35%

Examining this model:

Row #1 represents the net operating profit for the business. In other words, if total sales are $100,000 then the profit is 10% = $10,000. That means that the net profit per meal, which includes all expenses such as rent, insurance, waiters, etc., also equals 10% of the sales value. If the sale of a meal is $20.00 then the net profit per meal is $2.00, after all expenses are accounted for (row 8).

If you were to up-sell a portion of fries for just $1.00 (row B5) and the profit margin is 70¢ (row B8), then the new profit for the meal is $2.70 (row B9), which increases from the original profit of $2.00. The increase of 70¢ on the original $2.00 is 35% (70¢ ÷ $2.00).

Performance Indicators

A doctor will use a thermometer to test the temperature of your body. If your temperature is elevated it does not necessarily mean that the doctor will know what's wrong, but it will indicate that you are sick and the cause must be investigated.

A business works on the same principle. The business thermometer is called **Key Performance Indicators (KPI's)** and financial ratios.

KPI's can be in three forms: (1) Financial; (2) Managerial; and (3) Qualitative.

Financial: These KPI's are called financial ratios and examples include Gross Margin, Net Profit, Working Capital Ratios and Days Sales Outstanding. These ratios are extracted from the financial statement numbers and indicate the financial health of the business.

Managerial: Sometimes only part of these managerial KPI's are extracted from the financial statements - they are not based purely on the financial numbers. Some examples include sales per person, sales per square foot of space, unit sales per month and number of meals served.

Qualitative: These measurements are not numerical - they are usually based on opinions. Some examples include customer satisfaction, employee satisfaction and delivery speed.

Each of the above indicators tell a different story and is used to improve business performance.

Examples of Key Performance Indicators for specific industries are:

Manufacturing:
Gross Profit Margin
Inventory Turnover
Days Sales Outstanding
Revenue per Labour Dollar
Labour as a Percentage of Sales
Material Waste
Product Reject Rate

Retail:
Sales per square foot of space
Labour Percentage to Gross Sales
Sales Value per Invoice
Number of Sales per Day
Customer Conversion Rate
Inventory Shrinkage
Overtime Worked

Restaurants:
Gross Sales
Average Invoice Value
Number of Patrons Served
Table Turnover
Payroll to Sales Percentage
Food Overage
Food Sales as a % of Beverage Sales

Hotels:
Occupancy Rate
Customer Satisfaction
Employee Staff Turnover
Maintenance as a % of Sales
Employee Salaries as a % of
   Gross Sales
Conference Fees to Total Sales

AME | Learning

Exercises: Chapter 10

Exercise #1

MARK-UP vs. MARGIN

1. You operate your own business and need to calculate the amount of gross profit needed to pay for all your operating expenses.

Selling price	100	60	80	50	300	500
Cost of product	30	30	60	20	200	400
Gross Profit						
Gross Margin						

2. Calculate the percentage of mark-up required on the product that you buy.

Monthly expenses	5,000	8,000	20,000	15,000	5,000	6,000
Salary needed	3,000	5,000	4,000	5,000	2,000	5,000
Gross profit needed						
Cost of product	20,000	15,000	24,000	40,000	20,000	15,000
Mark-up %						

Exercise #2

DISCOUNTING

1. Complete the following discount chart. You sold 1,000 pizzas before discounting - how many must you sell after the discount of 20% to maintain the same Gross Profit?

1,000 pizzas sold before discount 20% discount	Original	New
Selling price per pizza	$12.00	
Cost per pizza	4.00	
Gross Profit	8.00	
Gross Margin %	67%	
% Increase in volume required		
New quantity of product to be sold		
Gross Profit before and after		
Total sales value for the offering		

2. Complete the following discount chart. The discount amount is 10%. You sold 500 pairs of shoes before the discount. How many pairs of shoes must be sold to maintain the same gross profit contribution after discounting.

500 pairs of shoes sold before discount 10% discount	Original	New
Selling price per pair of shoes	$120.00	
Cost per pair	60.00	
Gross Profit	60.00	
Gross Margin %	50%	
% Increase in volume required		
New quantity of product to be sold		
Gross Profit before and after		
Total sales value for the offering		

Exercise #3

UP-SELLING

1. You operate a fast food restaurant and encourage your waiters to sell an extra portion of fries. Calculate how much more profit each meal would generate with the up-sell.

	Assumptions	A	B
1	Net profit % for the restaurant	6.00%	Impact of Up-Sell relative to original Net Profit
2	Invoice value of original sale	$10.00	
3	Selling price of up-sell (fries)	$1.00	
4	Margin of up-sell	70.00%	
		Original Sales (pre-up-sell)	Value of Up-Sell
5	Average invoice value (original sale) from assumptions	$10.00	$1.00
6	Margin of up-sell (from assumptions)		
7	Net % of profit per sale (from assumptions)	6.00%	
8	Total net profit of original sale in dollars	$0.60	
9	Total net profit of original sale + up-sell		
10	Net profit increase % after the up-sell		

2. You operate a retail store that sells shoes and shoe care products. Calculate how much more profit each sale would generate if you were to up-sell shoe care products with each sale.

	Assumptions	A	B
1	Net profit % for the retail store	10.00%	Impact of Up-Sell relative to original Net Profit
2	Invoice value of original sale	$100.00	
3	Selling price of up sell (shoe care products)	$5.00	
4	Margin of up-sell	50.00%	
		Original Sales (pre-up-sell)	Value of Up-Sell
5	Average invoice value (original sale) from assumptions	$100.00	$5.00
6	Margin of up-sell (from assumptions)		
7	Net % of profit per sale (from assumptions)	10.00%	
8	Total net profit of original sale in dollars	$10.00	
9	Total net profit of original sale + up-sell		
10	Net profit increase % after the up-sell		

AME | Learning

Chapter 11
Financial Analysis

Financial Analysis

Analyzing Statements

What is financial analysis and why is it so important?

Remember that financial statements represent a historical event. If you exclude the notes to the financial statements (which are usually only included in audited financial statements) the statements will not provide answers. The purpose of the analysis is to help the reader ask the appropriate questions and understand which issues need to be addressed. Keep in mind that no single ratio will be able to provide the complete story. It's much like a puzzle in that you need all the pieces to see the whole picture.

The sequence of the analysis:

1. Revenues are Vanity - The business may generate lots of revenue, but that does not guarantee profit.

2. Profits are Sanity - The business may generate lots of profit, but that does not guarantee liquidity.

3. Cash Flow is Reality - Increased sales and profits do not guarantee cash in the bank.

This theme is used as a logical sequence when analyzing the health of a business.

The Accounting Map™

ASSETS	LIABILITIES	REVENUE & EXPENSES
CASH IN THE BANK	ACCOUNTS PAYABLE	① VARIOUS SOURCES OF REVENUE
③	UNEARNED REVENUE	COST OF GOODS SOLD 60%
ACCOUNTS RECEIVABLE	BANK LOAN	GROSS PROFIT 40%
INVENTORY	SHAREHOLDERS' LOAN	VARIOUS OPERATING EXPENSES 20%
		EBITDA 20%
PREPAID EXPENSES	OWNERS' EQUITY	INTEREST, TAX, DEPRECIATION, AMORTIZATION 15%
FIXED ASSETS		NET INCOME 5% ②

XYZ Company
BALANCE SHEET

	Last Year	This Year
Assets		
Cash	$23,615	$65,465
Accounts Receivable	71,500	157,500
Prepaid Expenses	12,000	18,000
Inventory	68,956	134,500
Total Current Assets	**176,071**	**375,465**
Fixed Assets	65,611	102,500
Less Accumulated Depreciation	-27,000	-44,000
Total Assets	**$214,682**	**$433,965**
Liabilities		
Accounts Payable	$37,560	$184,905
Current Portion of Bank Loan	12,000	24,000
Shareholders' Loans	30,000	30,000
Current Liabilities	**79,560**	**238,905**
Long Term Loans	48,000	72,000
Total Liabilities	**$127,560**	**$310,905**
Shareholders' Equity		
Opening Owner's Equity	$34,500	$87,122
Profit	52,622	35,938
Closing Shareholders' Equity	**$87,122**	**$123,060**
Liabilities + Equity	**$214,682**	**$433,965**

XYZ Company
INCOME STATEMENT

	Last Year	This Year
Sales	**$615,562**	**$960,300**
COGS	340,500	552,500
Gross Profit	**275,062**	**407,800**
Operating Expenses		
Advertising	$12,625	$18,500
Bank charges	1,456	1,850
Legal and professional	1,652	2,650
Management salaries	60,000	97,650
Office supplies	1,365	1,560
Rent	21,000	21,000
Repairs and maintenance	1,500	3,357
Other salaries	89,500	158,000
Telephone	986	1,045
Total Operating Expenses	**190,084**	**305,612**
EBITDA	**84,978**	**102,188**
Interest	2,356	12,250
Depreciation	12,000	17,000
Operating Profit Before Tax	**70,622**	**72,938**
Tax	18,000	37,000
Net Profit	**$52,622**	**$35,938**

First Impression

Examine the income statement on the previous page and you will see that:

· Sales have increased

· Gross profit has increased

· Net profit has increased

· Cash has increased

What is your first impression? It looks good, however, you will get quite a different picture when you actually analyze these statements.

REVENUES ARE VANITY!

Sales increased by $324,738. While it seems like a large increase, this number has little meaning on its own. We need to examine various levels of profitability in relation to sales.

PROFITS ARE SANITY!

Gross Profit

Gross Profit ÷ Revenue = Gross Margin (%)

Gross profit increased by $212,000. It appears that the company is performing better than last year. However, you will recall that gross margin represents the percentage of revenue left to pay for all other expenses. *The higher the percentage the better.* When converting gross profit to a percentage of revenue you will see the difference.

This paper represents 100% of your revenue. ⟶

By cutting away the COGS of say 60% you are left with 40% of the paper - this represents gross margin.

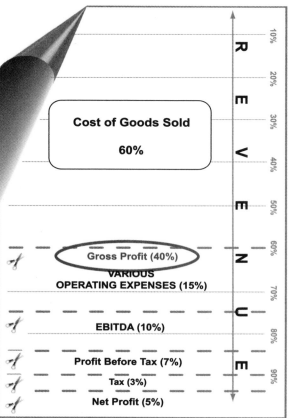

In other words, the less that is cut away relative to the whole piece pf paper (revenue), the more that remains (margin) to pay for all other expenses.

Gross Profit

	Last Year	This Year
Sales	$615,562	$960,300
COGS	340,500	552,500
Gross Profit	**$275,062**	**$407,800**
Gross Margin	45%	42%

Compared to 45% last year, there is only 42% of revenue remaining to pay for all other expenses.

A decrease in gross margin can be for various reasons:

▶ **Discounting** - can sufficient gross profit be sustained to cover costs when discounting? This can be a dangerous practice.

▶ **Product mix change** - selling more low margin product than high margin product.

▶ **Shrinkage** - inventory that is unaccounted for; the cost of goods that have not been sold (due to theft, goods signed for and not received, spoiled goods, etc.). Shrinkage is discovered by counting inventory - what should be in inventory vs what is in inventory equals a variance. The variance is recorded as a decrease in inventory, subsequently increasing Cost of Goods Sold and decreasing Gross Profit.

▶ **Higher cost of goods** - an increase in the cost of merchandise, without the ability to increase prices, will have an adverse affect on gross profit.

▶ **Clerical errors** - incorrect counting or ticket pricing.

Overhead Ratio (Operating Expenses)

Overhead Expenses ÷ Revenue = Overhead Margin

This measures the relative cost of operating the business (various controllable expenses such as labour, marketing, etc. as a % of sales). The lower the percentage the better.

When examining the operating expenses on the income statement (below the gross profit line) it is clear that management and other salaries increased as a percentage of revenue, increasing the total operating expenses relative to sales. This indicated that either the labour is less efficient or sufficient sales are not being generated relative to the cost.

This result will tell the manager to carefully evaluate the effectiveness of all the additional labour expense employed this year.

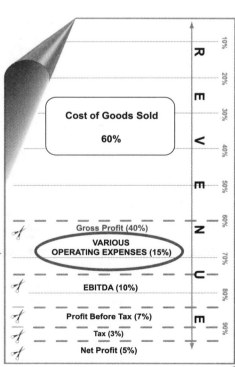

Overhead Ratio

Operating Expenses	Last Year		This Year	
Advertising	$12,625	2.05%	$18,500	1.93%
Bank charges	1,456	0.24%	1,850	0.19%
Legal and professional	1,652	0.27%	2,650	0.28%
Management salaries	60,000	9.75%	97,650	10.17%	Increased as a % of revenue
Office supplies	1,365	0.22%	1,560	0.16%
Rent	21,000	3.41%	21,000	2.19%
Repairs and maintenance	1,500	0.24%	3,357	0.35%
Other salaries	89,500	14.54%	158,000	16.45%	Increased as a % of revenue
Telephone	986	0.16%	1,045	0.11%
Total Operating Expenses	**$190,084**	30.88%	**$305,612**	31.82%	Increased as a % of revenue

EBITDA

Earnings Before Interest, Tax, Depreciation & Amortization ÷ Revenue

Notice that while the EBITDA dollar value improved the ratio relative to sales decreased, which means that the business is less efficient.

EBITDA

	Last Year	This Year
EBITDA	84,978	102,188
Revenue	615,562	960,300
	13.80%	**10.64%**

EBITDA

	Last Year		This Year	
Sales	$615,562		$960,300	
COGS	340,500		552,500	
Gross Profit	**$275,062**		**$407,800**	
Gross Margin		45%		42%
Operating Expenses				
Advertising	$12,625	2.05%	$18,500	1.93%
Bank charges	1,456	0.24%	1,850	0.19%
Legal and professional	1,652	0.27%	2,650	0.28%
Management salaries	60,000	9.75%	97,650	10.17%	Increased as a % of revenue
Office supplies	1,365	0.22%	1,560	0.16%
Rent	21,000	3.41%	21,000	2.19%
Repairs and maintenance	1,500	0.24%	3,357	0.35%
Other salaries	89,500	14.54%	158,000	16.45%	Increased as a % of revenue
Telephone	986	0.16%	1,045	0.11%
Total Operating Expenses	**$190,084**	30.88%	**$305,612**	31.82%	Increased as a % of revenue
EBITDA	**84,978**	13.80%	**102,188**	10.64%	**Decreased** as a % of revenue

Interest, tax, depreciation and amortization are expenses that cannot be controlled by most business operators (they are not generally considered direct operating expenses). These expenses can also be different between one location and another in the same business, because of the depreciation policies or tax rules unique to a state or province, or simply the unique borrowing conditions of a particular operator (which impacts interest).

Interest, tax, depreciation and amortization are therefore excluded from the profits to ensure a *level playing field* when comparing performances between one business and another in the same industry. It makes sense, therefore, to monitor profitability against those expenses that can be controlled.

It is common for a newspaper to quote an improvement in EBITDA without mentioning the interest and depreciation expenses. This can be dangerous. If a business has a very high debt load it can be very profitable at the EBITDA level, yet fail due to high interest rates that were not included in the profit calculation.

Note:

⮑   **Depreciation** relates to tangible assets - computers, machinery, vehicles, etc.

⮑   **Amortization** relates to intangible assets - goodwill, copyrights, patents, trademarks, etc.

Net Income

Net Income (Profit) ÷ Revenue = Profit Margin

This ratio determines the percentage of profit relative to revenue. In other words, everything that is left after all expenses are taken into account (it is often referred to as *the bottom line* - an increase or decrease to Owner's Equity).

Net Income	Last Year	This Year
Net Profit	52,622	35,938
Revenue	615,562	960,300
	8.55%	**3.74%**

Compare this profit margin from month-to-month, year-to-year and to your industry benchmark, because the standards vary from industry to industry.

Interest Coverage Ratio

EBITDA ÷ Interest

Lenders need to ensure that a business can service the interest on loans - it is necessary to make sufficient cash profit to pay for the interest (to be paid in cash). Although EBITDA is not strictly cash (most revenue and expenses are accrued), it is reasonable to assume that all revenue and expenses will involve cash within a few months.

The objective of this ratio is to ensure that there is at least $2.00 of profit for every $1.00 of interest to be paid (in other words, a 2 times interest coverage ratio is desirable). Last year the ratio was very healthy because EBITDA was strong and interest was low. This year interest expenses increased significantly while generating less EBITDA.

Interest Coverage Ratio	Last Year	This Year
EBITDA	84,978	102,188
Interest	2,356	12,250
	36.07	**8.34**

While the ratio is still within acceptable parameters, it has deteriorated significantly. This demonstrates that the company is not generating sufficient profit to support the interest paid on borrowings. Continuing this trend could result in the business being unable to pay the interest.

Linking the Income Statement to the Balance Sheet

Return on Equity

Net Profit ÷ Owner's Equity

Are the owners of the business getting an acceptable return on their investment? In other words, if the owners were to sell all the assets of the business and use the cash to pay all the debt, the remaining cash represents the Net Worth of the business (Owner's Equity).

The owner(s) has a choice: keep the money in the business or sell the interest and invest the cash elsewhere. Whether it is a decent return on the investment or not completely depends on the risk. For example, if you were to invest your money in a fixed deposit account in the bank you would receive very little interest because the risk is extremely low. If, however, you were to invest your money in a friend's new business, which has not yet proved to be successful, you would expect a much higher return for the risk. In fact there is decent chance you may even lose it all!

Generally speaking you will see about a 15% - 25% return on your investment in publicly-traded companies. The rate of return is expected to be much higher in private companies, as a result of the higher risk. In fact it's not unusual to see a 100% and more return on equity in small private companies.

The return will usually be calculated *before* tax because the owner must compare the return to, say, investing in a bank or another company that is taxed to the investor after being received.

There are several ways to calculate the ROE but the most common method is as follows:

➤ Add the Opening Owner's Equity to the Closing Owner's Equity and divide by 2.

➤ Divide the net profit by the result.

The logic of averaging the equity:

Not all the profit was made at one time. Keep in mind that an annual financial statement will report all the profit made over a year. You will not know at what point in time the profit was actually made so it's best to average it out. Take a look at the difference: ⟶

EXAMPLE:

Return on Equity (ROE)	
Opening Owner's Equity	100
Add Profit	50
Closing Owner's Equity	150
Profit	50
÷ Closing Equity	150
Return on Equity, without averaging, based on the closing balance	33%
Average Method	
Opening + Closing	250
÷ 2	125
Return on Equity	**40%**

CASH FLOW IS REALITY!

We now move over to the balance sheet only.

You are now aware that it is quite possible to make a healthy profit (according to the accrual system of accounting) but still run out of cash and go out of business despite success. To test the health of a business from a cash flow point of view, it is important to keep a watchful eye on liquidity ratios.

AME | Learning

Current Ratio

Currents Assets ÷ Current Liabilities

The Current Ratio (also called the *Working Capital Ratio*) tests the ability of the business to pay its debts over the next 12 months.

The business expects to convert all current assets into cash over the next twelve months. Current assets are those assets that will convert into cash through normal day-to-day operations of the business (i.e. accounts receivable, inventory, etc.). Fixed assets (i.e. buildings and machinery) could certainly be converted into cash, but it is an unlikely choice to simply pay the bills.

Current liabilities, on the other hand, represent all those liabilities that a business needs to *pay* within the next 12 months.

A safe current ratio is $2.00 worth of current assets for every $1.00 of current debt. This can change according to the industry (i.e. real estate).

Current Ratio

	Last Year	This Year
Current Assets	176,071	375,465
Current Liabilities	79,560	238,905
	2.21	1.57

This ratio was very healthy last year because current assets were more than twice the amount of current liabilities. This year, however, there is a problem in that the ratio is below the required 2:1. This could also prove to be a problem if the receivables are not collected and all the inventory is not sold. In that event, there is insufficient *reserve* to pay what is owing in the next 12 months.

How could this situation have been avoided? Perhaps the owner spent too much cash (current asset) on fixed assets, which are not liquid, resulting in a cash flow shortage. When examining the balance sheet it will be evident that fixed assets increased by more than $36,000, draining the cash needed to pay for the liabilities owing in the next 12 months.

Typically fixed assets (also known as long term assets) should be financed with long term debt (e.g. borrow money payable over 5 years).

Quick Ratio

Currents Assets (excluding Inventory and Prepaid Expenses) ÷ Current Liabilities

The Quick Ratio (also know as the Acid Test) determines the number of times the most liquid assets can cover immediate debts. It indicates the ability of the business to meet its immediate obligations. As inventory tends to take a long time to convert into cash and prepaid expenses are often not convertible into cash, they are excluded from this ratio.

If the ratio decreases dramatically from the Current Ratio and falls below 1:1, this indicates that the inventory level is too high. In other words, if the cash is not generated from accounts receivable then where *will* it come from?

You expect to convert $1.00 of the most liquid assets (accounts receivable and cash) for every $1.00 owing in the next 12 months without having to rely on selling inventory.

This ratio is a problem this year. Cash and Accounts receivable amount to less than 1:1 which means that there is likely to be a short term cash shortage. If the inventory had been sold, it would be in the form of accounts receivable or cash which would improve this ratio which illustrates the point made above the symptom of inventory possibly being mismanaged.

Quick Ratio	Last Year	This Year
Current Assets (AR and cash)	95,115	222,965
Current Liabilities	79,560	238,905
	1.20	0.93

Special note about this ratio: this ratio should be used to test the ability of the business to pay debts owing over the next 90 days. Current debt on the balance sheet does not indicate during which of the 12-month period the debts are owing, so it's important to establish when immediate debts are due.

How much more can the business borrow?

Debt to Equity Ratio

Total Liabilities ÷ Owner's Equity

This ratio is used by the lender to examine his/her risk versus the owner's risk. Lenders will want to know whether the owners subject themselves to at least twice the amount of risk. They will therefore assess the total amount owing (total liabilities) versus Owner's Equity.

Ordinarily, there should be no more than $1.00 of total liabilities for every $2.00 of Owner's Equity, or the other way around - the owners should have at least $2.00 of equity for each $1.00 of liabilities. This ratio can vary according to the industry. For example, it will be more tolerant in the real estate business, which usually deals with high mortgages (liabilities) and little equity.

Debt to Equity	Last Year	This Year
Total Debt	127,560	310,905
Owner's Equity	87,122	123,060
	1.46	2.53

Scenario #1: Total Liabilities (debt) ÷ Owner's Equity

In this first scenario we are using the debt to equity ratio versus the calculation below which is reversing it: equity to debt. They both have the same meaning, but one may be easier to read than the other depending on your point of view.

Scenario #2: Owner's Equity ÷ Total Liabilities (debt)

In this second scenario you will notice that in both years the owners had less risk than the lenders (total liabilities). In fact, the owners have taken less risk this year versus last year. In other words, the owner is risking $123,060 against the risk that banks and other suppliers are taking in the amount of $310,905. The ratio is therefore 0.40 or 40%.

Equity to Debt	Last Year	This Year
Owner's Equity	87,122	123,060
Total Debt	127,560	310,905
	0.68	0.40

If the debt to equity ratio is poor:

·   Making more profit will increase Owner's Equity

·   If the owner takes less salary, costs will decrease and profits will increase

·   Selling some of the equity will increase equity and increase cash

A bank may request the owner to postpone shareholders' loans. This means that the owner undertakes not to withdraw funds from his/her loans, which decreases liabilities and improves the ratio. It also means that the owner is taking more risk by leaving the loans in the business. In other words, the shareholders loans are considered as equity, which cannot be taken in the form of cash unless sold.

How well is your business being managed?

Managing inventory levels and the collection of accounts receivable is crucial to the successful management of a business.

The two main tests we will address are:

1.   Days Sales Outstanding ratio (also known as DSO)

2.   Inventory On Hand ratio (also known as the Inventory Turnover Ratio)

Days Sales Outstanding Ratio (DSO)

Accounts Receivable ÷ Revenue x 365 (days)

The longer that it takes to collect outstanding accounts, the lower the bank balance and the higher the risk of not collecting. There are also additional costs associated with late payments such as interest lost on the money and additional administration costs required to keep chasing the customers for payment.

This calculation indicates that the average collection of outstanding accounts from customers last year was 42 days. This year collections extended to 60 (59.8) days.

This is a very bad trend. It seems that to increase sales, sales people are extending credit terms to customers in addition to decreasing margin. This practice is both decreasing profits (as is apparent in the profitability ratios) and creating a potential cash flow problem.

DSO	Last Year	This Year
Accounts Receivable	71,500	157,500
Revenue	615,562	960,300
x 365 days	**42 days**	**60 days**

This represents the number of days the accounts receivable are outstanding.

Inventory On Hand Ratio

Inventory ÷ Cost of Goods Sold x 365 (days)

This ratio is largely dependent on the industry - always compare period-to-period and to other businesses in a similar industrial sector and be cautious to assess the inventory level according to cyclical changes. If assessing the inventory level of a store selling winter skis at the end of winter, you would expect the level to be low compared to the month prior to winter. Conversely, you would expect the inventory turnover to be no more than a couple of days in a bakery.

Inventory Turnover	Last Year	This Year
Inventory	68,956	134,500
Cost of Goods Sold	340,500	552,500
x 365 days	74 days	89 days

Last year, the inventory had lasted on an average of 74 (73.9) days. This year it will last for 89 (88.86) days. It would appear from this ratio that managers are not managing the inventory as well as they did last year. The higher the inventory, the lower the cash flow and increased costs such as:

· Interest lost on the money
· Insurance
· Shrinkage when some inventory goes bad, is stolen or becomes redundant
· Extra rent to store the inventory

Summary of Analysis

Profitability:

▶ It is clear that gross margin is decreasing, which needs to be addressed. It is likely that either prices are being discounted or the cost of the product has increased and it has not been recovered in the sales price. This is a dangerous trend.

▶ All operating expenses seem under control except for labour costs relative to sales. There is either too much of labour cost for the amount of sales being generated or they are not being efficient. The ratio of labour to sales needs to improve by at least 3%.

▶ EBITDA has decreased as a percentage, which is impacted by gross margin and labour. If these two ratios are corrected, the interest coverage ratio will also improve.

▶ Interest Coverage: This is a potential problem that needs to be watched, especially if the business needs to borrow more money. In this event interest will increase once again and unless EBITDA improves, could create a problem with the bank and their conditions of borrowing.

Liquidity and general control:

▶ Cash flow management has deteriorated significantly from last year.

▶ The current ratio and quick ratio indicate that too much cash was used to buy fixed assets.

▶ Accounts receivable terms have been extended. This is placing both a cash flow strain on the company and subjecting the business to credit risk. Sales people need to be trained not to give credit terms beyond the conditions of sale.

▶ Inventory is too high, which is subjecting the company to the risk of losing their inventory and starving the business of much needed cash.

Notes

AME | Learning

Exercises: Chapter 11

Exercise #1

FINANCIAL ANALYSIS

Using these financial statements, calculate the ratios on the following pages:

ABC Company
BALANCE SHEET

	Last Year	This Year
Assets		
Cash	$10,000	$2,000
Accounts Receivable	60,000	75,000
Prepaid Expenses	6,000	6,000
Inventory	68,000	92,000
Total Current Assets	**144,000**	**175,000**
Fixed Assets	50,000	90,000
Less Accumulated Depreciation	-20,000	-23,000
Total Assets	**$174,000**	**$242,000**
Liabilities		
Accounts Payable	$40,000	$62,000
Current Portion of Bank Loan	10,000	15,000
Shareholders' Loans	30,000	30,000
Current Liabilities	**80,000**	**107,000**
Long Term Loans	40,000	55,000
Total Liabilities	**$120,000**	**$162,000**
Shareholders' Equity		
Opening Owner's Equity	$20,000	$54,000
Profit	34,000	26,000
Closing Shareholders' Equity	**$54,000**	**$80,000**
Liabilities + Equity	**$174,000**	**$242,000**

ABC Company
INCOME STATEMENT

	Last Year	This Year
Sales	**$420,000**	**$640,000**
COGS	270,000	430,000
Gross Profit	**150,000**	**210,000**
Operating Expenses		
Advertising	$1,000	$1,500
Bank charges	500	1,200
Legal and professional	1,500	1,400
Salaries	80,000	129,000
Office supplies	600	1,400
Rent	15,000	15,000
Repairs and maintenance	1,000	1,200
Telephone	400	1,100
Total Operating Expenses	**100,000**	**151,800**
EBITDA	**50,000**	**58,200**
Interest	1,000	3,200
Depreciation	3,000	6,000
Operating Profit Before Tax	**46,000**	**49,000**
Tax	12,000	23,000
Net Profit	**$34,000**	**$26,000**

NOTES:

Gross Margin

Description	Last Year	This Year
Ratio:		

Overhead Ratio (Operating Expenses)

Description	Last Year	This Year
Ratio:		

EBITDA %

Description	Last Year	This Year
Ratio:		

Net Income (Profit Margin)

Description	Last Year	This Year
Ratio:		

Interest Coverage Ratio

Description	Last Year	This Year
Ratio:		

Return on Equity (ROE)

Description	Last Year	This Year
Ratio:		

Current Ratio

Description	Last Year	This Year
Ratio:		

Quick Ratio

Description	Last Year	This Year
Ratio:		

Debt to Equity

Description	Last Year	This Year
Ratio:		

NOTES:

_____

_____

_____

_____

_____

_____

_____

_____

_____

_____

_____

_____

_____

_____

_____

_____

_____

_____

NOTES:

Days Sales Outstanding (DSO)

Description	Last Year	This Year
x 365 days:		

Inventory On Hand Ratio

Description	Last Year	This Year
x 365 days:		

Notes

AME | Learning

Chapter 12

Internal Controls & Cash Management

Internal Controls & Cash Management

► Definition of Controls
► Types of Controls

Definition of Controls

Controls are measures, procedures, performance indicators, and other methods used to check and regulate business operations systematically. These procedures can include cash controls, budgetary controls, credit controls, working procedures, inventory control, production processes, hiring policies and quality measures.

The purpose of internal controls is to provide reasonable assurance regarding the achievement of objects relating to

- effectiveness and efficiency of operations
- reliability of financial reporting
- compliance with applicable laws and regulations.

Each internal control is designed to

- align objectives of the business
- safeguard assets
- prevent and detect fraud and error
- encourage good management
- allow action to be taken against undesirable performance
- reduce exposure to risks, and
- ensure proper financial reporting

Under an adequate system of internal control, each business transaction is

- complete
- accurate
- authorized
- valid
- real (i.e. it exists).

In addition, when internal controls are present, errors in the system are automatically identified and corrected; duties are segregated; and financial reports are timely, and in accordance with GAAP.

Generally, internal controls can be classified as preventive (i.e. to stop an incident before it happens), or detective (i.e. to discover an incident after it happens). Obviously, it is better to prevent incidents than to discover them after they occur.

Try this exercise ... Think about doing something dishonest. You may think of shoplifting merchandise from a retail store; writing a cheque when you have no money in the bank, going 50 km over the speed limit, etc.

Now, think about how someone would stop you from completing your dishonest act. Shoplifting? What about those ever-present cameras; electronic tags; security guards?

Writing an NSF cheque? Vendors may ask you to wait until the cheque clears before giving you the merchandise. The vendor may send out a "collection agent".

Want to speed? Consider radar, unmarked police cars, "good" citizens reporting you.

All of the above are in the realm of internal controls.

Imagine the numerous reasons a motor vehicle may be involved in an accident:

1.   The driver fell asleep or lost control because of speeding - the driver's fault.

2.   The brakes failed - the mechanic's fault.

3.   The other car drove through a red light - someone else's fault.

4.   A tree fell on the car - just plain bad luck!

In all these scenarios something different caused the accident. Operating and controlling a business is not dissimilar to this metaphor. Consider the following:

Michael purchased a family restaurant, which he managed himself, buying supplies, paying bills and opening and closing each day. He was doing so well that he decided to buy another location in another suburb of the city. He promoted an employee, who had worked with him for the past 3 years, to manage the old location while he focused on setting up the new location.

Business was great. The old location seemed to be maintaining the sales numbers, the new location was catching on fast and Michael was really happy. He decided that it was time that he and his wife Jennifer take a vacation.

Michael was not a numbers guy and disliked anything to do with accounting. He operated a simple hands-on business and his bookkeeper updated the books each month to ensure that taxes were paid and payroll was taken care of on time. Other than these two functions, the bookkeeper relied on the accountant to complete the financial statements at the end of each year and complete Michael's annual tax return.

Not long after Michael returned from his vacation he received a call from one of his suppliers to say that a cheque that he had issued a few days before was returned by the bank because of insufficient funds in Michael's account. Michael was not only furious, he was extremely embarrassed. He had to transfer money from his savings account to cover the shortfall and immediately started looking into what might have happened.

Since Michael knew very little about accounting, he contacted his accountant to investigate the matter. An entire year had passed since the accountant had worked with Michael's financial statements, so the investigation was no easy task. After some time, this is what was discovered:

1. After counting inventory, it was discovered that gross margin had dropped by more than 8%.

2. Cash was only being deposited every few days, rather than daily, and the cash receipts did not match the cash register.

3. Payroll was considerably higher, relative to sales, than it had been in previous years.

4. His trusted manager was stealing food supplies and selling them for cash. This increased the food costs, which decreased gross margin.

5. It appeared that he was paying ghost employees - he was making payments to casual labour that turned out to be himself.

6. Some of the servers were 'sweethearting' customers - meaning that friends were being served with free meals or extras at no charge.

Michael nearly went bankrupt as a result of this fraud, but with the help of his accountant he implemented various controls to prevent this from happening again.

Compare this scenario with the car accident metaphor.

♦ The driver's fault - clearly Michael (the business owner) had no control over the vehicle.

♦ The mechanic's fault - the restaurant was a good business and did not fail because of a poor economy.

♦ Someone else's fault - if the bookkeeper had been more competent, he could have warned Michael of the problems before they got out of hand.

♦ Just plain bad luck - perhaps, because his manager was dishonest, or maybe this could have been avoided if Michael had performed a better background check on the manager before he was hired.

One thing was for sure: the problem was avoidable.

The business recovered, but only because of the accountant's help and because Michael learned to understand the business aspects of operating his restaurants. The controls that were implemented by the accountant included:

1. **Cash control policies:**
   a. Cash had to be deposited daily and match the cash register. These were checked weekly
   b. No cheques could be issued without copies of purchase orders and matching invoices and proof of delivery
   c. Petty cash had to be reconciled weekly and signed by Michael
   d. Payroll was to be paid directly into employees accounts and weekly spot checks had to be made to ensure that staff was working the hours for which they were being paid.
   e. Each month the bookkeeper had to do a bank reconciliation and check with Michael for anything that seemed out of the ordinary.

f. The accountants prepared a simple cash flow spreadsheet template for the bookkeeper to submit to Michael each month.

2. **Management controls:**

Each month Michael learned to study performance ratios including:

a. Gross Margin - counting inventory each month

b. Revenue for labour dollar

c. Average sales value per meal

Different types of businesses require different controls and levels of control. For example, a large bank would require very stringent controls relating to cash management, whereas a manufacturing company would need a high level of control over inventory. Banks do not use inventory and most manufacturers do not handle cash.

There are various principles that are consistent with most types of businesses. A detailed description of specific cash controls, audit trails and accounting procedures is outside the scope of this course. However, there are certain key principles that are important to know. Following are details regarding various types of controls.

Physical cash controls

Many businesses work with physical cash such as restaurants, retail stores and fast food outlets. If all employees were honest, most of these controls would not be necessary. However, in reality, working with bank notes can be very tempting and so it is important to ensure that adequate controls are in place to discourage theft.

An employer needs a system to keep track of the money from the time it leaves the customer's hands until the time it is deposited in the bank. A restaurant operator, for example, would require the following list of cash controls in order to limit cash loss:

1. Written cash/credit handling policy: forms are provided for employees to use to record refunds given to customers and credits for mistakes made. This form shows the time, date, amount and employee's signature.

2. Limited access to the safe: the safe should be kept locked at all times. Most safes have envelope size areas which allow for money drops if necessary (drop safes).

3. The opening and closing cash, used to make change for customers, should be the same at all times. The money must be counted at the open and close of business, dated and signed by the employee.

4. Paid-outs (e.g. small amounts that are paid out such as staff tea/coffee, stamps, small stationery items) should be entered on a form with the time, date, signature and receipt stapled to it. Paid-outs should be deducted from a petty cash fund if possible and not from the daily deposits or cash drawers.

5. Cash drops after each shift: one person should be responsible for each shift deposit. They must enter a log with the amount of the deposit, total sales for the day, date, time and signature and place it in an envelope with the deposit to be dropped into the safe.

6. Daily bank deposits: daily deposits are separated and included with the bank deposit slips and daily cash reports.

7. Maintain a key and safe combination access log: keys are numbered and a log is kept with information on the person having the key.

8. Written standard cash register procedures: what types of cheques are accepted (no out of town cheques), what type of ID is required, etc.

9. Registers with a cumulative register reading: this is like an odometer on a car, keeping a running total of the sales, coupons, etc. These readings are to be incorporated into the daily sales report.

10. Use registers that allow the transaction amounts to be visible to the cashier and the customers. Secret shoppers take note of these transactions to make sure the employees are not under-ringing sales.

11. Sales should always be entered in to the register at the time of the transaction and a cash receipt should be given to the customer.

12. Cashiers should place the customer's money on the register ledge until the change is made. This confirms the amount given by the customer, without question.

13. Cash registers should not be left unattended. Money should not be exchanged from register to register if multiple registers are used.

14. Z readings: This clears the register of the previous days sales. This reading should be done daily and attached to the daily cash report.

15. Bank deposit follow ups: this will ensure that monies have been deposited into the correct account. Bank statements should be reviewed line by line and checked for accuracy with regard to deposits. Banks do make mistakes.

Control Over Cheques and Deposits

Many companies such as consulting firms, legal firms, manufacturers, etc. handle very little cash. However, there are many examples of money theft by employees that do not involve bank notes. Some examples include schemes such as:

♦ A manager authorizing payment to an imaginary supplier for goods never received - the supplier happens to be himself.

♦ An employee authorizing an over-payment to a supplier who then shares the overpayment with the employee.

♦ Over-paying staff who share the overtime with the manager.

♦ Paying staff who do not even exist.

♦ Doing deals with suppliers by accepting bribe money - the bribe money is simply added to the cost of the product.

There have been enough schemes discovered to fill a book. These schemes to steal from a business can be avoided, for the most part, with the right controls. Keep in mind that when two or more people are in collusion, it's more difficult to avoid.

AME | Learning

There is, however, such a thing as over control. For example: Using an elaborative system to track the use of stationery that costs $500 per month to manage. If the company is only using $1,000 worth of stationery per month it would make no sense to implement such an elaborate control. Controls should be commensurate with the risk of loss. The more elaborate the control, the higher the cost.

Control Over Discount Policies

An area subject to abuse in many organizations is discount policy. Discounts can be given to customers who are not actually eligible for discounts.

To control discounts, the first step is to write down the discount policy. The policy should be disseminated to both staff and customers.

A central concept in controlling discount policy is authorization. The policy must clearly state who is authorized to give discounts; and to what extent. The authorization may be limited by amount (i.e. person A can give a discount on sales to $500, person B is allowed to give discounts on sales from $500 - $1,000, and so on), product, or by some other limit.

Computers can be used to enforce discount policy. Consider an organization that uses point-of-sale terminals and scans in the UPC from the customer purchase. In such instances, the sale price is determined from the POS database. Each salesperson "signs in" to the terminal. Within the computer program that operates the terminal, there is information that defines each salesperson's discount authority. If a salesperson tries to record an unauthorized discount, the program will either disallow it (preventive control), or produce a control list on a regular basis that shows unauthorized discounts (detective control). The control list must be reviewed on a regular basis by a responsible official, at which time appropriate action may be taken.

Which employees should be given authority to give discounts? This is a subject for hiring policy, and the personnel department. It may be policy that new hires are not allowed to give any discounts. As an employee gains experience the discount level could be increased. An observation about hiring can be made at this point. When hiring, a background check is an internal control that must be included as a compulsory part of the hiring process. If the background check reveals that the potential employee has a criminal record, or was fired because they gave unauthorized discounts to customers, the company would need to reconsider the hire.

The computer procedure outlined above is applicable to non-retail operations as well as retail operations. In all cases, the computer should either prevent unauthorized discounts, or failing that, detect unauthorized discounts.

For very small operations using a manual system, the owner is a key part of control over discounts. On a regular basis the owner must review invoices and determine that only authorized discounts are processed.

Control Activities

Control activities take many forms: policies, procedures, approvals, verification, reconciliations, performance reviews, security measures, and segregation of duties. When developing control activities, management must consider not only costs, but also the flow of transactions.

Employees are unlikely to carry out a control activity if it is difficult to perform, or interferes with the natural flow of a transaction.

Information and Communication

The information system of a company must be designed to identify, capture, and communicate relevant information on a timely basis to the decision-makers in the company. Old information is as good as no information. Armed with essential information, managers can effectively carry out their responsibilities and maintain accountability for the company assets.

Monitoring

Monitoring company processes and assessing quality are part of normal management and supervisory activities. When the system is not working as designed, corrective action can be initiated. Here are some examples of control sheets that could be implemented to avoid some of the more common theft schemes:

Sales and Receivables	Yes	No	N/A
Are invoices sent out as soon as possible rather than at month end?			
Are there controls to ensure that all goods and services are billed?			
Are there controls to ensure that invoices are accurate?			
Are payment terms, including due date and charges for overdue accounts, clearly stated on the invoice?			
Are special instructions from customers followed?			
Are old accounts reviewed?			
Is credit approved before goods are shipped?			
Does credit evaluation consider credit history, references and credit agencies rating?			
Is there a process in place for dealing with delinquent accounts?			
Is DSO (Days Sales Outstanding) calculated regularly and tracked over time?			
Is an aging of accounts receivable reviewed by management monthly?			
Are accounts receivables metrics compared to other companies in the same industry?			
Are accounts receivable write-offs approved by management?			
Is there a process in place to control, approve and track credit notes?			
Are cash (currency) receipts controlled by a cash register or similar device?			
Is there adequate division of duties in the processing of cash receipts (eg. the accounts receivable clerk should not be preparing invoices or opening the mail)?			
Is the credit department completely independent of the sales department?			
Is senior management involved, where appropriate, in the collection process?			

Banking and Cash Management	Yes	No	N/A
Are cash receipts deposited daily?			
Are there controls to ensure that all cash receipts are deposited?			
Is activity through the bank accounts reviewed daily?			
Is positive pay or negative pay used to prevent or detect fraudulent items?			
Do cheques have anti-forgery features?			
Are bank charges reviewed at least annually?			
Do all cheques require two signatures?			
Are signing officers independent of cheque preparation?			
Are there special procedures for approving large cheques?			
Are excess funds automatically transferred to reduce overdrafts daily?			
Are there adequate controls over non-local currency bank accounts?			
Are all bank accounts reconciled monthly?			
Are bank charges reasonable?			
Are there good controls over petty cash?			
Are there good controls over employee expense reimbursements?			
Is direct deposit used for payroll payments?			
Is electronic access used to monitor all bank accounts?			
Are there strong controls over electronic banking?			
Is there a cash forecasting process in place?			

Accounts Payable and Disbursements	Yes	No	N/A
Is there an approved list of vendors?			
Is there adequate approval from management before items are ordered from suppliers?			
Are suppliers costs being checked to ensure that they are competitive?			
Are vendor invoices checked against purchase orders and receiving reports to ensure the items have actually been received?			
Are all discounts for prompt payment taken?			
Is there adequate division of duties in the processing of payments?			
Are accounts payable metrics compared to other companies in the same industry?			

Cash Flow and Operations Management	Yes	No	N/A
Is there a cash flow budget and is it up-to-date and reviewed by management?			
Is there an operating budget (revenue and expenses) and is it up-to-date and reviewed by management?			
Are monthly financial statements and management reports prepared promptly?			
Is insurance coverage reviewed at least semi-annually?			
Are statistics such as sales, gross margin and profit per employee tracked monthly and compared to budget?			
Are there controls in place over the hiring of employees or consultants?			

In Summary

All controls have limitations and are subject to human behaviour. Some problems may arise simply through honest error or naivety, while others involve blatant theft. Human errors can arise because employees are not properly trained or they are fatigued due to the amount of work burden. Controls have little impact in these cases.

However, there are many clever thieves such as the executives of Enron, WorldCom and BreEx, who are experts at working around systems. Unfortunately they are often caught only after serious damage has already been done. Many problems can be avoided by hiring right and ensuring that sound background checks are done before hiring new people.

A final note about internal controls; they don't always work! You may make an error in judgment, like hiring a new employee without doing a background check. The employee could turn out to be dishonest, and steal from you before your discover what happened. Not all transactions can be covered in a policy manual; it is important to hire staff that are honest and know how to handle unusual situations. Collusion occurs when two or more people work together to initiate a fraud. Because it is very difficult to prevent collusion, it is important that only honest and reliable people are hired. Management override can destroy any internal control that has been set up. Procedures should not be changed without discussing the control with the authority that set up the control. When controls are not a natural part of a procedure (i.e. they must be performed in addition to everything else), they are often ignored. When setting up internal controls, try to have them flow "naturally" from the transaction. Internal controls need to be strong; each control should do what it is supposed to. If you discover that an internal control is not working, review it carefully, and determine where it can be strengthened.

Notes

AME | Learning

Exercise: Chapter 12
Business Case

Business Case

Controls

Craig and Amanda, a married couple, operate three small retail stores that specialize in kitchenware. Along with directly selling to customers who visit their stores, they also wholesale to other businesses on credit terms (accounts receivable). While they do have competition, they sell unique products many of which are custom designed for them. The stores themselves are creatively laid out and attract the medium to high spending consumer. Historically, they have been customer focused and offer a high level of product quality and service.

Craig oversees the day-to-day store operations and marketing. Amanda, being the artistic one, spends most of her time with store layout, new product development and merchandising. Neither of them has any accounting experience or business background and rely heavily on their bookkeeper, Mary, who has been with them from the start. Mary's responsibilities are more than just bookkeeping. She often interviews new hires, negotiates salaries and has signing authority on the bank account. Until recently, Craig and Amanda rarely fired employees because they worked closely with all their staff members. However since opening their second store and now especially since opening the third store there has been a significant staff turnover due to inexperience. In one case a cashier was fired after having been caught giving away free product to a friend when paying for other goods that were bought.

Each month Mary provides an income statement and balance sheet to Craig and Amanda who focus mostly on the gross revenue line. The business is cyclical in nature with big peak and valley sales. Mary explained to the owners that the statements were based on accruals and that is why some months show a loss. She told them that she liked to do some creative accounting to reduce their tax liability. Mary persuaded Craig and Amanda that they did not need to go through the expense of hiring an external accounting firm since she did all the accounting work, including the annual tax returns.

Jerry, one of the managers has been with the company for 3 years and is a big help to Craig. He cashes up in the evenings, supervises inventory counts for all the stores and has authority to hire and fire. (Mary happens to be married to Jerry.) There are no standard controls in the business because Mary feels that with a small, owner-managed business there is no need to go to the expense of introducing fancy systems.

Ever since they started their third store, gross sales for the company has been increasing, but there never seems to be enough cash to pay bills or for the owners to draw for personal use. It reached a point where vendors started to call and complain about late payments. This worried Craig and Amanda as they now need to approach the bank to apply for a larger loan. With Mary convincing them that this is all just temporary, Craig and Amanda have offered their home as security for the loan.

Completely frustrated, Craig and Amanda finally decide to hire a chartered accountant to help them through this problem.

Acting as the accountant, analyze the financial statements on the next page and answer the following questions:
1. Analyze financial ratios and comment on the possible reasons for the change to these ratios.
2. When addressing each ratio, identify the possible risks that might occur if the trend continues.
3. Recommend some change to controls that will improve the organization's results and mitigate further risk.

[Answers to this business case are to be handed in separately.]

Here are the financial statements, representing the past two years, for the companies owned by Craig and Amanda:

Balance Sheet
as at December 31, 20xx

Assets	Last Year	This Year
Cash	$25,000	$2,000
Accounts Receivable	20,000	30,000
Prepaid Expenses	6,000	10,000
Inventory	93,000	167,000
Total Current Assets	**144,000**	**209,000**
Fixed Assets	70,000	110,000
Less Accumulated Depreciation	-20,000	-32,000
Total Assets	**$194,000**	**$287,000**
Liabilities		
Accounts Payable	$33,000	$88,000
Current Portion of Bank Loan	10,000	30,000
Shareholders' Loans	30,000	40,000
Current Liabilities	**73,000**	**158,000**
Long Term Loans	40,000	80,000
Total Liabilities	**$113,000**	**$238,000**
Shareholders' Equity		
Opening Owner's Equity	$20,000	$81,000
Profit	61,000	-32,000
Closing Shareholders' Equity	**$81,000**	**$49,000**
Liabilities + Equity	**$194,000**	**$287,000**

Income Statement

	Last Year	This Year
Sales	**$720,000**	**$980,000**
COGS	320,000	480,000
Gross Profit	**400,000**	**500,000**
Operating Expenses		
Advertising	1,000	2,000
Bank charges	500	1,200
Legal and professional	1,500	1,400
Store managers' salaries	120,000	190,000
Sales people salaries	90,000	140,000
Accounting & admin salaries	70,000	90,000
Rent	15,000	26,000
Repairs and maintenance	1,000	1,200
Insurance	1,200	18,000
Miscellaneous	6,800	15,200
Total Operating Expenses	**307,000**	**485,000**
EBITDA	**93,000**	**15,000**
Interest	6,000	9,000
Depreciation	3,000	15,000
Operating Profit Before Tax	**84,000**	**-9,000**
Tax	23,000	23,000
Net Profit	**$61,000**	**-$32,000**

Business Case Framework

Framework to use to solve Accounting Made Easy™ Business Cases

Following is a step-by-step guideline to analyze and resolve a business case:

➤ **Step 1:** After carefully reading the business case, identify and list the relevant facts.

➤ **Step 2:** Analyze facts and identify key issues in the organization relating to:

⇨ Organizational

Micro:

♦ Structure

♦ Culture [ethics / communication / trust / customer centric, etc.]

♦ Employees [staff turnover, conflict of interest, work satisfaction, etc.]

♦ Operational Controls

♦ Customers / Vendors

Macro:

♦ Market / Competition

♦ Society / Environmental [controllable and uncontrollable]

♦ Economy

⇨ Management

♦ Management Style

♦ Ownership

⇨ Financial

♦ Study the financial statements and identify reasons for increases or decreases in financial performance.

♦ Analyze statements using financial ratios and key performance indicators utilizing frameworks studied in the course. List reasons for the increase/decrease in these ratios and identify the issues related to them.

➤ **Step 3:** Critically analyze the relevant facts and issues and identify the root cause or underlying problem.

➤ **Step 4:** Utilizing your knowledge gained over the period of this course, evaluate the problem and propose your recommendations.

[View illustration on the next page.]

Framework to solve
Accounting Made Easy™
Business Cases

Organization Business Case

Relevant Facts

Example - Situation
i.   Market share
ii. Management Structure
iii. Current controls in place
iv. Financial situation

Step 1
Identify & list relevant facts

Issues

Example - Issues
i.   Conflict of interest
ii. Lack of budgets
iii. Insufficient financial controls
iv. Cashflow and profitability

Step 2
Analyze facts and identify key issues

Underlying problem

Example - Underlying problem
i.   Lack of communication
ii. Insufficient employee training
     • Sales negotiating skills
     • Inventory management
     • Accounts receivable

Step 3
Critically analyze the relevant facts and issues and identify the root cause

Step 4

Evaluate Problem & Propose Recommendations

Example - Recommendations
i.   Financial   - Owner to stop paying dividends until cashflow improves
ii. Management   - Stop discretionary discounts
                           - Provide sales negotiating training to improve margins
iii. Organizational - Monitor key performance indicators and ratios
                           - Provide inventory management and cash collection training

Notes

AME | Learning

Chapter 13
Debits & Credits

Debits & Credits

Formal accounting is based on the Debit and Credit system. This system means that a Debit is recorded on the left-hand side and a Credit is recorded on the right-hand side of an account. Remember the accounting equation: Assets = Liabilities + Owner's Equity. For this equation to work there must be a Debit for every Credit to ensure that the balance sheet stays in balance.

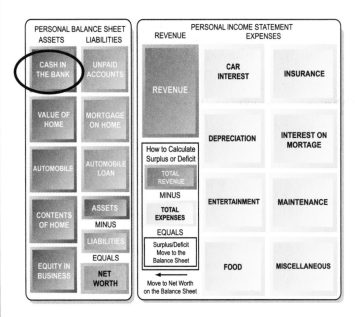

Examples:

Using the *Debit & Credit Dictionary* (on the next page) and this *Accounting Map*™ diagram, follow the flow of these examples:

1. You receive a salary cheque:
   - increase **Cash in the Bank** (Debit)
   - increase **Revenue** (Credit)

2. You reduce a debt (i.e. Bank Loan):
   - decrease **Bank Loan** (Debit)
   - decrease **Cash in the Bank** (Credit)

3. You purchase an asset (i.e. Inventory) for cash:
   - increase **Inventory** (Debit)
   - decrease **Cash in the Bank** (Credit)

REMEMBER:

1. *Newton's Third Law:* entries are always made in pairs.

2. Using *common language* you can have:

   - an increase and an increase (such as cash and revenue);

   - a decrease and a decrease (such as paying your credit card); or

   - a decrease and an increase (such as buying an asset).

   These transactions will **always** correspond to a Debit or a Credit

3. The transactions are **always** opposite to each other. For every Debit there must be a Credit and vice versa.

The foundations of modern accounting were developed in 14th century Italy. Luca Pacioli, a Franciscan Monk and mathematics scholar, left the monastery and wrote "Everything About Arithmetic, Geometry and Proportion", a book which outlined the method of double-entry bookkeeping. Pacioli's book was translated into 5 languages within its first century of publication. This acccounting method, which came to be known as the "Italian method" was soon used worldwide.

Debit and Credit Dictionary:

THE BALANCE SHEET

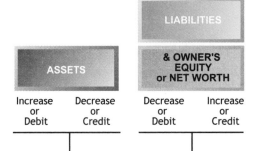

THE INCOME STATEMENT

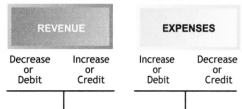

This [D]rives Me [C]razy!

Debits (DR) on the LEFT.

Credits (CR) on the RIGHT.

Quick tips to remember:

- An **increase** in an **asset** (i.e. cash, Accounts Receivable, etc.) is a **Debit**.
  Therefore, a **decrease** in an **asset** is a **Credit**.

- An **increase** in an **expense** is a **Debit**.
  Therefore, a **decrease** in an **expense** is a **Credit**.

Note: For every debit there must be a credit and vice versa.

Exercise #1

To familiarize yourself with Debit and Credit transactions, complete the worksheet on the facing page using the transactions below. Record the account for each pair of transactions and note whether the result is a Debit or Credit to that account. Also note whether the result is an increase or decrease.

1.	Cash sales (*completed for you as an example*)	$6,300
2.	Charge entertainment expenses to your credit card	2,500
3.	Pay cash for maintenance to your building	1,000
4.	Buy a computer - to be paid for next month	1,500
5.	Pay interest on your student loan	200
6.	Pay a portion of the student loan principal	500
7.	Pay staff salaries	2,000
8.	Pay back a portion of your bank loan (principal only)	1,000
9.	Arrange for another student loan	3,000
10.	Depreciation of equipment	500
11.	Pay interest portion of your bank loan	100
12.	Pay cash for monthly rent expenses	2,200
13.	Pay cash for telephone expenses	150
14.	Receive interest on your savings account	80
15.	Pay cash for car insurance	500
16.	Sell furniture for cash	800
17.	Charge a newspaper advertisement to your credit card	450
18.	Your lawyer invoices you for services rendered	950
19.	Pay cash for miscellaneous living expenses	400
20.	Pay accounts payable	1,300

	Account Name	Inc or Dec	Debit	Credit
1	Cash	increase	$6,300	
	Revenue	increase		$6,300

Notes

AME | Learning

Chapter 14
Technical Accounting

Technical Accounting

- ▸ Technical Accounting
- ▸ Account Code Integrity
- ▸ Completing Financial Statements
- ▸ Chart of Accounts
- ▸ Bank Reconciliations
- ▸ Compound Entries
- ▸ Handling Account Errors

- ▸ Sales Discounts Allowed
- ▸ Sales Returns & Allowances
- ▸ Accrued Liabilities
- ▸ Payroll Deductions
- ▸ Petty Cash
- ▸ Shareholders' Equity
- ▸ Intangible Assets, Amortization & Goodwill

This chapter covers items not dealt with in detail in the rest of this textbook.

Technical Accounting

Completing manual records of accounting is a laborious process. In today's modern world of technology, the reality is that computers perform the accounting functions. However, a bookkeeper/accountant will be required to prepare the computer accounting system to ensure that the system is properly set up. The initial set-up must represent all the appropriate activities of the business so that the business managers can operate efficiently using the information provided to them by the accountant. To help you understand how the process works, you will complete various exercises using the old fashioned manual method, simulating what is actually happening within a computerized accounting system.

Learning this technical level of accounting is not only for those students wishing to become accountants. For you to function effectively and logically as a data entry clerk, sales person or manager, it is very important to understand the underlying principles that drive a computer accounting system. Here is an example:

Let's say that a customer pays you $1,200 in the form of a deposit for services to be rendered over the next twelve months. Someone who is not familiar with the principles of accounting, from a technical point of view, would probably enter an invoice into the system representing a sale for the $1,200. The results would be:

Increase in Sales of $1,200 (with no related expenses)

Increase in Profit of $1,200

Increase in Cash of $1,200

Your first thought might be to spend the cash profits of $1,200. *What is wrong with this?* Here's the reality: The full entry should **not** have been a sale. You should have simply issued a cash receipt since you have not yet earned your right to the cash. Remember - you have not yet provided the service. So the accounting entry should have been an increase in cash and an increase in unearned revenue.

This kind of mistake is common in the workplace and can often lead to disastrous results.

An understanding of technical accounting is crucial to making the correct entries in your computerized accounting system. If you enter garbage into the computer, you will get garbage out!

Account Code Integrity

When working with a set of accounts in a manual or computer system, each account is given a unique number. There is a method to numbering these accounts, which are recorded as a **Chart of Accounts**. The Chart of Accounts is a listing of all the accounts being used by a business, accompanied by a specific reference number.

To set up a Chart of Accounts, you must first define the various accounts to be used by the business. Each account should have an identifying number. For very small businesses, three-digit account numbers may be sufficient, although more digits are desirable in order to allow for new accounts to be added as the business grows. With more digits available, new accounts can be added while maintaining the logical order or sequence. Complex businesses may have *thousands* of accounts and require longer account numbers!

It is worthwhile to put thought into assigning your account numbers in a logical way and following specific industry standards. An example of how the digits might be coded are as follows:

> **Account Numbering**
> 1000 - 1999: **Asset** accounts
> 2000 - 2999: Liability accounts
> 3000 - 3999: Equity accounts
> 4000 - 4999: Revenue accounts
> 5000 - 5999: Expense accounts

Separating each account by several numbers will allow many new accounts to be added while maintaining the same logical order. Note that the account numbering follows the order of the financial statements: Balance Sheet - Assets, Liabilities, and Equity; Income Statement - Revenue accounts, then Expense accounts.

Defining Accounts

Different types of businesses will have different accounts. For example, to report the cost of goods sold in a manufacturing business, there will be various accounts for manufacturing costs, whereas a retailer will have accounts for the purchase of its stock merchandise. Many industrial associations publish recommended charts of accounts for their respective industries in order to establish a consistent standard of comparison among firms in their industry. Accounting software packages often come with a selection of predefined account charts for various types of businesses.

Some accounts must be included due to tax reporting requirements. For example, some tax authorities require that travel, entertainment, advertising, and several other expenses be tracked using individual accounts. (You should check the appropriate tax regulations and generate a complete list of such required accounts.)

Other accounts should be set up according to vendor. If the business has more than one bank account, for example, the chart of accounts might include an account for each of them.

There is a trade-off between simplicity and the ability to make historical comparisons. Initially keeping the number of accounts to a minimum has the advantage of making the accounting system simple. Start with a small number of accounts and then, as certain accounts acquire significant balances, they can be split into smaller, more specific accounts. However, following this strategy makes it more difficult to generate consistent historical comparisons. For example, if the accounting system is set up with a miscellaneous expense account that later is broken into more detailed accounts, it would be difficult to compare those detailed expenses with the past expenses of the same type. In this respect, there is an advantage in organizing the chart of accounts with a higher level of detail from the beginning.

Account Order

Balance sheet accounts tend to follow a standard format that lists the most liquid assets first. Revenue and expense accounts tend to follow the standard format of first listing the items most closely related to the operations of the business. For example, sales would be listed before non-operating income such as interest earned on savings.

Chart of Accounts

We are using a health club business as an example:

You will notice that we are skipping 5 numbers at a time. The reason for this is to allow for another account of a similar nature to be inserted in between which will ensure that all similar accounts are grouped together. For example, if you were to open another bank account, the new account may be coded as 102.

You will also notice that the Expenses are listed in alphabetic order, making it easier to locate accounts.

Many companies are adopting XBRL (Extensible Business Reporting Language) when assigning account numbers. XBRL

Account Description	Account #
ASSETS - Category 1	
Cash	101
Accounts Receivable	105
Prepaid Expenses	110
Inventory	115
Fixed Assets - Equipment	120
Accumulated Depreciation	130
LIABILITIES - Category 2	
Accounts Payable	200
Unearned Revenue	205
Bank Loan	210
Equipment Loan	215
OWNER'S EQUITY - Category 3	
Capital Account	300
Owner's Investment	305
Owner's Drawings	310
Income Summary	315

Account Description	Account #
REVENUE - Category 4	
Membership Sales	400
EXPENSES - Category 5	
Advertising	500
Bad Debts	505
Insurance	510
Maintenance	515
Miscellaneous	520
Office Supplies	525
Professional Fees	530
Rent	535
Salaries & Bonuses	540
Salary Benefits	541
Telephone	545
Travel	550
Depreciation	555
OTHER REVENUE & EXPENSES	
Interest Earned on Savings	405
Discounts Received	410
Interest & Bank Charges	560
Loss on Disposal of Equipment	565

is a global standard that facilitates the exchange of financial information. The XBRL organization has developed a "standard" set of account numbers that are used when recording financial information.

AME | Learning

Completing Financial Statements

These are the basic steps to maintain a formal set of financial statements, which manually simulates computer generated financial statements. We will take you through them one step at a time.

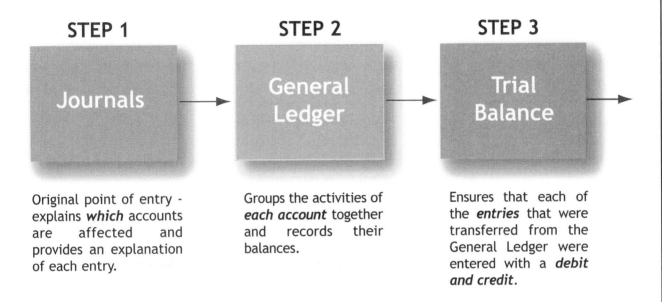

STEP 1

Journals

Original point of entry - explains **which** accounts are affected and provides an explanation of each entry.

STEP 2

General Ledger

Groups the activities of **each account** together and records their balances.

STEP 3

Trial Balance

Ensures that each of the **entries** that were transferred from the General Ledger were entered with a **debit and credit**.

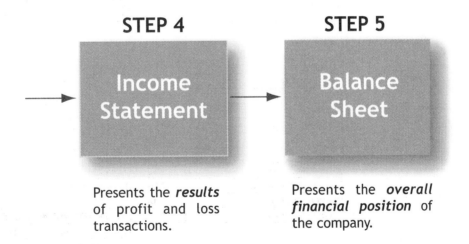

STEP 4

Income Statement

Presents the **results** of profit and loss transactions.

STEP 5

Balance Sheet

Presents the **overall financial position** of the company.

291

General Journal

The *General Journal* is the first step in recording transactions — it is also referred to as the *book of original entry*. The journal is used to record every pair of transactions (debit and credit) and the purpose of the transaction. This process is called **journalizing**.

The General Journal provides a complete, organized record of all the transactions of the business. Recording all the transactions in one place reduces the risk of potential errors and makes it easier to track any mistakes.

The format of the General Journal is relatively standard and generally includes the following items:

❶ *Date*: enter the current year at the top of the first column and then the month and day of the transaction — the journal entries are in chronological order (by date)

❷ *Account Title & Explanation*: there are three lines per transaction, as follows:
   a. the first line is the name of the account that is being **debited**
   b. the second line is the name of the account that is being **credited** (the credit line is indented slightly - this is a long-standing standard for accountants)
   c. the third and last line is a very brief explanation of the reason for the transaction

❸ **General Ledger No. (also referred to as *Reference or Posting Reference*)**: enter the number assigned to the account from the Chart of Accounts (e.g. Cash = 101, Rent Expense = 302, etc.) *after* the amount has been recorded in the general ledger

❹ *Debit or Credit*: enter the amount of the transaction in the appropriate column — is it a debit for that amount or a credit?

❺ *Leave a blank space between journal entries*.

GENERAL JOURNAL		❸		J1
DATE: 20XX ❶	ACCOUNT TITLE AND EXPLANATION	GL NO.	DEBIT	CREDIT
Jan. 1	Rent	535	$2,000	
	Cash ❷	101		$2,000
	Paid rent for month of January			

Reference Numbers

The general journal, general ledger and trial balances are all linked. It is very important to cross reference all the entries, thereby tracing the flow of information.

After the general journal entries have been completed, the general ledger account number to which the various entries will be *posted* should be entered into the GL No. column. Conversely, each entry in the general ledger should be cross-referenced to the general journal. The general journal usually has a reference number at the top of the page (for example J1, J2 etc.) This page number is entered into the reference column in the general ledger.

Companies may choose to use specialized journals in addition to the general journal. Specialized journals may be used to record transactions of a certain type, e.g. Sales, Purchases, Receipts, Disbursements, Payroll, etc.

General Ledger

All the activities for the month have been recorded into the General Journal. What you do not know at this point is to what extent the accounts have been affected. In other words, there have been several transactions relating to cash, but at this time, you do not know the actual cash balance. The accounts need to be sorted into a manageable format - each account is assigned a separate page where *all* transactions affecting that account will be recorded.

You will need to record the date of the transaction, a short explanation, the journal page where the transaction originated, the amount, whether it was a debit or credit and the new balance.

Each entry must be posted (recorded) to the relevant ledger account. These ledgers are combined to form a General Ledger that is used for preparing financial statements and other reports. The posting of journal entries to the ledgers must be done as soon as possible — preferably daily or on a monthly basis, but may also be done on a weekly basis. The individual account balances must be **current** when the financial statements are prepared and therefore it is imperative that the posting be made on a regular basis.

Referring to the transactions on the previous page, the posting to the General Ledger is completed as follows (note the General Ledger is for Rent Expense and Cash):

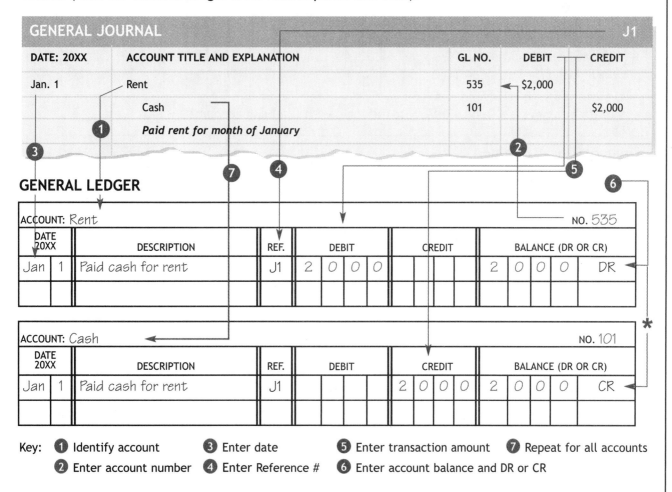

Key:
- ❶ Identify account
- ❸ Enter date
- ❺ Enter transaction amount
- ❼ Repeat for all accounts
- ❷ Enter account number
- ❹ Enter Reference #
- ❻ Enter account balance and DR or CR

✱ See an explanation for DR and CR balances on the next page.

Note that the recording of a description in the description column of a general ledger account is optional. Most entries do not include a description in the description column of the general ledger. The column is reserved for *unusual items*.

The Logic of Debit and Credit Balances

The logic of debt and credit balances when looking at a general ledger is all based on the transaction. For example, an increase to expenses corresponds to a debit, therefore the higher the expenses, the higher the debit balance. So, as long as you have expenses you will always see a debit balance. On the other hand, an increase in sales corresponds to a credit. Therefore your general ledger sales balance will always be a credit.

Here are some examples:

ACCOUNT: Revenue - Membership Sales   NO. 400

DATE 20XX		DESCRIPTION	REF.	DEBIT	CREDIT	BALANCE (DR OR CR)	
Jan	1	Opening Balance	J1			2 0 0 0	CR
Jan	14	Sell membership to Joe Bloggs	J1		2 0 0	2 2 0 0	CR
Jan	18	Sell membership to Cathy Bloom	J1		2 5 0	2 4 5 0	CR
Jan	20	Sell membership to John Boomer	J1		2 5 0	2 7 0 0	CR

An increase in assets is a Debit - let's test the logic with the bank account:

ACCOUNT: Bank Account (Cash)   NO. 101

DATE 20XX		DESCRIPTION	REF.	DEBIT	CREDIT	BALANCE (DR OR CR)	
Jan	1	Opening Balance	J1			5 0 0 0	DR
Jan	14	Sell membership to Joe Bloggs	J1	2 0 0		5 2 0 0	DR
Jan	18	Sell membership to Cathy Bloom	J1	2 5 0		5 4 5 0	DR
Jan	20	Sell membership to John Boomer	J1	2 5 0		5 7 0 0	DR
Jan	22	Sell a machine for cash	J1	6 0 0		6 3 0 0	DR
Jan	23	Collect Accounts Receivable	J1	8 0 0		7 1 0 0	DR
Jan	24	Pay Accounts Payable	J1		8 0 0	6 3 0 0	DR
Jan	26	Pay Wages	J1		2 0 0 0	4 3 0 0	DR

See the logic? As sales increase so does the credit balance, resulting in a closing balance that is a credit. Conversely, when using cash, the transaction itself is a debit or a credit but the **remaining balance** is still a debit (positive balance).

Note that the recording of a description is optional (see note at top of page).

Trial Balance

Remember that for every Debit (DR) entry, there must be a Credit (CR) entry and vice versa. To ensure that this rule has been adhered to, we need to create a **trial balance** to ensure that all the debits equal all the credits. Some accountants choose to total the debit and credit columns in journals as well, as an added control to ensure that the debits equal credits. This is demonstrated in the General Journal (J12) on page 296. (The trial balance is also used as an internal report for the preparation of financial statements.)

A trial balance that balances does *not* indicate that all the entries are correct. Here are some examples:

a. You could have credited cash and debited assets instead of debiting an expense. The trial balance will balance, but the financial statements will be wrong.

b. The journal entry may not have been recorded at all.

c. The journal entry may have been posted twice.

d. Incorrect amounts may have been posted for both the DR and CR entry.

It is pretty easy to make a mistake and stay in balance. Locating errors can be a frustrating experience, so it's very important to ensure that entries are made correctly *the first time*.

The trial balance is made up of several components:

Date: for the month ended (month, day, year).

Account title: name of the account.

Debit or Credit: the account balance and whether it is a debit or credit (see next page).

Illustration of the Process

Here is the procedure for entering the following transactions for December, 20XX:

▶ Dec. 1: Collect and deposit $10,000 in cash sales (increase cash & increase sales)

▶ Dec. 2: Pay $5,000 for staff payroll (decrease cash & increase salaries expense)

STEP 1 - General Journal

Enter the transactions into the General Journal and check that the debit and credit columns balance.

GENERAL JOURNAL				J12
DATE 20XX	ACCOUNT TITLE AND EXPLANATION	GL NO.	DEBIT	CREDIT
Dec 1	Cash	101	10,000	
	Revenue - Membership Sales	400		10,000
	Cash sales			
Dec 2	Salaries & Bonuses	540	5,000	
	Cash	101		5,000
	Pay staff payroll			
	Total		15,000	15,000

STEP 2 - General Ledger

Now transfer (post) the amounts to the General Ledger from the General Journal.

ACCOUNT: Cash   **NO.** 101

DATE 20XX		DESCRIPTION	REF.	DEBIT	CREDIT	BALANCE (DR OR CR)
Dec	1	Cash Sales	J12	10 0 0 0		10 0 0 0 DR
Dec	2	Payroll	J12		5 0 0 0	5 0 0 0 DR

ACCOUNT: Revenue - Membership Sales   **NO.** 400

DATE 20XX		DESCRIPTION	REF.	DEBIT	CREDIT	BALANCE (DR OR CR)
Dec	1	Cash Sales	J12		10 0 0 0	10 0 0 0 CR

ACCOUNT: Salaries & Bonuses   **NO.** 540

DATE 20XX		DESCRIPTION	REF.	DEBIT	CREDIT	BALANCE (DR OR CR)
Dec	2	Payroll	J12	5 0 0 0		5 0 0 0 DR

STEP 3 - Trial Balance

Create a Trial Balance to ensure that the debits and credits from the General Journal were posted to the correct debit and credit columns in the General Ledger. (The ledgers have been repeated to make it easier to illustrate the cross-reference).

ACCOUNT: Cash   NO. 101

DATE 20XX		DESCRIPTION	REF.	DEBIT	CREDIT	BALANCE (DR OR CR)
Dec	1	Cash Sales	J12	10 0 0 0		10 0 0 0 DR
Dec	2	Payroll	J12		5 0 0 0	5 0 0 0 DR

ACCOUNT: Revenue - Membership Sales   NO. 400

DATE 20XX		DESCRIPTION	REF.	DEBIT	CREDIT	BALANCE (DR OR CR)
Dec	1	Cash Sales	J12		10 0 0 0	10 0 0 0 CR

ACCOUNT: Salaries & Bonuses   NO. 540

DATE 20XX		DESCRIPTION	REF.	DEBIT	CREDIT	BALANCE (DR OR CR)
Dec	2	Payroll	J12	5 0 0 0		5 0 0 0 DR

Health Pro XYZ
Trial Balance
December 31, 20xx

ACCOUNT TITLES	DR.	CR.
Cash	5,000	
Fixed Assets		
Accumulated Depreciation		
Accounts Payable		
Capital Account		
Revenue - Membership Sales		10,000
Advertising		
Insurance		
Salaries & Bonuses	5,000	
Rent		
Maintenance		
Telephone		
Total	**10,000**	**10,000**

All the debits should be equal to all the credits.

Examples of Transactions

Example #1

Here is an example of the sequence of the transactions in completing a set of financial statements.

Transactions for this example:

Date	Details	Amount
Jan 1st	Sell memberships for cash	3,000
Jan 2nd	Issue cheques for payroll	500
Jan 3rd	Pay rent using pre-authorized payment	300
Jan 4th	Buy equipment on account	1,000
Jan 5th	Pay Accounts Payable	500

Remember the sequence:

1. Complete the GENERAL JOURNAL

2. Post to the GENERAL LEDGER

3. Create a TRIAL BALANCE

Chart of Accounts →

Account Description	Account #
ASSETS - Category 1	
Cash	101
Accounts Receivable	105
Prepaid Expenses	110
Inventory	115
Fixed Assets - Equipment	120
Accumulated Depreciation	130

Account Description	Account #
LIABILITIES - Category 2	
Accounts Payable	200
Unearned Revenue	205
Bank Loan	210
Equipment Loan	215

Account Description	Account #
OWNER'S EQUITY - Category 3	
Capital Account	300
Owner's Investment	305
Owner's Drawings	310
Income Summary	315

Account Description	Account #
REVENUE - Category 4	
Membership Sales	400

Account Description	Account #
EXPENSES - Category 5	
Advertising	500
Bad Debts	505
Insurance	510
Maintenance	515
Miscellaneous	520
Office Supplies	525
Professional Fees	530
Rent	535
Salaries & Bonuses	540
Salary Benefits	541
Telephone	545
Travel	550
Depreciation	555

Account Description	Account #
OTHER REVENUE & EXPENSES	
Interest Earned on Savings	405
Discounts Received	410
Interest & Bank Charges	560
Loss on Disposal of Equipment	565

STEP 1:

Here is the completed General Journal:

GENERAL JOURNAL				J1
DATE: 20XX	**ACCOUNT TITLE AND EXPLANATION**	**GL NO.**	**DEBIT**	**CREDIT**
January 1	Cash	101	3,000	
	Revenue - Membership Sales	400		3,000
	Sell memberships for cash			
January 2	Salaries & Bonuses	540	500	
	Cash	101		500
	Payroll for the week			
January 3	Rent	535	300	
	Cash	101		300
	Paid for rent for the month			
January 4	Fixed Assets - Equipment	120	1,000	
	Accounts Payable	200		1,000
	Bought equipment - pay next month			
January 5	Accounts Payable	200	500	
	Cash	101		500
	Paid last month's Accounts Payable			

STEP 2:

Using the General Journal transactions on the previous page, the following are the entries posted to the General Ledger.

ACCOUNT: Cash — NO. 101

DATE 20XX		DESCRIPTION	REF.	DEBIT				CREDIT			BALANCE (DR OR CR)				
Jan	1	Sell memberships for cash	J1	3	0	0	0				3	0	0	0	DR
Jan	2	Payroll for the week	J1					5	0	0	2	5	0	0	DR
Jan	3	Paid rent	J1					3	0	0	2	2	0	0	DR
Jan	5	Paid Accounts Payable	J1					5	0	0	1	7	0	0	DR

ACCOUNT: Fixed Assets - Equipment — NO. 120

DATE 20XX		DESCRIPTION	REF.	DEBIT				CREDIT			BALANCE (DR OR CR)				
Jan	4	Bought equipment on account	J1	1	0	0	0				1	0	0	0	DR

ACCOUNT: Accounts Payable — NO. 200

DATE 20XX		DESCRIPTION	REF.	DEBIT				CREDIT			BALANCE (DR OR CR)				
Jan	4	Bought equipment on account	J1					1	0	0	0	1	0	0	0	CR
Jan	5	Paid Accounts Payable	J1		5	0	0					5	0	0	CR

ACCOUNT: Revenue - Membership Sales — NO. 400

DATE 20XX		DESCRIPTION	REF.	DEBIT				CREDIT			BALANCE (DR OR CR)				
Jan	1	Sell memberships for cash	J1					3	0	0	0	3	0	0	0	CR

ACCOUNT: Rent — NO. 535

DATE 20XX		DESCRIPTION	REF.	DEBIT				CREDIT			BALANCE (DR OR CR)				
Jan	3	Paid rent	J1		3	0	0					3	0	0	DR

ACCOUNT: Salaries & Bonuses — NO. 540

DATE 20XX		DESCRIPTION	REF.	DEBIT				CREDIT			BALANCE (DR OR CR)				
Jan	2	Payroll for the week	J1		5	0	0					5	0	0	DR

STEP 3:

The **closing account balances** from the General Ledger are transferred to the Trial Balance. The following worksheet facilitates the preparation of financial statements. The worksheet is essentially a trial balance with four additional columns; a pair of columns for the income statement, and a pair of columns for the balance sheet.

TRIAL BALANCE - WORKSHEET - MONTH ENDED JANUARY 31, 20XX						
	TRIAL BALANCE		INCOME STATEMENT		BALANCE SHEET	
ACCOUNT TITLES	DR	CR	DR	CR	DR	CR
Cash	1,700				1,700 ❶	
Fixed Assets	1,000				1,000 ❷	
Accounts Payable		500			❸	500
Revenue - Membership Sales		3,000		3,000 ❹		
Rent	300		300 ❺			
Salaries & Bonuses	500		500 ❻			
Totals	3,500	3,500	800	3,000	2,700	500
Profit (Loss)			2,200 ❼			
Owner's Equity					❽	2,200
Total	3,500	3,500	3,000	3,000	2,700	2,700

Remember that the total of all debits and credits must be equal. The difference between the revenue column (CR) and the expense column (DR) on the Income Statement is the profit or loss. If the credits exceed the debits the result is a profit. If debits exceed credits the result is a loss.

TRIAL BALANCE - JANUARY 31, 20XX		
	TRIAL BALANCE	
ACCOUNT TITLES	DR	CR
Cash	1,700	
Fixed Assets	1,000	
Accounts Payable		500
Revenue - Membership Sales		3,000
Rent	300	
Salaries & Bonuses	500	
Totals	3,500	3,500
Profit (Loss)		
Owner's Equity		
Total	3,500	3,500

By "plugging" the difference between the revenues and expenses (debits and credits) the trial balance will balance. Notice the profits increased together with Owner's Equity resulting in a balanced balance sheet.

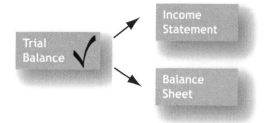

STEPS 4 and 5:

Preparing the financial statements: The trial balance is not laid out in a friendly manner for the reader. It is therefore useful to create an easily understandable document in the form of a balance sheet and income statement. The totals come from the trial balance worksheet.

You have learned to post the transactions from the general journal to the general ledger and ensure that for every debit there was a credit by adding up the trial balance. So what do we do with this information? The balances from each of the general ledger accounts needs to be presented in a logical manner so that management can use the information to manage the business.

INCOME STATEMENT
FOR MONTH ENDING JANUARY 31, 20XX

Revenue - membership fees	$3,000	❹
Expenses		
Rent	300	❺
Salaries and Bonuses	500	❻
Total Expenses	800	
Net Income	$2,200	❼

STATEMENT OF OWNER'S EQUITY
FOR MONTH ENDING JANUARY 31, 20XX

ⓐ	Owner's Equity at January 1	$	0
ⓑ	Add additional investments		0
ⓒ	Add Net Income		2,200
ⓓ	Subtract Owner's Drawings		0
ⓔ	Closing Owner's Equity		$2,200 ❽

BALANCE SHEET
AS AT JANUARY 31, 20XX

ASSETS		
Cash	$ 1,700	❶
Accounts Receivable	0	
Prepaid Expenses	0	
Inventory	0	
Fixed Assets - Equipment	1,000	❷
Total Assets	$ 2,700	
LIABILITIES		
Accounts Payable	$ 500	❸
Unearned Revenue	0	
Bank Loan	0	
Equipment Loan	0	
Total Liabilities	$ 500	
OWNER'S EQUITY	$ 2,200	
Liabilities + Equity	$ 2,700	

Statement of Owner's Equity

The Statement of Owner's Equity reports any changes in equity over the reporting period.

ⓐ It begins with the opening owner's equity at the beginning of the period.

ⓑ It will increase with any additional capital the owner invests into the business.

ⓒ It will increase or decrease by the profit or loss on the income statement.

ⓓ It reflects any decrease from withdrawals by the owner (drawings).

ⓔ The final closing balance is then transferred to the owner's equity section of the balance sheet.

Example #2 - Adjustments

Once you have finished recording the routine financial transactions you still need to adjust various accounts to record transactions such as depreciation, bank charges shown on the bank statement and to correct mistakes, etc.

These entries are recorded on the worksheet in a separate column called *adjustments*. Once the adjustments have been entered, the new balances are transferred to the **Adjusted Trial Balance**. After completion of the trial balance, the income statement and balance sheet entries are separated just like you did in the first exercise to allow you to calculate a profit or loss.

Here is an example of the Adjusted Trial Balance:

Health Pro XYZ
TRIAL BALANCE - WORKSHEET
January 31, 20xx

ACCOUNT TITLES	UNADJUSTED TRIAL BALANCE DR	CR	ADJUSTMENTS DR	CR	ADJUSTED TRIAL BALANCE DR	CR	INCOME STATEMENT DR	CR	BALANCE SHEET DR	CR
Cash										
Fixed Assets - Equipment										
Accounts Payable										
Capital Account										
Revenue - Membership Sales										
Rent										
Salaries & Bonuses										
Telephone										
Totals										
Interest & Bank Charges										
Depreciation										
Total Adjusted										
PROFIT (LOSS)										

STEP 1:

Here is the General Journal showing two adjustments:

GENERAL JOURNAL				J2
DATE: 20XX	ACCOUNT TITLE AND EXPLANATION	GL NO.	DEBIT	CREDIT
February 1	Cash	101	5,000	
	Capital Account	300		5,000
	Deposit your own cash into the business			
February 2	Fixed Assets - Equipment	120	1,000	
	Cash	101		1,000
	Buy computers for cash			
February 3	Cash	101	3,000	
	Revenue - Membership Sales	400		3,000
	Membership sales for cash			
February 4	Telephone	545	300	
	Accounts Payable	200		300
	Telephone bill to be paid next month			
February 5	Salaries & Bonuses	540	800	
	Cash	101		800
	Issue cheques for payroll			
February 6	Rent	535	1,000	
	Cash	101		1,000
	Pay rent by cheque			
Adjustments:				
February 28	Depreciation	555	100	
	Fixed Assets - Equipment	120		100
	Depreciate fixed assets			
February 28	Interest & Bank charges	560	20	
	Cash	101		20
	Record bank charges from bank statement			

STEP 2:

Here are the postings to the General Ledger:

ACCOUNT: Cash   NO. 101

DATE 20XX		DESCRIPTION	REF.	DEBIT	CREDIT	BALANCE (DR OR CR)	
Feb	1	Deposit your cash in business	J2	5 0 0 0		5 0 0 0	DR
Feb	2	Buy computers for cash	J2		1 0 0 0	4 0 0 0	DR
Feb	3	Revenues for cash	J2	3 0 0 0		7 0 0 0	DR
Feb	5	Pay for labour with cheque	J2		8 0 0	6 2 0 0	DR
Feb	6	Pay for rent with cheque	J2		1 0 0 0	5 2 0 0	DR
Feb	28	Record bank charges	J2		2 0	5 1 8 0	DR

ACCOUNT: Fixed Assets - Equipment   **NO.** 120

DATE 20XX		DESCRIPTION	REF.	DEBIT				CREDIT				BALANCE (DR OR CR)				
Feb	2	Buy computers for cash	J2	1	0	0	0					1	0	0	0	DR
Feb	28	Depreciate fixed assets	J2						1	0	0		9	0	0	DR

ACCOUNT: Accounts Payable   **NO.** 200

DATE 20XX		DESCRIPTION	REF.	DEBIT			CREDIT			BALANCE (DR OR CR)			
Feb	4	Record telephone bill	J2				3	0	0	3	0	0	CR

ACCOUNT: Capital Account   **NO.** 300

DATE 20XX		DESCRIPTION	REF.	DEBIT				CREDIT				BALANCE (DR OR CR)				
Feb	1	Deposit cash in business	J2					5	0	0	0	5	0	0	0	CR

ACCOUNT: Revenue - Membership Sales   **NO.** 400

DATE 20XX		DESCRIPTION	REF.	DEBIT				CREDIT				BALANCE (DR OR CR)				
Feb	3	Revenues for cash	J2					3	0	0	0	3	0	0	0	CR

ACCOUNT: Rent   **NO.** 535

DATE 20XX		DESCRIPTION	REF.	DEBIT				CREDIT				BALANCE (DR OR CR)				
Feb	6	Pay rent with cheque	J2	1	0	0	0					1	0	0	0	DR

ACCOUNT: Salaries & Bonuses   **NO.** 540

DATE 20XX		DESCRIPTION	REF.	DEBIT			CREDIT			BALANCE (DR OR CR)			
Feb	5	Pay for labour with cheque	J2	8	0	0				8	0	0	DR

ACCOUNT: Telephone   **NO.** 545

DATE 20XX		DESCRIPTION	REF.	DEBIT			CREDIT			BALANCE (DR OR CR)			
Feb	4	Record telephone bill	J2	3	0	0				3	0	0	DR

ACCOUNT: Depreciation   **NO.** 555

DATE 20XX		DESCRIPTION	REF.	DEBIT			CREDIT			BALANCE (DR OR CR)			
Feb	28	Depreciate fixed assets	J2	1	0	0				1	0	0	DR

ACCOUNT: Interest & Bank Charges   **NO.** 560

DATE 20XX		DESCRIPTION	REF.	DEBIT			CREDIT			BALANCE (DR OR CR)			
Feb	28	Record bank charges	J2		2	0					2	0	DR

Step 3:

The closing account balances from the General Ledger are transferred to the Trial Balance worksheet.

Health Pro XYZ
TRIAL BALANCE
Worksheet for the period ended February 28, 20xx

ACCOUNT TITLES	UNADJUSTED TRIAL BALANCE		ADJUSTMENTS		ADJUSTED TRIAL BALANCE		INCOME STATEMENT		BALANCE SHEET	
	DR	CR	DR	CR	DR	CR	DR	CR	DR	CR
Cash	5,200			20	5,180				5,180 ❶	
Fixed Assets - Equipment	1,000			100	900				900 ❷	
Accounts Payable		300				300			❸	300
Capital Account		5,000				5,000			❿	5,000
Revenue - Membership Sales		3,000				3,000	❹	3,000		
Rent	1,000				1,000		1,000 ❺			
Salaries & Bonuses	800				800		800 ❻			
Telephone	300				300		300 ❼			
Totals	8,300	8,300	0	120	8,180	8,300	2,100	3,000	6,080	5,300
Interest & Bank Charges			20		20		20 ❽			
Depreciation			100		100		100 ❾			
Total Adjusted			120	120	8,300	8,300	2,220	3,000	6,080	5,300	ⓒ
PROFIT (LOSS)							780 ⓫			780	ⓓ
							3,000	3,000	6,080	6,080

ⓐ

ⓑ

ⓐ This represents the UNADJUSTED trial balance, as illustrated in the first exercise. It is not complete because it does not include the adjustments - depreciation and bank charges - which still need to be entered.

ⓑ Below the unadjusted trial balance totals, new accounts are added for adjusting entries as required. As adjusting entries are entered, some amounts are recorded on these new lines, while other amounts are recorded in accounts already shown on the worksheet. For example, the debit to bank charges requires a new account (Bank charges and interest), while the credit is made to an already existing account (Cash).

ⓒ Now that we have the final totals having made sure that every debit has an associated credit, we can then calculate a profit or loss.

ⓓ Once the profit (loss) has been calculated the formal financial statements must be prepared.

Steps 4 & 5:

Preparing the formal financial statements, as follows:

HEALTH PRO XYZ
INCOME STATEMENT
FOR MONTH ENDING FEBRUARY 28, 20XX

Revenue - membership fees	$3,000	**4**
Expenses		
Rent	1,000	**5**
Salaries and Bonuses	800	**6**
Telephone	300	**7**
Bank charges & interest	20	**8**
Depreciation	100	**9**
Total Expenses	**2,220**	
Operating Profit	**$ 780**	

STATEMENT OF OWNER'S EQUITY
FOR MONTH ENDING FEBRUARY 28, 20XX

Owner's Equity at February 1	$ 0	
Add additional investments	5,000	**10**
Add Net Income	780	**11**
Subtract Owner's Drawings	0	
Closing Owner's Equity	**$5,780**	

HEALTH PRO XYZ
BALANCE SHEET
AS AT FEBRUARY 28, 20XX

ASSETS		
Cash	$ 5,180	**1**
Accounts Receivable	0	
Prepaid Expenses	0	
Inventory	0	
Fixed Assets - Equipment	900	**2**
Total Assets	**$ 6,080**	
LIABILITIES		
Accounts Payable	$ 300	**3**
Unearned Revenue	0	
Bank Loan	0	
Equipment Loan	0	
Total Liabilities	**$ 300**	
OWNER'S EQUITY	**$ 5,780**	
Liabilities + Equity	**$ 6,080**	

Bank Reconciliations

Even though banks use computers, errors may exist in their computer programs. People generate much of the data included in your bank account, and people can record incorrect amounts, charge amounts to the wrong bank account, and process amounts that do not belong in your bank account.

In fact, the banks rely on you to point out errors to them. If an amount is incorrectly charged to your bank account the bank expects you to report the error to them, usually within thirty days of receiving the bank statement. The problem is, many people assume that because their statements are computer-produced they cannot contain errors. As a result, many bank errors go undetected.

A simple internal control is to check your bank statement. To do this, you compare the items in your records (journals and ledgers) to the items shown on the bank statement. The process is called a **bank reconciliation.**

Some items correctly shown on the bank statement may not appear in your records and, on the other hand, some items in your records may not appear on the bank statement. The bank reconciliation process ensures that both your records and the bank's records agree. Here is an example of two typical transactions that may disagree with your records:

1. A bank automatically deducts bank charges, such as interest charged to you and a fee for maintaining your account. This is how banks make money.

2. A bank may automatically *deposit* interest into your account that you have *earned* in return for having a cash balance in your account.

You will not know the value of these transactions until you receive your bank statement, as follows:

			ABC BANKING		
Harold Z. Smythe					
20 Easy Street					
Victoria, BC					
V9A 1P1				ACCOUNT NUMBER: **0136911**	
STATEMENT OF		FROM	TO		PAGE
Personal Chequing Account		**Sept 1, 20XX**	**Sept 30, 20XX**		1
DESCRIPTION	WITHDRAWALS	DEPOSITS		DATE	BALANCE
Balance Forward			09	01	1,256.00
❶ Deposit		500.00	09	03	1,756.00 ✓
❷ Cheque #24	87.00		09	04	1,669.00 ✓
❸ Cheque #25	200.00		09	06	1,469.00 ✓
❹ Bank machine withdrawal	100.00		09	08	1,369.00 ✓
❺ Cheque #26	325.00		09	15	1,044.00 ✓
⑥ Automatic withdrawal - rent	450.00		09	30	594.00 ✓
⑦ Bank charges	10.00		09	30	584.00
⑧ Interest earned on savings		30.00	09	30	614.00

Numbers **1 to 5** match with your own General Ledger records. Numbers **6 to 8** do not match.

⑥ *Automatic withdrawal:* There are certain pre-approved withdrawals that are automatically deducted from your account by the bank. As you know about these you can enter them into your system and they should not have to be reconciled at the end of the month. Some typical examples include rent, insurance, car payments, bank loans and charities. However, if you had forgotten to enter this on your records the bank statement would have brought this to your attention.

⑦ *Bank charges:* This is an example of an expense that is deducted from your bank account automatically. Although you may be aware that the charges will occur, you will not know the amount each time. In this case you will have to record these charges by decreasing (crediting) cash and increasing (debiting) bank charges, which will now match (reconcile) your books with the bank's records.

⑧ *Interest earned on savings:* This is an example of a payment made to you that was not recorded during the month because even though you may have known that the payment was due to you, you would not have known the amount. In this case you will have to record the interest by increasing (debiting) cash and increasing (crediting) interest revenue, which again will reconcile with the bank's records.

Now you will reconcile to the bank statement using your personal bank book (or general ledger). Review each entry on the bank statement on the previous page and place a checkmark in the "Clear" column representing a match, indicating that the bank statement entry matches the entry on your general ledger. Make a corresponding tick mark on the bank statement. Items that remain unticked, either on the bank statement of your company's records are reconciling items.

DATE 20XX		DESCRIPTION	DEBIT				CREDIT				BALANCE				CLEAR
\multicolumn{16}{l}{ACCOUNT: Bank Account}
Sep	1	Opening balance									1	2	5	6	
Sep	3	Deposit salary cheque	5	0	0						1	7	5	6	✔
Sep	4	Cheque #24 - groceries						8	7		1	6	6	9	✔
Sep	6	Cheque #25 - car insurance					2	0	0		1	4	6	9	✔
Sep	8	Bank machine withdrawal					1	0	0		1	3	6	9	✔
Sep	15	Cheque #26 - car payment					3	2	5		1	0	4	4	✔
Sep	30	Automatic withdrawal - rent					4	5	0			5	9	4	✔

Remember that your bank balance, according to YOUR records, must match the balance on the bank statement. It does happen, from time to time, that there may be an incorrect entry on the bank statement. In other words, money could have been incorrectly withdrawn or a deposit made into your account which does not belong to you. In this event there is nothing to change on your books, you simply must contact the bank to correct the error.

In this exercise, you should assume that the items listed on the bank statement, but not recorded on your general ledger so far, are in fact correct.

Your general ledger shows a bank balance of $594.00 on September 30th (⑥ on the previous page). However, the bank statement shows a balance of $614.00 (⑧ on the previous page). In other words you think that you have $20 less than you actually have in your account.

Now you need to enter the missing transactions from the bank statement onto your records to complete the match. Here are the transactions:

Entry ⑦ on the bank statement - bank charges - *debit Interest & Bank Charges and credit Cash*:

ACCOUNT: Interest & Bank Charges — No. 560

DATE 20XX		DESCRIPTION	DEBIT	CREDIT	BALANCE
Sep	30	Bank service charges	1 0		1 0

ACCOUNT: Cash — No. 101

DATE 20XX		DESCRIPTION	DEBIT	CREDIT	BALANCE
Sep	30	Bank service charges		1 0	1 0

Entry ⑧ on the bank statement - interest earned on savings - *debit Cash and credit Interest Earned on Savings*:

ACCOUNT: Cash — No. 101

DATE 20XX		DESCRIPTION	DEBIT	CREDIT	BALANCE
Sep	30	Interest earned on savings	3 0		3 0

ACCOUNT: Interest Earned on Savings — No. 405

DATE 20XX		DESCRIPTION	DEBIT	CREDIT	BALANCE
Sep	30	Interest earned on savings		3 0	3 0

Summary of reconciliation:

The difference between your closing bank balance of $594.00 and the bank's closing balance of $614.00 amounts to $20.00. If you examine the entries that you just made, you will see that you recorded a withdrawal of $10.00 (bank charges) and a deposit of $30.00 (interest), the difference being $20.00, which correctly increases your balance to $614.00.

ACCOUNT: Bank Account

DATE 20XX		DESCRIPTION	DEBIT	CREDIT	BALANCE	CLEAR
Sep	30	Opening balance			5 9 4	
Sep	30	Bank service charges		1 0	5 8 4	✓
Sep	30	Interest earned on savings	3 0		6 1 4	✓

Compound Entries

A transaction that affects 3 or more accounts is called a compound journal entry. In the example below, we record the reduction of a bank loan in the amount of $900 (March and April), as well as interest of $100 on the loan. We could make 2 separate payments: (1) loan reduction $900 (figure 1.1) and (2) interest $100 (figure 1.2), but it is more practical to make one payment in the amount of $1,000. The challenge is in recording the payment. The loan reduction (principal amount) relates to balance sheet accounts only, while the interest portion impacts the balance sheet and the income statement. The common account for both payments is the bank account (cash). Therefore, we complete a compound entry as shown in figure 1.3 below.

figure 1.1

GENERAL JOURNAL				J4
DATE: 20XX	ACCOUNT TITLE AND EXPLANATION	GL NO.	DEBIT	CREDIT
	Bank loan		900	
	Cash			900
	Paid bank loan			

figure 1.2

GENERAL JOURNAL				J4
DATE: 20XX	ACCOUNT TITLE AND EXPLANATION	GL NO.	DEBIT	CREDIT
	Interest		100	
	Cash			100
	Paid interest on bank loan			

figure 1.3

GENERAL JOURNAL				J4
DATE: 20XX	ACCOUNT TITLE AND EXPLANATION	REF.	DEBIT	CREDIT
	Bank loan		900	
	Interest		100	
	Cash (includes both loan reduction and interest payment)			1,000
	Paid bank loan with interest			

Handling Account Errors

Accounting errors do occur. The question is, what's the best way to deal with them?

When you correct errors, you want to ensure that you can identify what happened when reviewing the records at a later date. To that end, the best way to handle errors is to (1) reverse the original entry; and (2) record the correct entry.

For example:

Let's say you made a credit card purchase for $1,200, but recorded the purchase as $1,000. Here's the original entry:

Description	Debit	Credit
Purchases	1,000	
Accounts Payable		1,000
Purchased speakers on credit card		

DR Purchases   **CR Accounts Payable**

You later realize that you recorded an incorrect amount, so you will have to reverse the original entry, as follows:

Description	Debit	Credit
Accounts Payable	1,000	
Purchases		1,000
Reverse entry for purchase of speakers on credit card		

DR Accounts Payable   **CR Purchases**

Now record the correct entry of $1,200:

Description	Debit	Credit
Purchases	1,200	
Accounts Payable		1,200
Correct entry for purchase of speakers on credit card		

DR Purchases   **CR Accounts Payable**

Sales Discounts Allowed

When a discount is offered to customers who agree to pay earlier than when their accounts are due, it is called a **discount allowed**.

Accounting for Discounts Allowed

There are 2 methods for recording a discount allowed:
1. Decrease (DR) revenue, or
2. Increase (DR) discount expense.

These methods both have the same operating profit result, so the choice will depend on the circumstances.

Let's say a customer is offered a volume discount *after* they purchase a certain volume. In this case, revenue would probably decrease, because the discounted amount would be applied at the time of the initial sale (contra account). If, however, the customer takes a discount for early payment, it would not affect the initial sales value. In this case, the discount would be regarded as a discount expense.

Ethical Problem - Cash Discounts

The following situation relates to discounts earned by a business partnership, which are discounts allowed by the supplier company.

During the month of May, a supplier approaches one of the business partners, John, and offers to give him cash equal to 3% of the purchases the business made from his company. The salesman indicated that the cash would be handed over to John in an envelope, meaning that it would not have to be reported in the books of the business, or even to the government for tax purposes.

Should the offer be accepted? Why or why not?

John has a duty to be honest with his business partner, Phil. If John is not honest and if Phil were to find out, how could he trust John in other areas of the business? (Remember that when you enter into a partnership, you are liable for your partner's debts). Phil may even decide to dissolve the partnership!

Who does John cheat if he accepts this money? He would be cheating his business partner as well as the government. The expenses of their business will be overstated, which understates the company's income and reduces taxable income. Also, if John does not report the income, he will be incorrectly reporting his income.

This example may not seem too bad, but if enough people in John's position are unethical, tax rates would have to be increased in order to make up for the shortfall. Taxes supply essential services, like health care and highways. If the government cannot raise taxes it must reduce services and then nobody wins.

Scenario #1: Recording Discount as an Expense

Original sales entry:	Debit	Credit
Accounts Receivable	100	
Sales		100
Sold services on account		

DR Accounts Receivable	CR Sales

Customer pays only $98 due to the 2% discount allowed:		
Cash	98	
Accounts Receivable		98
Received payment		

DR Cash	CR Accounts Receivable

Account for the discount by increasing discount expense:		
Discounts allowed (expense)	2	
Accounts Receivable		2
Discounts allowed		

DR Discounts Allowed	CR Accounts Receivable

Combining the two entries with a compound entry:		
Cash	98	
Discounts allowed (expense)	2	
Accounts Receivable		100
Received payment with discount		

DR Cash	CR Accounts Receivable
DR Discounts Allowed	

Scenario # 2: Reducing Sales

Original entry:	Debit	Credit
Accounts Receivable	100	
Sales		100
Sold services on account		

DR Accounts Receivable	CR Sales

Customer pays only $98 due to the 2% discount allowed:		
Cash	98	
Accounts Receivable		98
Received payment		

DR Cash	CR Accounts Receivable

Account for the discount by decreasing sales:		
Sales	2	
Accounts Receivable		2
Discounts allowed		

DR (Reduce) Sales	CR Accounts Receivable

Result: Sales are now reflected as $98. No change to expenses and the account receivable is cleared.

Internal Controls - Purchase Discounts

A surplus of cash can be used to pay suppliers early to benefit from discounts.

An objective of internal control is the effective and efficient use of resources. So how are purchase discounts tied in with internal controls?

Purchases can be recorded as gross (the price charged before discount) or net (the price actually paid after discount).

A policy should be established that *all purchase discounts will be taken*, and the person paying the bills should be advised of this policy. A policy should also be established that missed discounts will be recorded in a *discounts lost* (expense) account. As a result, if the policy regarding taking all purchase discounts is not followed, the transaction will be highlighted in the *discounts lost* account.

Here is an example:

Purchases are recorded at the net amount. For example, the company buys $1,000 worth of a product on terms 2%/n 10 days. In other words, if the account is paid within 10 days after either receiving the goods or the date of the invoice (whichever has been agreed upon) then 2% may be deducted from the account. The purchase is recorded like this:

Description	Debit	Credit
Purchases	980	
Accounts Payable		980

To record purchase $1,000 2%/10n/30 - net amount $980

Now assume that the person responsible missed the discount date. The entry would look like this:

Description	Debit	Credit
Accounts Payable	980	
Discounts lost	20	
Cash		1,000

To record payment (missed discount date)

When the bill is presented to accounting for payment it must be accompanied by the invoice. The accounting clerk will see that the discount is lost and must approve the journal entry. At this point the invoice is marked as paid.

Here are the control points:

· "All discounts will be taken" policy is established

· Original invoice is approved by accounting

· Cheque is presented to the owners for signature - original invoice is presented again

· Owners approve the "discount lost" entry

· Original invoice is marked as paid

When they approve the "discount lost" entry, the owners have an opportunity to review the policy with the person responsible for paying the bills.

Accounting for Discounts Earned

An alternative to recording discounts as *lost* is to record discounts as *earned*. Both have the same operating profit result. Your choice depends on the circumstances. For example, let's say that your supplier offers you a volume discount *after* you have purchased a certain amount of products or services. In this event, you would probably decrease the expense/asset, since the purchase would not have been recorded at the higher value if the discounted amount has been invoiced initially (contra account). In this case, you would regard the discount as *discounts earned* (revenue) and would record it as follows:

Original purchase entry:

Description	Debit	Credit
Inventory	$100	
Accounts Payable		$100
Purchased Inventory on account		

Debit: Inventory
Credit: Accounts Payable

You pay only $98 due to the 2% discount allowed:

Description	Debit	Credit
Accounts Payable	$98	
Cash		$98
Payment issued		

Debit: Accounts Payable
Credit: Cash

Accounting for the discount by increasing discounts earned:

Description	Debit	Credit
Accounts Payable	$2	
Discounts Earned		$2
Discounts allowed by supplier		

Debit: Accounts Payable
Credit: Discounts Earned

Combining the two entries with a compound entry:

Description	Debit	Credit
Accounts Payable	$100	
Discounts Earned (revenue)		$2
Cash		$98
Made payment payment with discount		

Which method of accounting for discounts should be used? It depends on the circumstances. If a company consistently takes discounts and occasionally misses a discount, then recording purchases net and highlighting *discounts lost* makes sense. If the company rarely takes discounts, then *discounts earned* should be used.

When should assets or expenses be credited instead of discounts earned? It only makes sense to credit assets/expenses if the effect is material (significant).

All methods of recording discounts are allowable under GAAP. The choice is up to the owners of the business. However, once a method has been selected it must remain in place (consistency principle).

Reducing an asset or expense (in this case, an asset):

Original entry:

Description	Debit	Credit
Inventory	$100	
Accounts Payable		$100
Purchased inventory on account		

You pay only $98 resulting from the 2% discount allowed:

Description	Debit	Credit
Accounts Payable	$98	
Cash		$98
Issued payment		

Accounting for the discount by reducing the asset:

Description	Debit	Credit
Accounts Payable	$2	
Inventory		$2
Reduce Inventory		

Result: Inventory is now reflected as $98. The Accounts Payable account is cleared.

Credit Card Sales

Most businesses today accept credit cards. Credit card sales are treated like cash sales. The difference lies in the fact that the credit card companies charge the sellers a fee for the *privilege* of accepting their credit cards. The fee is a percent of credit card sales during the period. The fee is not fixed and is negotiable between the credit card company and the business. Generally speaking, the more credit cards a company processes the lower the fee.

In addition, most credit cards are processed electronically (i.e. automatically deposited in the bank). Those businesses that still process credit card chits by hand accumulate the chits, total the amount and the chits are then deposited in the bank just like cash.

Recording Credit Card Sales

Assume that your company accepts credit cards and had credit card sales of $1,000 for the period.

Description	Debit	Credit
Cash	$1,000	
Sales		$1,000
To record credit card sales		

Debit	Credit
Cash	Sales

Recording the Credit Card Fee

Assume that the credit card company charges a fee of 2½% of credit card sales processed during the month ($1,000 above). The bank automatically deducts the money out of your company's bank account at the end of the period.

Description	Debit	Credit
Bank charges and interest	$25	
Cash		$25
To record credit card sales fees (2½% x $1,000 = $25)		

Debit	Credit
Bank Charges and Interest	Cash

Sales Returns and Allowances

From time to time, businesses will sell goods that are then returned to them for various reasons:

· wrong colour or size
· wrong amount delivered
· customer changed their mind
· defective goods

When goods are returned (if they cannot be returned to stock) the business will have to either dispose of them, or sell them at a loss. In order to avoid the hassle of taking the goods back, repackaging them (if it can be done) and displaying them again, a business may offer the customer an allowance. The allowance is a reduction in price. The purpose of the reduction is to convince the customer to keep the goods.

To track the amount of sales returns and allowances, businesses set up accounts to accumulate and compare them with total sales from time to time. There is no *normal* amount/percent of sales returns and allowances. But the owner will have a *breaking point* at which it is believed that there are too many sales returns or too much of an allowance. At that point, the owner will investigate to determine the cause of excessive returns and allowances. Corrective action can then be taken.

Recording a Sales Return

When recording a sales return, a credit is given to the customer and the goods are returned to stock with the appropriate inventory adjustment.

For example: A customer returns goods with a retail value of $2,000. The cost of the goods to the business was $1,000.

Description	Debit	Credit
Sales Returns and Allowances	$2,000	
Accounts Receivable		$2,000
Credit note issued for excess goods delivered		

Debit	Credit
Sales Returns and Allowances	Accounts Receivable

Remember that the cost of the goods, having been returned, will increase (debit) the inventory. COGS will decrease (credit) due to the decrease in sales.

Description	Debit	Credit
Inventory	$1,000	
Cost of Goods Sold		$1,000
Return of goods to inventory		

Inventory	COGS

Recording a Sales Allowance

Recording a sales allowance is similar to recording a sales return, except that there is no adjustment to inventory.

For example: A customer bought goods for $1,000. The delivered goods were of the wrong colour. The business offers a 15% allowance if the customer keeps the goods. The customer accepts.

Description	Debit	Credit	Debit	Credit
Sales Returns and Allowances	$150		**Sales Returns and Allowances**	**Accounts Receivable**
Accounts Receivable		$150		

Sales allowance - wrong colour goods delivered - 15% of $1,000

Accrued Liabilities

Using a new hockey rink business as an example (a partnership), called *Rinks-O-Ice*, here are some year-end issues facing this business:

1. At the end of the fiscal year, the revenue and expense accounts are cleared out in anticipation of starting the next fiscal year. The resulting profit or loss for the year will be transferred to the retained earnings account.

2. Prior to the year-end date, the owners may have discussions with the company lawyer. The lawyer will not send the bill until after year-end.

3. The owners decide that they want an audit performed on their first year of operations and hire a public accountant to complete the audit. There are three days between the last payday and the company year-end. An account must be set up to record the three day's of pay.

   Note: All of the preceding are accrued liabilities.

4. During the month a young skater trips on a mat and suffers a concussion. The skater's parents maintain that the child tripped because the mat was placed improperly. The parents are suing *Rinks-O-Ice* for $1 million for negligence. The owners consult their lawyer, who advises them that the matter of negligence is not clear-cut and that the corporation will have to go to court. At year-end it is not clear whether or not *Rinks-O-Ice* would be successful in defending itself against the accusation of negligence.

5. *Rinks-O-Ice* has to pay corporate income taxes. The taxes have been recorded each month, assuming that taxable income is equal to the income as shown on the company's income statement. This, however, is not the real situation, and the taxable income does differ from the income shown on the financial statements. Accordingly, taxes payable will be more or less than the amount shown on the financial statements. Sometimes the difference in taxes is payable, or recoverable, in the future.

Part of the difference in taxes is due to the way the company calculates amortization. The tax department allows companies to calculate amortization using a method similar to the declining balance method.

6. In addition to the usual month end adjusting entries, the company recorded interest receivable on the bank balance.

Internal Controls

We are reminded of the internal control benefits of the trial balance.

A trial balance ensures that accounts balance. A post-closing trial balance ensures that only asset, liability and equity accounts remain after the closing process.

As part of the year-end review procedures, the owners of *Rinks-O-Ice* review the post-closing trial balance to assure themselves that all the revenue and expense accounts have been closed. Normal procedure would be for the owners to initial the post-closing trial balance to indicate approval.

Accrued liabilities are amounts payable for which a bill or invoice has not yet been received, or the amount is not yet payable. Examples of accrued liabilities are audit, legal fees and accrued payroll.

Audit fees relate to the current year, but the audit will not be performed until after the year-end. If the matching principle is to be followed, an account for the audit fees must be set up.

Payday is on a certain day of the week. If the year-end occurs on a date other than the pay date, an account will have to be set up to reflect the amount earned by employees between the last payday and year-end.

For example:

Audit fees are estimated to be $1,000. The lawyer spent 2 hours in discussions with the owners at an hourly rate of $100. Payday is Friday of each week, paying employees up to the Friday of the preceding week. The payroll for one week (5 days) is $3,000. The year-end falls on a Wednesday.

Following the above, the company owes three days pay ($3,000 x 3/5) or $1,800.

All of the above need to be set up in an entry recording the accrued liability:

Description	Debit	Credit
Audit and legal fees	$1,200	
Payroll	1,800	
Accrued liabilities		$3,000

To record year end accrued liabilities

Audit and Legal Fees

Payroll

Accrued Liabilities

Contingent Liabilities

A contingent liability depends on a future event that may or may not happen. In the case of *Rinks-O-Ice*, the corporation has been sued for $1 million and the matter must be taken to court. The company's lawyer advises the owners of *Rinks-O-Ice* that the outcome of the case cannot be predicted. Thus they cannot reasonably predict whether or not they will owe the million dollars. Fortunately *Rinks-O-Ice* has liability insurance. Under the terms of the insurance contract, they would actually be liable to pay the first $100,000 if the lawsuit is successful.

Because the outcome of the lawsuit is unknown, the owners *do not* have to accrue the $100,000. However, since the amount is material (in relation to the existing assets of the company), it should be disclosed in the notes to the financial statements as follows:

> **Contingent liability**
>
> *Rinks-O-Ice* is being sued for $1 million regarding a case of alleged negligence. Legal counsel advises that the outcome of the case cannot be predicted. Insurance coverage limits the payout to $100,000.

Payroll Deductions

Salary Benefits

Every business is required to pay the government various employee benefits. These benefits include Employment Insurance (the government will pay you a certain percentage of your salary if you become unemployed), Workers' Compensation (a government sponsored injury insurance plan), Pension Plans (so that you can receive a pension when you retire) and various other deductions that apply according to the laws in various countries, states or provinces.

In addition to these deductions, an employer is also required to deduct income tax from your earnings. The amount that your employer agrees to pay you is called **gross earnings**. The amount that you take home after deductions is called **net earnings**. Deductions are recorded in a separate general ledger account to enable an employer to keep track of the deductions.

For ease of reference, we will simply call them all *salary benefits*. This lesson will show you how to record the deductions, and the subsequent payment of the deductions.

Gross Wages

Gross wages is the amount of wages before any deductions. For example, say that the hourly rate is $10.00. That means in order to generate wages of $1,500, employees would have to work 150 hours (150 hr. x $10.00 per hour = $1,500 gross wages).

DEBIT Salaries & Bonuses $xxxx	CREDIT Cash $xxxx

Payroll Deductions

The reality of life is that you have to pay taxes, employment insurance, pension, medical and many other deductions. Sometimes employers contribute additional amounts on behalf of an employee (e.g. employment insurance and pension). The result is that the employee receives less than the gross pay amount. The amount received is called **net pay** and it is calculated by subtracting deductions from gross pay.

For example:

Gross Pay	$1,500
Payroll Deductions	300
Net Pay	**$1,200**

[This amount is an example only and does not represent an actual deduction amount.]

To record payroll (wages, salaries) with deductions - using the example above - you need to do the following:

· Remove the amount of **net** pay from cash and record it as Salaries & Bonuses (expense)
· Record the amount of deductions as Salary Deductions Payable (liability until actually paid)
· Record the amount of deductions as Salary Benefits (expense)

Although you are learning about deductions, this "Deductions Payable" account will not be used for this course and therefore you will not find this account on your Accounting Map™.

Employer's Portion of Expenses

Often, the government requires employers to match or contribute the deductions made from their employee's salary. This is an expense to the business.

To record this additional expense:

· Debit Salaries & Bonuses (expense)
· Credit Salary Deductions Payable (liability)

DEBIT Salaries & Bonuses $xxx

CREDIT Salary Deductions Payable $xxx

Continuing with our example, the amount deducted from gross pay was $300. Let's assume that the government requires additional contributions by the business of $100. This means that expenses and the amount payable to the government *both* increase by $100.

Paying the Deduction Liability

Amounts deducted from payroll are owing to the government and others. The amounts are required by law and contract to be paid, usually the month following the deduction.

To record the payment of the liability, you need to do the following:

· Reduce the bank account (asset).
· Remove the amount of the liability from the Salary Deductions Payable account (liability).

In our example, the transaction to be recorded is the payment of net wages ($1,200), recording the liability of $300, and recording the employer's matching portion of deductions ($100).

Petty Cash

A business may at times require small amounts of cash to pay for *petty* (small) expenses such as parking, postage stamps, courier fees, etc. Rather than issuing a payment each time, a business will set up a Petty Cash Fund in order to pay these small amounts in cash.

Petty Cash is usually operated on an imprest system, meaning that the amount of cash on hand plus any expenses reimbursed to date is equal to the amount of the Petty Cash Fund set up.

Setting up a petty cash fund:

1. An individual is designated as the *petty cashier* or *petty cash custodian*. The petty cash custodian is responsible for the safekeeping of the cash, ensuring that it is disbursed for legitimate payments and that a record of the petty cash activities is maintained. The cash is usually stored in a petty cash box in a safe place.

2. The custodian needs to estimate how much cash is required for the next week, 2 weeks or month, depending upon how often it needs to be replenished. Let's use $100 as the estimation for this exercise. The $100 is expected to last a week.

3. The accounting transaction will be: increase (debit) Petty Cash and decrease (credit) Cash.

4. As cash is disbursed from the petty cash box, the person receiving the cash will sign a petty cash receipt or petty cash ticket as illustrated below.

RECEIVED IN PETTY CASH	
Date: *September 5, 20xx*	

Description	Amount	
Lunch	8	00
TOTAL	8	00

_____
Received By

Rebecca McGillivray
Approved By

5. When the cash is nearly used up, the fund should be reimbursed. To complete this procedure the Petty Cash Custodian is required to:

   a. Create a summary of all the activities by grouping all the types of expenses together with a subtotal of each category. Let's say that the total is $83.00.

   b. All the expenses should be added up and deducted from the original $100 *float* that was deposited in the Petty Cash box at the commencement of the petty cash period.

   c. The physical amount of cash left in the petty cash box *should be* equal to $17.00 (the opening balance of $100.00 less the $83.00 expenses) as listed on the summary.

Petty Cash Summary Slip

Period: December 10th - December 17th

Opening Balance		$100.00
Parking		
Dec 10	$10.00	
Dec 12	6.00	
Dec 14	5.00	$21.00
Freight in		
Dec 10	$18.00	
Dec 11	6.00	$24.00
Office Supplies		
Dec 13	$ 7.00	
Dec 16	13.00	$20.00
Gasoline		
Dec 14	$18.00	$18.00
Total Disbursements		$83.00
Cash over and short		$ 2.00
Total to be reimbursed to Petty Cash		$85.00

Opening balance less disbursements

6. In the case of an overage or shortage of cash, the difference will be added or deducted from the *Cash Over and Short* account. For example: In the diagram (*previous page*) the custodian discovered a shortage of $2.00. This could have occurred due to a number of reasons including miscounting change, overcharging someone, etc. This will result in an increase in disbursements.

7. The Petty Cash custodian presents the completed Petty Cash Summary Slip, together with supporting vouchers to the cashier (person who writes cheques). The cashier verifies the Summary Slip by reviewing the supporting vouchers. The cashier prepares a cheque and gives it to the Petty Cash custodian. To ensure that the vouchers are not presented again, each voucher is stamped "paid".

8. The Petty Cash custodian cashes the cheque, and reimburses the Petty Cash Fund by placing the cash box. At this point in time, the amount of the Petty Cash Fund is equal to its original amount of $100.

Posting Petty Cash to the General Ledger

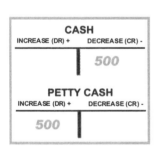

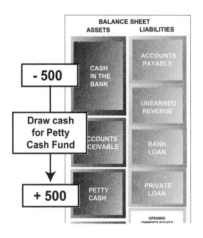

When drawing cash from the daily bank account for the petty cash fund, the cash remains an asset: the T-Account entry is to decrease cash (credit) and increase petty cash (debit).

At this time equity remains unchanged.

When an expense is incurred, it is first paid by removing cash from the Petty Cash box and replacing the amount of cash with a voucher (receipt) worth the same amount. No change to Petty Cash (Petty Cash Fund account) is recorded when each individual voucher is paid. Just before the Petty Cash Fund is reimbursed in our example, there are vouchers (Parking $21, Freight-in $24, Office Supplies $20, Gasoline $18, Cash Short $2) worth $85 and Cash of $15. When the Petty Cash Summary is presented, the Petty Cash Custodian exchanges the vouchers for a cheque worth $85. The Petty Cash Custodian cashes the cheque and puts the $85 in the Petty Cash box, returning the total cash in the Petty Cash box to $100. No change to Petty Cash is recorded when the cheque is issued and the cash placed in the Petty Cash box.

When the bookkeeper records the cheque there is *still no change to the Petty Cash account*. The cheque is recorded with a debit to various expenses (Parking, freight-in, office supplies, gasoline, cash short), and a credit to Cash (Bank).

It is important to note that the *only* time the Petty Cash account in the ledger is used is when the account is set up (or increased or decreased). When the vouchers are reimbursed by the cashier, the resulting cheque is recorded by debiting expenses, and crediting Cash (Bank).

If, when counting the Petty Cash fund, the total vouchers plus cash on hand is less than the original amount set up for the fund, there is "Cash Short". On the other hand if the total vouchers plus cash on hand total more than the original amount of the fund, there is "Cash Over". The Petty Cash custodian is held accountable for shortages and overages.

It is common practice to maintain a spreadsheet of the various expenses so that each month the General Ledger can be updated with the correct allocation of expenses. Following is an example:

ABC DISTRIBUTORS
PETTY CASH EXPENSES PAID
For the Month of July 20xx

Description	Receipt #	Amount	GST	Office	Travel	Meals	Marketing
Photo Developing	1	8.07	0.49				7.58
Taxis	2	65.00			65.00		
Meals	3	33.00	0.93			32.07	
Batteries	4	11.00	6.23				4.77
Photocopying - brochures	5	23.32	1.32				22.00
Photocopying - general	6	3.05		3.05			
Parking	7	1.87			1.87		
Parking	8	10.26			10.26		
Parking	9	3.00			3.00		
Parking	10	4.00			4.00		
Parking	11	6.50			6.50		
Parking	12	7.00			7.00		
Parking	13	6.00			6.00		
Parking	14	3.94			3.94		
Parking	15	1.00			1.00		
Gas	16	10.00			10.00		
Meals	17	8.10	0.43			7.67	
Travel	18	49.01	2.58	46.43			
TOTAL		$254.12	$11.98	$49.48	$126.24	$32.07	$34.35

Cash will be credited by this amount.

Each of these TOTAL amounts will be debited to the respective GL expense accounts.

Petty Cash Control

Petty cash funds can be a convenient way to buy small items. However, the funds also provide opportunities for abuse. It is therefore important to regulate the use of the petty cash fund to ensure that it is not mishandled. Here are 3 tips to ensure that petty cash is used appropriately:

1. Determine specific guidelines regarding when and how petty cash may be used.

2. Consistently maintain any documentation on the use of petty cash.

3. Review the regulations regularly with your employees.

1. **Determining specific guidelines:**

   The first step to ensuring that your petty cash is used in the right way is to establish the various ways in which it is supposed to be used. Determine what purchases can be made with purchase orders or purchase cards. Then make a list of other types of purchases that may have to be made at some point. This will provide a starting place for drawing up a list of requirements for the use of petty cash. High value items and regular types of purchases such as payroll, inventory, paying accounts payable, independent contractors, fixed assets, etc., should never be purchased through the petty cash fund. The fund should be strictly reserved for small ("petty") expenses.

2. **Maintain documentation:**

   It is impossible to keep accurate records unless you have a uniform documentation system. Establish an easy-to-use system and follow it scrupulously. The most common and the easiest way is by keeping track of all receipts, whether register receipts or written invoices. Each receipt should have the date of purchase, the name of the company or vendor, a list of the items or services purchased, the price of each item, and the total cost. Also ensure that:

   a) The person who made the purchase signs the receipt.

   b) All receipts are filed correctly so that they can be checked if there are any discrepancies.

3. **Review regulations with employees:**

   Ensure that petty cash is used appropriately by having a clear and precise method for reporting petty cash. Designate a particular person to whom all petty cash purchases must be submitted. File these reports. Set a particular date for which all petty cash reports for the month are due.

   If nobody knows what the regulations are, then the ability to abuse the petty cash fund becomes easier. Keep everyone up-to-date and do not allow for bending the rules.

Shareholders' Equity

On page 98, *Financing a Business*, it was noted that there are many ways of financing a business. Each financial structure method (Sole Proprietorship, Partnership, Limited Company, Joint Venture) has its own advantages and disadvantages. This section deals with the *Limited Company* form of organization.

When a limited company is set up, it requires two main accounts, Share Capital, and Retained Earnings. When a limited company is set up, the government issues its Letters Patent. The Letters Patent are essentially the birth certificate of the company.

Share Capital may be further sub-divided into the types of shares issued; the major types of shares are common shares and preferred shares.

The Retained Earnings account presents the profits that a company has earned to date, less any amounts that have been paid out (dividends) to shareholders.

Share Capital

As noted above, share capital may be composed of common shares and preferred shares.

When a limited company is started, potential shareholders exchange cash, assets, or services for shares. Today, most common shares do not have a par (stated) value. However, the number of common shares to be issued may be limited by the incorporating documents (letters patent) of the corporation.

When shares are issued for cash, the company decides on the number of shares to be issued. For example, if a company decides to issue 1,000 shares for $100 on January 10th, the journal entry would be as follows:

GENERAL JOURNAL				
DATE: 20XX	ACCOUNT TITLE AND EXPLANATION	GL NO.	DEBIT	CREDIT
January 10	Cash		$100	
	Common Shares			$100
	Issued 1,000 shares for cash			

The company may also issue shares for assets received. For example, a person may exchange a building valued at $1 million for 10,000 shares on January 10th. The value of the building, and the number of shares would be arrived at by agreement between the company and the person giving the building to the company.

GENERAL JOURNAL

DATE: 20XX	ACCOUNT TITLE AND EXPLANATION	GL NO.	DEBIT	CREDIT
January 10	Building		$1,000,000	
	Common Shares			$1,000,000
	Issued 10,000 shares in exchange for building valued at $1,000,000			

A third possibility is that the company could issue shares in exchange for services. For example, a lawyer performing work for the set-up of the company may think that the company would be a good investment, and be willing to accept common shares instead of cash. For this example, assume that the legal fees are $5,000 and that 100 shares are issued. Note, once again, that the number of shares is not pre-determined, and is arrived at by agreement between the company and the person who supplies the services.

GENERAL JOURNAL

DATE: 20XX	ACCOUNT TITLE AND EXPLANATION	GL NO.	DEBIT	CREDIT
January 10	Legal fees		$5,000	
	Common Shares			$5,000
	Issued 100 shares in exchange for legal services			

If the shares issued were preferred shares, the preceding entries would be similar, except that the name of the shares would be Preferred Shares.

The company should maintain a Share sub-ledger showing the number of shares held by each shareholder.

Common Shares and Preferred Shares

Preferred Shares may have several "preferences" attached to them. However the main features of preferred shares are usually:

▶ preferred shares receive a regular dividend each year
▶ preferred dividends must be paid before dividends are paid to common shares

There are many other types of preferences, however, they are beyond the scope of this text. As well, there may be several classes of preferred shares, each class with its own preferences.

Common Shares have certain rights associated with them. The major right is the right to vote at company meetings. There are several other rights associated with common share ownership, but, again, the explanation is beyond the scope of this text. Common shares only receive dividends when dividends are declared. Common shares receive dividends after preferred shares have received their dividends.

Retained Earnings

When the revenue and expense accounts are closed in a proprietorship, the profit or loss for the year is closed to the Owner's Equity account. When the company is a limited company, the profit or loss for the year is closed to the retained earnings account. The retained earnings account contains all the profits that the company has earned from the date that it first started business, minus any dividends paid to shareholders.

Dividends

People become shareholders because they expect to receive a return from their investment in a company. The return will be in the form of dividends.

At the end of each period, the directors of the company will decide if they have enough cash and retained earnings available to pay shareholders dividends. If the directors feel there is enough retained earnings and cash to pay dividends, they will declare a dividend of a certain amount per share. The directors establish a *Record Date* on which the share records are reviewed to determine who owns how many shares.

For example, assume that the directors declare a dividend of $1.00 per share on 1,000 outstanding common shares (there are no preferred shares) on January 31st. The dividend is to be paid on February 15th. The entry would be as follows:

GENERAL JOURNAL

DATE: 20XX	ACCOUNT TITLE AND EXPLANATION	GL NO.	DEBIT	CREDIT
January 31	Retained Earnings		$1,000	
	Dividends Payable			$1,000
	Declared dividend of $1 per share on 1,000 shares			

Note that the Retained Earnings account is debited. Some companies would debit a "Dividends Declared" account, which would subsequently be closed to Retained Earnings.

On the date of record, no journal entry is required; the directors will determine *who* gets the dividends on that date.

On the date of dividend payment, the following entry is recorded. ⟶

GENERAL JOURNAL

DATE: 20XX	ACCOUNT TITLE AND EXPLANATION	GL NO.	DEBIT	CREDIT
February 15	Dividends Payable		$1,000	
	Cash			$1,000
	Paid dividend payable			

Corporations are not required to pay dividends unless the board of directors of the corporation decide to do so.

Financial Statement Presentation of Shareholders' Equity

Generally Accepted Accounting Principles require limited companies to show the number of shares of each class that are authorized, issued and fully paid.

The number of shares authorized can be found in the incorporating documents (Letters Patent) of a company. The number of shares issued can be found by examining the share sub-ledger.

When shares are issued, the person to whom the share is issued, may not pay the full value for the shares received. In such cases, the shares would not be fully paid.

Shown below is the Shareholders' Equity section from *Research in Motion's* (RIM) 2007 financial statements:

Shareholders' Equity		
Capital stock (note 12)		
Authorized — unlimited number of non-voting, cumulative, redeemable, retractable preferred shares; unlimited number of non-voting, redeemable, retractable Class A common shares and an unlimited number of voting common shares Issued — 185,871,144 voting common shares (March 4, 2006 — 186,001,765)	**2,099,696**	2,068,869
Retained earnings (deficit)	359,227	(100,174)
Paid-in capital	36,093	28,694
Accumulated other comprehensive loss (note 17)	(11,516)	(1,974)
	2,483,500	1,995,415
	$3,088,949	$2,314,349

Note the following items:

▸ there is an unlimited number of non-voting, redeemable, retractable preferred shares
- · the preferences for these shares are redeem-ability, and retractability
- · these shares have no voting privileges

▸ there is an unlimited number of non-voting, redeemable, retractable Class A common shares
- · the shares cannot vote
- · the preferences are redeem-ability and retractability
- · the shares are termed Class A

- there is an unlimited number of voting shares
  - these shares can vote
- there are 185,871,144 voting common shares issued; as noted on the previous line, there is an unlimited number authorized
- the retained earnings is a credit balance this year, but was a debit balance last year (meaning that as of last year, the company had more yearly losses than profits).
- GAAP also covers other items such as *Paid-in capital* and *Accumulated other comprehensive losses* (beyond the scope of this text).

In addition to Capital Stock details, as noted above, companies must also disclose the details of increases and decreases in Capital Stock, and details of changes in Retained Earnings.

Here is *RIM's* explanation of changes in the number of shares of Capital Stock outstanding:

	Number Outstanding (000's) Common Shares
Balance as at February 28, 2004	184,830
Exercise of stock options	4,655
Balance as at February 26, 2005	189,485
Exercise of stock options	2,837
Common shares repurchased pursuant to Common Share Repurchase Program	(6,320)
Balance as at March 4, 2006	186,002
Exercise of stock options	3,042
Conversion of restricted share units	7
Common shares repurchased pursuant to Common Share Repurchase Program	(3,180)
Balance as at March 3, 2007	185,871

Shown on the next page is *RIM's* explanation of the changes in Retained Earnings. Obviously, *RIM's* explanation of changes in retained earnings is far and beyond anything that you have to prepare at this time. However, if you examine the statement very carefully, you can see that Retained Earnings is increased by profits (*RIM* didn't pay any dividends). All the other items shown on the statement are examples of items that a large, publicly-traded limited company may encounter.

Research in Motion - 2007 Financial Statements

	Capital Stock	Paid-In Capital	Retained Earnings (Deficit)	Accumulated Other Comprehensive Income (Loss)	Total
Balance as at February 28, 2004 — as previously reported	$1,829,388	$ —	$(119,206)	$ 11,480	$1,721,662
Adjustment to opening shareholders's equity (note 4)	172,062	60,170	(233,005)	—	(773)
Balance as at February 28, 2004 — as restated (note 4)	2,001,450	60,170	(352,211)	11,480	1,720,889
Comprehensive income (loss):					
Net income	—	—	205,612	—	205,612
Net change in unrealized gains on investments Issued — 186,001,765 voting common shares (February 26, 2005 — 189,484,915) available for sale	—	—	—	(18,357)	(18,357)
Net change in derivative fair value during the year	—	—	—	8,446	8,446
Amounts reclassified to earnings during the year	—	—	—	(4,340)	(4,340)
Shares issued:					
Exercise of stock options	54,151	—	—	—	54,151
Transfers to capital stock from stock option exercises	25,269	(25,269)	—	—	—
Share-based payment	—	2,899	—	—	2,899
Excess tax benefits from share-based compensation (note 12 (b))	—	3,777	—	—	3,777
Deferred income tax benefit attributable to fiscal 2004 financing costs	8,727	—	—	—	8,727
Balance as at February 26, 2005 — as restated (note 4)	$2,089,597	$ 41,577	$(146,599)	$ (2,771)	$1,981,804
Comprehensive income (loss):					
Net income	—	—	374,656	—	374,656
Net change in unrealized gains on investments available for sale	—	—	—	(5,888)	(5,888)
Net change in derivative fair value during the year	—	—	—	18,029	18,029
Amounts reclassified to earnings during the year	—	—	—	(11,344)	(11,344)
Shares issued:					
Exercise of stock options	23,269	—	—	—	23,269
Transfers to capital stock from stock option exercises	18,984	(18,984)	—	—	—
Share-based payment	—	2,551	—	—	2,551
Excess tax benefits from share-based compensation (note 12 (b))	—	3,550	—	—	3,550
Common shares repurchased pursuant to Common Share Repurchase Program	(62,981)	—	(328,231)	—	(391,212)
Balance as at March 4, 2006 — as restated (note 4)	$2,068,869	$ 28,694	$(100,174)	$ (1,974)	$1,995,415
Comprehensive income (loss):					
Net income	—	—	631,572	—	631,572
Net change in unrealized gains on investments available for sale	—	—	—	11,839	11,839
Net change in derivative fair value during the year	—	—	—	(13,455)	(13,455)
Amounts reclassified to earnings during the year	—	—	—	(7,926)	(7,926)
Shares issued:					
Exercise of stock options	44,534	—	—	—	44,534
Transfers to capital stock from stock option exercises	18,055	(18,055)	—	—	-
Share-based payment	—	19,454	—	—	19,454
Excess tax benefits from share-based compensation (note 12 (b))	—	6,000	—	—	6,000
Common shares repurchased pursuant to Common Share Repurchase Program	(31,762)	—	(172,171)	—	(203,933)
Balance as at March 3, 2007	$2,099,696	$ 36,093	$ 359,227	$ (11,516)	$2,483,500

See notes to the consolidated financial statements.

Intangible Assets, Amortization, and Goodwill

Thus far in this text, we have discussed only tangible assets. Tangible assets are things you can see, lift up, move around, etc. Examples of tangible assets are land, buildings, equipment, and computers. Generally speaking, tangible assets cost a lot of money, and last a (reasonably) long time.

Intangible assets, on the other hand, are composed mainly of their purchase price, or legal fees. Patents, copyrights, and trademarks are examples of intangible assets.

Example:

ABC company purchased patent rights for a revolutionary machine from A. Einstein for $500,000 cash on April 1.

GENERAL JOURNAL

DATE: 20XX	ACCOUNT TITLE AND EXPLANATION	GL NO.	DEBIT	CREDIT
April 1	Intangible Asset - Patents		$500,000	
	Cash			$500,000
	Purchase of Patent from A. Einstein			

Intangible assets with a definite life (e.g. Patents and Copyrights) are amortized on a straight-line basis over their remaining useful life.

Example:

The Patent purchased in the previous example will expire in five years. The year end of the company is March 31.

GENERAL JOURNAL

DATE: 20XX	ACCOUNT TITLE AND EXPLANATION	GL NO.	DEBIT	CREDIT
March 31	Amortization - Intangible Asset - Patents		$100,000	
	Intangible Asset - Patents			$100,000
	Amortization of Patent for one year (1 x 500,000/5)			

Note that the credit is to the asset account that records the original cost.

Goodwill

Goodwill is an intangible asset that usually arises on the purchase of a company. Goodwill is the difference between the price paid and the net value of the assets purchased. It is usually attributed to the fact that the company has a "good name" with the public, its customers, and its suppliers, and has been around for many years.

Example:

John Doe purchases XYZ limited for $1,000,000 on January 1st. The December 31st statements of XYZ limited show assets of $1,500,000 and liabilities of $700,000. That means the net book value of XYZ is $800,000 (1,500,000 - 700,000). The difference between the purchase price and the net book value of XYZ is goodwill.

GENERAL JOURNAL				
DATE: 20XX	ACCOUNT TITLE AND EXPLANATION	GL NO.	DEBIT	CREDIT
January 1	Assets		$1,500,000	
	Goodwill		200,000	
	Liabilities			$ 700,000
	Cash			1,000,000
	Purchase of XYZ Limited for $1,000,000 cash			

Note that in an actual purchase, the various assets purchased (inventory, building, land, vehicles, etc.) would be debited with the appropriate amounts totalling $1,500,000. Similarly, the liabilities assumed (accounts payable, bank loan, etc.) would be credited to the appropriate accounts, totalling $700,000.

Goodwill has an indefinite life. When intangible assets have an indefinite life no amortization is recorded unless the asset is impaired in value. In practical terms, this means that there is usually no amortization recorded in intangible assets with an indefinite life.

Example:

Consider the above company which purchased XYZ Limited. XYZ, when purchased, manufactured a unique product. The company continued successfully for 5 years. At that time scientists developed a new product that would make XYZ's product obsolete in a few years. That meant that XYZ was no longer a viable company, and it is unlikely that XYZ could be sold at a favourable price. In short, the value of XYZ's goodwill is impaired. The owners estimated that the amount of impairment was $100,000, and record the impairment at the year end date (December 31).

GENERAL JOURNAL

DATE: 20XX	ACCOUNT TITLE AND EXPLANATION	GL NO.	DEBIT	CREDIT
December 31	Impairment of Intangible Assets		$100,000	
	Goodwill			$100,000
	To record impairment of goodwill			

Note the following:

▸ Impairment of Intangible Asset is an expense, and will appear on the income statement

▸ $100,000 is management's estimate of the impairment. The owners know that they have a few years before their product becomes totally obsolete. They will write down the value of goodwill to zero over the remaining time.

Notes

AME Learning

Exercises: Chapter 14

Exercise #1

Technical Accounting

Chart of Accounts - check off the appropriate category into which the various accounts belong:

ACCOUNT	ASSETS	LIABILITIES	REVENUE	EXPENSES	EQUITY
Sales					
Car					
Cash					
Computer					
Telephone bill					
Gas					
Insurance					
Bank Loan					
Owner's Drawings					
Prepaid Expenses					
Unearned Revenue					
Discounts Received					
Depreciation					
Office Supplies					
Interest Paid					
Discounts Allowed					
Equipment					
Accounts Payable					
Capital Account					

Using the chart below, enter the sequence in which financial statements are processed - using numbers 1 to 5:

Trial Balance	
General Ledgers	
General Journal	
Balance Sheet	
Income Statement	

Exercise #2

Short Answer

1. Explain the role of the General Journal.

    _____

    _____

    _____

    _____

2. Explain the role of the General Ledger.

    _____

    _____

    _____

    _____

3. Explain the role of the Trial Balance.

    _____

    _____

    _____

    _____

4. Explain the role of the Income Statement.

    _____

    _____

    _____

    _____

5. Explain the role of the Balance Sheet.

    _____

    _____

    _____

    _____

Exercise #3

Multiple Choice

Please circle the correct answer.

1. It is important for people who are not accountants to understand the basic principles of accounting.

    a. True
    b. False

2. It is important to understand basic accounting principles using a manual system before trying to understand a computerized accounting program.

    a. True
    b. False

3. Everything that you need to do in a manual accounting system can also be done by a computer.
    a. True
    b. False

4. Every Chart of Accounts listing is the same for every business.
    a. True
    b. False

5. When a balance sheet balances it indicates that the amounts shown are all correct.
    a. True
    b. False

6. A balanced trial balance always means that all the entries were entered.
    a. True
    b. False

7. A balanced trial balance means that for every debit there is another debit.
    a. True
    b. False

8. A balanced trial balance means that for every debit there is another credit.
    a. True
    b. False

Exercise #4

DR or CR?

Using the table below, enter the correct debit and credit entries. (The first entry has been completed for you.)

TRANSACTION	DEBIT	CREDIT
Deposit cash sales	*Cash*	*Sales*
Pay for rent with cheque #058		
Record professional fees billed to be paid next month		
Pay Accounts Payable		
Deposit unearned revenue		
Deposit Owner's Capital		
Record depreciation		
Buy assets with a loan		
Borrow money from the bank		
Pay interest with cash		
Record interest received from a supplier by way of a credit note		
Pay bank loan principal		
Record unearned revenue as earned for this month		
Refund unearned revenue to a customer		
Correct an entry - travel expense was incorrectly recorded as salaries		
Record the cash payment from a customer who owed money from a few months ago		
Correct an entry - a sale recorded as Accounts Receivable should have been recorded as cash		
Equipment was sold for less than the amount recorded in the fixed assets ledger account		

Exercise #5

Can you Balance?

Using the chart below, enter the correct amounts into the appropriate balance sheet accounts. When you have finished entering the amounts, record the correct value of Owner's Equity.

1.   Cash $5,000

2.   Unearned Revenue $2,000

3.   Vehicle $8,000

4.   Loan on vehicle $3,000

5.   Accounts Receivable $1,000

6.   Prepaid Expenses $1,000

7.   Bank Loan $5,000

ACCOUNT NAME	ASSET $ AMOUNT	LIABILITY $ AMOUNT
Cash		
Unearned Revenue		
Accounts Receivable		
Vehicle Loan		
Prepaid Expenses		
Bank Loan		
Vehicle		
Owner's Equity		
Total Assets		
Total Liabilities		
Total Liabilities + Owner's Equity		

Exercise #6

Petty Cash

What would the T-Account entries be to set up a petty cash float of $200.00?

Account Name: _____

(DEBIT)	(CREDIT)

Account Name: _____

(DEBIT)	(CREDIT)

Review the following petty cash receipts and complete the petty cash summary on the next page.
Note: there is a cash shortage of $6.00. →

RECEIVED IN PETTY CASH

Date: *September 1, 20xx*

Description	Amount	
Parking	12	00
TOTAL	12	00

Received By / *Rebecca McGillivray* Approved By

RECEIVED IN PETTY CASH

Date: *September 5, 20xx*

Description	Amount	
Lunch	8	00
TOTAL	8	00

Donna Jones Received By / *Rebecca McGillivray* Approved By

RECEIVED IN PETTY CASH

Date: *September 10, 20xx*

Description	Amount	
Photocopying - Quick Copy	3	00
TOTAL	3	00

Received By / *Rebecca McGillivray* Approved By

RECEIVED IN PETTY CASH

Date: *September 12, 20xx*

Description	Amount	
Gas	20	00
TOTAL	20	00

Received By / *Rebecca McGillivray* Approved By

RECEIVED IN PETTY CASH

Date: *September 15, 20xx*

Description	Amount	
Stamps for mailout	15	00
TOTAL	15	00

Norman Saunders Received By / *Rebecca McGillivray* Approved By

RECEIVED IN PETTY CASH

Date: *September 24, 20xx*

Description	Amount	
Office stationery	22	00
TOTAL	22	00

Received By / *Rebecca McGillivray* Approved By

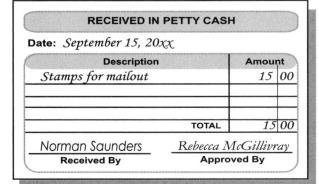
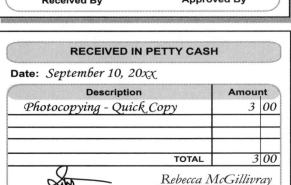

Complete the following petty cash summary:

Petty Cash Summary Slip

Period:

Opening Balance			$
Item	**Date**	**Amount**	**Balance**
Total Disbursements			$
Cash over and short			
Total to be reimbursed to Petty Cash			$

Exercise #7

Completing Financial Statements

We are providing two *separate* exercises.

On the blank forms provided on the next few pages, enter the transactions into the General Journal, post to the General Ledger and create a Trial Balance. When you have finished these steps, create an income statement and balance sheet.

Use the following Chart of Accounts:

Account Description	Account #
ASSETS - Category 1	
Cash	101
Accounts Receivable	105
Prepaid Expenses	110
Inventory	115
Fixed Assets - Equipment	120
Accumulated Depreciation	130
LIABILITIES - Category 2	
Accounts Payable	200
Unearned Revenue	205
Bank Loan	210
Equipment Loan	215
OWNER'S EQUITY - Category 3	
Capital Account	300
Owner's Investment	305
Owner's Drawings	310
Income Summary	315

Account Description	Account #
REVENUE - Category 4	
Membership Sales	400
EXPENSES - Category 5	
Advertising	500
Bad Debts	505
Insurance	510
Maintenance	515
Miscellaneous	520
Office Supplies	525
Professional Fees	530
Rent	535
Salaries & Bonuses	540
Salary Benefits	541
Telephone	545
Travel	550
Depreciation	555
OTHER REVENUE & EXPENSES	
Interest Earned on Savings	405
Discounts Received	410
Interest & Bank Charges	560
Loss on Disposal of Equipment	565

Exercise 7(a): Transactions

Jan 1   Deposit owner's capital in the amount of $3,000

Jan 2   Cash membership sales of $5,000

Jan 3   Pay rent of $1,000 with a cheque

Jan 4   Use direct deposit to record staff wages of $2,000

Jan 5   Pay cash for Accountant fees of $300

Jan 6   Buy equipment for $3,000 - to be paid in 3 months time

Jan 7   Record a bill for repairs in the amount of $500 that needs to be paid next month

GENERAL JOURNAL				J1
DATE 20XX	ACCOUNT TITLE & EXPLANATION	GL NO.	DEBIT	CREDIT

GENERAL JOURNAL				J2
DATE 20XX	ACCOUNT TITLE & EXPLANATION	GL NO.	DEBIT	CREDIT
TOTAL				

Complete the General Ledger

JANUARY

ACCOUNT: *CASH*   NO. *101*

DATE 20XX	DESCRIPTION	REF.	DEBIT	CREDIT	BALANCE (DR OR CR)

ACCOUNT: NO.

DATE 20XX	DESCRIPTION	REF.	DEBIT	CREDIT	BALANCE (DR OR CR)

ACCOUNT: NO._____

DATE 20XX	DESCRIPTION	REF.	DEBIT	CREDIT	BALANCE (DR OR CR)

ACCOUNT: NO.

DATE 20XX	DESCRIPTION	REF.	DEBIT	CREDIT	BALANCE (DR OR CR)

ACCOUNT:						NO.
DATE 20XX	DESCRIPTION	REF.	DEBIT	CREDIT	BALANCE (DR OR CR)	

ACCOUNT:						NO.
DATE 20XX	DESCRIPTION	REF.	DEBIT	CREDIT	BALANCE (DR OR CR)	

ACCOUNT:						NO.
DATE 20XX	DESCRIPTION	REF.	DEBIT	CREDIT	BALANCE (DR OR CR)	

ACCOUNT:						NO.
DATE 20XX	DESCRIPTION	REF.	DEBIT	CREDIT	BALANCE (DR OR CR)	

ACCOUNT:						NO.
DATE 20XX	DESCRIPTION	REF.	DEBIT	CREDIT	BALANCE (DR OR CR)	

Complete the Trial Balance Worksheet

TRIAL BALANCE WORKSHEET - MONTH ENDING JANUARY 31, 20XX							
Account # and Title		Adjusted Trial Balance		Income Statement		Balance Sheet	
		DR	CR	DR	CR	DR	CR
	Totals						
	Profit (Loss)						
	Owner's Equity						
	Totals						

Complete the Formal Financial Statements

INCOME STATEMENT - MONTH ENDED JANUARY 31, 20XX		
Total Revenue		
Expenses		
Total Expenses		
Profit (Loss)		

STATEMENT OF OWNER'S EQUITY @ JANUARY 31, 20XX		
Closing Owner's Equity		

BALANCE SHEET - AS AT JANUARY 31, 20XX	
ASSETS:	
Total Assets	
LIABILITIES:	
Total Liabilities	
OWNER'S EQUITY	
LIABILITIES + OWNER'S EQUITY	

Exercise 7(b): Transactions

Feb 1   Deposit owner's capital in the amount of $10,000

Feb 2   Purchase Fixed Assets $4,000 - use debit card

Feb 3   Sales billed to Accounts Receivable $5,000

Feb 4   Deposit UNEARNED revenues $1,800

Feb 5   Pay rent $1,500

Feb 6   Record legal fees to be paid next month in the amount of $300

Feb 7   Use direct deposit to record labour $1,200

Feb 8   Pay the local tax authorities payroll benefits for $150

Feb 9   Prepay insurance in the amount $1,200

Feb 10   Pay Accounts Payable $200

Feb 11   Deposit payments from customers who owed money in the amount of $2,000

Adjustments:

Feb 28   Record depreciation in the amount of $400

Feb 28   Recognize $100 of prepaid insurance as an expense for this month

Feb 28   Recognize $150 of unearned revenue as earned for his month

GENERAL JOURNAL				J2
DATE 20XX	ACCOUNT TITLE & EXPLANATION	GL NO.	DEBIT	CREDIT

GENERAL JOURNAL				J3
DATE 20XX	ACCOUNT TITLE & EXPLANATION	GL NO.	DEBIT	CREDIT

GENERAL JOURNAL				J4
DATE 20XX	ACCOUNT TITLE & EXPLANATION	GL NO.	DEBIT	CREDIT
TOTAL				

Complete the General Ledger for Exercise 7(b)

ACCOUNT: *CASH* NO. *101*

DATE 20XX		DESCRIPTION	REF.	DEBIT	CREDIT	BALANCE (DR OR CR)

ACCOUNT: NO.

DATE 20XX		DESCRIPTION	REF.	DEBIT	CREDIT	BALANCE (DR OR CR)

ACCOUNT: NO.

DATE 20XX		DESCRIPTION	REF.	DEBIT	CREDIT	BALANCE (DR OR CR)

ACCOUNT: NO.

DATE 20XX		DESCRIPTION	REF.	DEBIT	CREDIT	BALANCE (DR OR CR)

ACCOUNT:						NO.
DATE 20XX	DESCRIPTION	REF.	DEBIT	CREDIT	BALANCE (DR OR CR)	

ACCOUNT:						NO.
DATE 20XX	DESCRIPTION	REF.	DEBIT	CREDIT	BALANCE (DR OR CR)	

ACCOUNT:						NO.
DATE 20XX	DESCRIPTION	REF.	DEBIT	CREDIT	BALANCE (DR OR CR)	

ACCOUNT:						NO.
DATE 20XX	DESCRIPTION	REF.	DEBIT	CREDIT	BALANCE (DR OR CR)	

ACCOUNT:						NO.
DATE 20XX	DESCRIPTION	REF.	DEBIT	CREDIT	BALANCE (DR OR CR)	

ACCOUNT:						NO.
DATE 20XX	DESCRIPTION	REF.	DEBIT	CREDIT	BALANCE (DR OR CR)	

ACCOUNT: _____ NO. _____

DATE 20XX		DESCRIPTION	REF.	DEBIT	CREDIT	BALANCE (DR OR CR)

ACCOUNT: _____ NO. _____

DATE 20XX		DESCRIPTION	REF.	DEBIT	CREDIT	BALANCE (DR OR CR)

ACCOUNT: _____ NO. _____

DATE 20XX		DESCRIPTION	REF.	DEBIT	CREDIT	BALANCE (DR OR CR)

ACCOUNT: _____ NO. _____

DATE 20XX		DESCRIPTION	REF.	DEBIT	CREDIT	BALANCE (DR OR CR)

Complete the Trial Balance Worksheet for Exercise 7(b)

TRIAL BALANCE - WORKSHEET - FEBRUARY 28, 20XX											
		UNADJUSTED TRIAL BALANCE		ADJUSTMENTS		ADJUSTED TRIAL BALANCE		INCOME STATEMENT		BALANCE SHEET	
#	ACCOUNT TITLES	DR	CR	DR	CR	DR	CR	DR	CR	DR	CR
	Totals										
	Adjustments										
	Total Adjusted										
	PROFIT (LOSS)										

Complete the Formal Financial Statements for Exercise 7(b)

INCOME STATEMENT - MONTH ENDED FEBRUARY 28, 20XX		
Total Revenue		
Expenses		
Total Expenses		
Profit (Loss)		

STATEMENT OF OWNER'S EQUITY @ FEBRUARY 28, 20XX		
Closing Owner's Equity		

BALANCE SHEET - AS AT FEBRUARY 28, 20XX	
ASSETS:	
Total Assets	
LIABILITIES:	
Total Liabilities	
OWNER'S EQUITY	
LIABILITIES + OWNER'S EQUITY	

Exercise #8

Bank Reconciliation

Perform a bank reconciliation using the following bank statement and general ledger.

➢ Review each entry on the bank statement and clear them against the general ledger account.

➢ Record any missing or incorrect transactions from the bank statement onto your records (*for the purpose of this exercise, the bank statement is correct*).

➢ Confirm that the closing balance on both the general ledger account and the bank statement are a match.

DOUGLAS BANK

Account Owner
2 Yonge Street
Toronto, ON
M5A 7Z7

ACCOUNT NUMBER: **23456789**

STATEMENT OF **Personal Chequing Account**	FROM **May 1, 20XX**	TO **May 31, 20XX**		PAGE **1**
DESCRIPTION	WITHDRAWALS	DEPOSITS	DATE	BALANCE
Balance Forward			05 01	2,050.00
Deposit		800.00	05 03	2,850.00
Cheque #036	150.00		05 04	2,700.00
Cheque #037	275.00		05 06	2,425.00
Automatic withdrawal	425.00		05 06	2,000.00
Bank machine withdrawal	100.00		05 08	1,900.00
Cheque #038	65.00		05 15	1,835.00
Automatic withdrawal	850.00		05 31	985.00
Bank charges	10.00		05 31	975.00
Interest earned on savings		25.00	05 31	1,000.00

ACCOUNT: Bank Account

DATE 20XX		DESCRIPTION	DEBIT			CREDIT			BALANCE				CLEAR
May	1	Opening balance							2	0	5	0	
May	3	Deposit salary cheque	8	0	0				2	8	5	0	
May	4	Cheque #036 - XBox games				1	5	0	2	7	0	0	
May	6	Cheque #037 - car insurance				2	7	5	2	4	2	5	
May	6	Automatic withdrawal - car lease				3	8	0	2	0	4	5	
May	8	Bank machine withdrawal				1	0	0	1	9	4	5	
May	15	Cheque #038 - movie/snacks					6	5	1	8	8	0	
May	31	Automatic withdrawal - rent				8	5	0	1	0	3	0	

ACCOUNT:

DATE 20XX		DESCRIPTION	DEBIT	CREDIT	BALANCE

ACCOUNT:

DATE 20XX		DESCRIPTION	DEBIT	CREDIT	BALANCE

ACCOUNT:

DATE 20XX		DESCRIPTION	DEBIT	CREDIT	BALANCE

ACCOUNT:

DATE 20XX		DESCRIPTION	DEBIT	CREDIT	BALANCE

ACCOUNT:

DATE 20XX		DESCRIPTION	DEBIT	CREDIT	BALANCE

Bank Account balance = $_____

Bank Statement balance = $_____

Exercise #9

Payroll Deductions

Please circle the correct answer.

1. What does the term "Gross Wages" mean?
   a. Amount of wages before deductions
   b. Amount of wages after deductions
   c. The amount of hours worked

2. List 3 types of payroll deductions:
   (1) _____
   (2) _____
   (3) _____

3. What does the term "Net Pay" mean?
   a. Amount of wages after deductions
   b. Amount of wages before deductions
   c. Annual salary amount

4. If your net pay is $1,200 and your payroll deductions were $300, how much was your gross pay?
   a. $900
   b. $1,500
   c. $1,100

5. An employer is required by the government to contribute amounts to government plans in addition to the amounts deducted from employees.
   a. True
   b. False

6. To whom are the payroll deductions paid?
   a. The employer
   b. The employee
   c. The government and others

Practical Insights

Practical Insights

DEBITS & CREDITS - BANK VERSION

As strange as it may seem, the bank's reference to Debits and Credits is the exact opposite of your records. For example, when you deposit cash into *your* bank account on *your* records you would record that deposit as a Debit (increasing an asset). However, when the bank records the transaction, they consider the bank account as *theirs*, which means they are Debiting *their* account and Crediting yours. That is why you will see the word "Credit" on the bank statement for an increase in *your* bank account. Some banks have recognized this confusion and will reflect a Debit on your bank statement as a "Withdrawal" and a Credit as a "Deposit", which of course makes everything much clearer.

Exactly the same principle applies to "debit cards". When you use your debit card for a purchase, you are actually crediting (decreasing) your bank account. So, in effect, your debit card is a "credit card" - it is a *cash* credit card as opposed to a *charge* credit card. To make complete sense your debit card should actually be called a "Cash Card" and your credit card should actually be called a "Charge Card".

Here's the logic: When you purchase something, you either pay for it or you don't! If you pay for it, you are crediting (decreasing) cash and if you do not pay for it, you are crediting (increasing) unpaid accounts. Both are *credit*. The other side of the transaction is to debit (increase) the expense, which does not change.

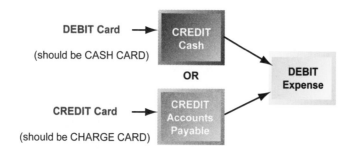

"Credit" means you either decrease cash or increase debt.

AME | Learning

SOURCE DOCUMENTS

The source document is the original record of a transaction. During an audit (inspection) source documents are used as evidence that a particular business transaction occurred. Examples of source documents include:

▶ Cash receipts

▶ Credit card receipts

▶ Cash register tapes

▶ Cancelled cheques

▶ Customer invoices (Sales invoices)

▶ Supplier invoices

▶ Purchase orders

▶ Time cards

▶ Deposit slips

▶ Notes for loans

▶ Payment stubs for interest

At a minimum, each source document should include the date, the amount, and a description of the transaction. When practical, beyond these minimum requirements, source documents should contain the name and address of the other party to the transaction.

When a source document does not exist, for example, when a cash receipt is not provided by a vendor or is misplaced, a document should be generated as soon as possible after the transaction, using other documents such as bank statements to support the information on the generated source document.

Once a transaction has been journalized (entered into the system), the source document should be filed and made retrievable so that transactions can be verified, should the need arise at a later date.

Notes

Chapter 15

Closing the Books

Closing the Books

▶ Closing Entries
▶ Net Income Summary
▶ Year-End Trial Balance
▶ Year-End Summary

Closing Entries

Throughout a year in business you will maintain the books and use the information from the financial statements to measure the state of the business. At the end of an accounting period (in this case one year) you must complete the full year accounting cycle. What you are doing is finalizing the financial statements so that you can measure the business activities for the period.

In order to *close the books* for this accounting period, you must perform certain functions. Each function is designed to clear out revenue, expense and withdrawal accounts (known as *temporary accounts*) to start a fresh accounting period. Since the income statement reports net income (profit or loss) for a single accounting period (shows revenue less expenses for that period only) you need to begin the next accounting period with zero balances.

> **REMINDER NOTE:**
>
> The account balances on the **Balance Sheet** are **PERMANENT**. This means that Balance Sheet accounts (Assets, Liabilities, Owner's Equity) are ongoing, with the closing balances at the end of one accounting period carried forward to the next accounting period.
>
> The account balances on the **Income Statement** are **TEMPORARY**. This means that Income Statement accounts (revenue and expenses) accumulate throughout the accounting period but are cleared at the end of the period. The accounts are cleared using *closing entries*.

Once the income statement has been finalized at the end of the accounting period (the year) a new accounting period starts. First the balances from the income statement accounts (revenue and expenses) which have accumulated for the entire period are transferred to Owner's Equity. The profit (or loss) made in this accounting period now belongs to the owner of the business. The income statement will then start fresh for the new accounting period.

All of the revenue and expenses of a business actually belong to the owner. The owner has the benefit of the revenue and is responsible for the expenses. When the revenue and expense accounts are closed for the year, it is confirmation that a review of the accounts is complete and the amounts are ready to transfer to the Owner's Equity account. In order to do this, there is one temporary step: transfer all of the account balances to a **Net Income Summary** account and then transfer the balance of this account to Owner's Equity.

AME | Learning

The reason for this temporary Net Income Summary account is so that you can easily identify how much was added to Owner's Equity during the year by the profits the business generated. (Distinguishing between any increase in Owner's Equity from money put in the business versus an increase from profits.) This is an optional step in closing the books - it is not mandatory. This summary is simply a very efficient method of identifying how much of the increase in Owner's Equity was due to profits.

The first step is to enter the year-to-date amount of the revenue or expense account as a minus item on each account (clear the accounts) and put the same amount as a plus item on the Owner's Equity account. You are then ready to start seeing what income is being generated for the next accounting period (for the next year).

The steps to take in clearing out the revenue and expense accounts are as follows:

1. **Close the Revenue accounts** - transfer to the Net Income Summary account

2. **Close the Expense accounts** - transfer to the Net Income Summary account

3. **Close the Income Summary account** to Owner's Equity account

4. **Close the Drawings account** to Owner's Equity account

Steps 1 to 3 are performed in order to determine the profit (or loss) generated for the year to be transferred (or given) to the owner - who may now either leave it in the business or take it out of the business for personal use. Step 4 simply recognizes the amounts withdrawn during the year, which also reduces the equity in the business.

Net Income Summary

In order to move the revenue and expense accounts to Owner's Equity *and* find out what the profit or loss is, as part of the process, accountants use a "net income summary". (This account may also be called a "profit & loss account", an "income summary", etc. The name of the account may be different, depending on the preference of the person setting up the account, but the principle remains the same.)

The balances of the revenue accounts (*credit* balances) are moved to the net income summary and placed in the CREDIT column.

The balances of the expense accounts (*debit* balances) are moved to the net income summary and placed in the DEBIT column.

At this point, the balance in the net income summary tells you whether you have a profit or a loss. A credit balance means that there were more revenues than expenses - a profit. A debit balance in the account means that there was a loss.

After you verify that the profit or loss amount is correct, you can then move the total balance from the net income summary account to Owner's Equity.

The following is an illustrative *example* of the steps to closing the books. There are 15 expense accounts (which will have a debit balance at the end of the period) and 6 revenue accounts (which will have a credit balance at the end of the period). These need to have a zero balance in preparation for the next accounting period. You therefore need to credit all expense accounts and debit all revenue accounts (bringing them to zero). **Note:** We are only using a few accounts for the purpose of this illustration:

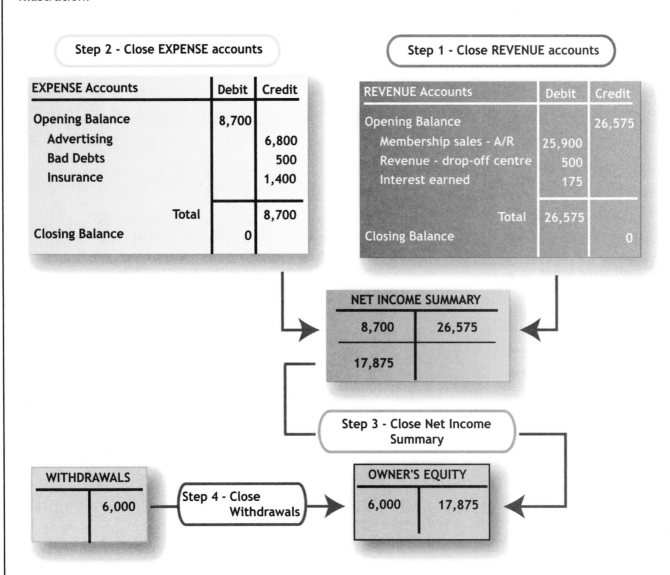

On the next few pages we will take you through the steps one at a time.

The Year-End Trial Balance

Throughout the accounting period (the year) you complete financial statements at the end of each month in order to determine the profit (loss) each month.

At the end of the accounting period, you must use the cumulative totals for the entire year. (Remember that the Balance Sheet is a permanent, ongoing record so the totals at year-end **are** the totals on December 31st.)

The year-end Trial Balance is as follows:

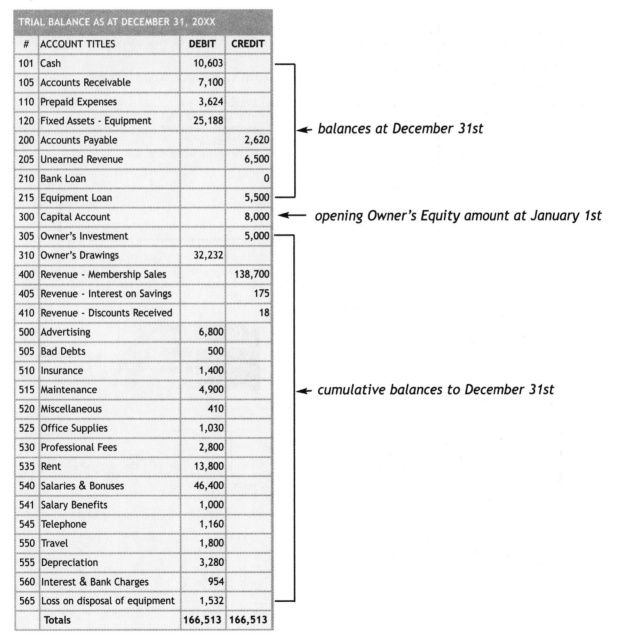

#	ACCOUNT TITLES	DEBIT	CREDIT
101	Cash	10,603	
105	Accounts Receivable	7,100	
110	Prepaid Expenses	3,624	
120	Fixed Assets - Equipment	25,188	
200	Accounts Payable		2,620
205	Unearned Revenue		6,500
210	Bank Loan		0
215	Equipment Loan		5,500
300	Capital Account		8,000
305	Owner's Investment		5,000
310	Owner's Drawings	32,232	
400	Revenue - Membership Sales		138,700
405	Revenue - Interest on Savings		175
410	Revenue - Discounts Received		18
500	Advertising	6,800	
505	Bad Debts	500	
510	Insurance	1,400	
515	Maintenance	4,900	
520	Miscellaneous	410	
525	Office Supplies	1,030	
530	Professional Fees	2,800	
535	Rent	13,800	
540	Salaries & Bonuses	46,400	
541	Salary Benefits	1,000	
545	Telephone	1,160	
550	Travel	1,800	
555	Depreciation	3,280	
560	Interest & Bank Charges	954	
565	Loss on disposal of equipment	1,532	
	Totals	166,513	166,513

TRIAL BALANCE AS AT DECEMBER 31, 20XX

← *balances at December 31st*

← *opening Owner's Equity amount at January 1st*

← *cumulative balances to December 31st*

Step 1: Close the Revenue Accounts

Use the general journal to close the revenue accounts. Revenue accounts are normally credit balances.

When you close the revenue accounts, you want to make the balance in each revenue account zero. In order to do that, you need to **debit** the revenue accounts. The corresponding credit is made to the net income summary account.

TRIAL BALANCE AS AT DECEMBER 31, 20XX			
#	ACCOUNT TITLES	DEBIT	CREDIT
101	Cash	10,603	
105	Accounts Receivable	7,100	
110	Prepaid Expenses	3,624	
120	Fixed Assets - Equipment	25,188	
200	Accounts Payable		2,620
205	Unearned Revenue		6,500
210	Bank Loan		0
215	Equipment Loan		5,500
300	Capital Account		8,000
305	Owner's Investment		5,000
310	Owner's Drawings	32,232	
400	Revenue - Membership Sales		138,700
405	Revenue - Interest on Savings		175
410	Revenue - Discounts Received		18
500	Advertising	6,800	
505	Bad Debts	500	
510	Insurance	1,400	
515	Maintenance	4,900	
520	Miscellaneous	410	
525	Office Supplies	1,030	
530	Professional Fees	2,800	
535	Rent	13,800	
540	Salaries & Bonuses	46,400	
541	Salary Benefits	1,000	
545	Telephone	1,160	
550	Travel	1,800	
555	Depreciation	3,280	
560	Interest & Bank Charges	954	
565	Loss on disposal of equipment	1,532	
	Totals	166,513	166,513

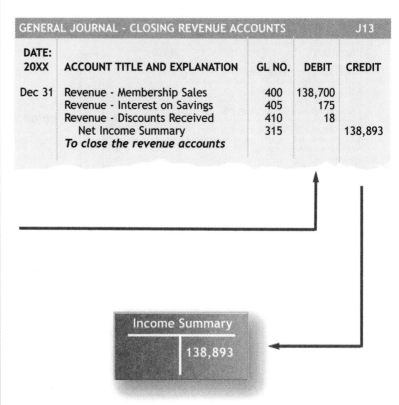

GENERAL JOURNAL - CLOSING REVENUE ACCOUNTS				J13
DATE: 20XX	ACCOUNT TITLE AND EXPLANATION	GL NO.	DEBIT	CREDIT
Dec 31	Revenue - Membership Sales	400	138,700	
	Revenue - Interest on Savings	405	175	
	Revenue - Discounts Received	410	18	
	Net Income Summary	315		138,893
	To close the revenue accounts			

Income Summary

138,893

Step 2: Close the Expense Accounts

In a fashion similar to closing the temporary revenue accounts, you also need to close the expense accounts. Since expense accounts are normally debit balances, you need to credit the expense accounts in order to reduce them to a zero balance. The corresponding entry is a debit to the summary.

#	ACCOUNT TITLES	DEBIT	CREDIT
101	Cash	10,603	
105	Accounts Receivable	7,100	
110	Prepaid Expenses	3,624	
120	Fixed Assets - Equipment	25,188	
200	Accounts Payable		2,620
205	Unearned Revenue		6,500
210	Bank Loan		0
215	Equipment Loan		5,500
300	Capital Account		8,000
305	Owner's Investment		5,000
310	Owner's Drawings	32,232	
400	Revenue - Membership Sales		138,700
405	Revenue - Interest on Savings		175
410	Revenue - Discounts Received		18
500	Advertising	6,800	
505	Bad Debts	500	
510	Insurance	1,400	
515	Maintenance	4,900	
520	Miscellaneous	410	
525	Office Supplies	1,030	
530	Professional Fees	2,800	
535	Rent	13,800	
540	Salaries & Bonuses	46,400	
541	Salary Benefits	1,000	
545	Telephone	1,160	
550	Travel	1,800	
555	Depreciation	3,280	
560	Interest & Bank Charges	954	
565	Loss on disposal of equipment	1,532	
	Totals	166,513	166,513

TRIAL BALANCE AS AT DECEMBER 31, 20XX

GENERAL JOURNAL - CLOSING EXPENSE ACCOUNTS				J13
DATE: 20XX	ACCOUNT TITLE AND EXPLANATION	GL NO.	DEBIT	CREDIT
Dec 31	Net Income Summary	315	87,766	
	Advertising	500		6,800
	Bad Debts	505		500
	Insurance	510		1,400
	Maintenance	515		4,900
	Miscellaneous	520		410
	Office Supplies	525		1,030
	Professional Fees	530		2,800
	Rent	535		13,800
	Salaries & Bonuses	540		46,400
	Salary Benefits	541		1,000
	Telephone	545		1,160
	Travel	550		1,800
	Depreciation	555		3,280
	Interest & Bank Charges	560		954
	Loss on disposal of equipment	565		1,532
	To close the expense accounts			

Net Income Summary

87,766	138,893

Step 3: Close the Income Summary account to Owner's Capital account

You will now move the net income for the year to Owner's Equity because these funds belong to the owner. The funds have not been put directly to Owner's Equity during the year in order to monitor how the business was doing. Once you have finalized the business activities for the year, you can move these funds to the place they really belong - the Owner's Equity account - and you can start monitoring the detailed operations for the next year on a fresh income statement (starting with zero balances).

In order to make this transfer, you will close the net income summary account by recording the journal entry that reduces the balance of the Income Summary to a zero balance. Check first, however, to make sure that the balance of the Income Summary agrees with your income statement from January 1st to December 31st.

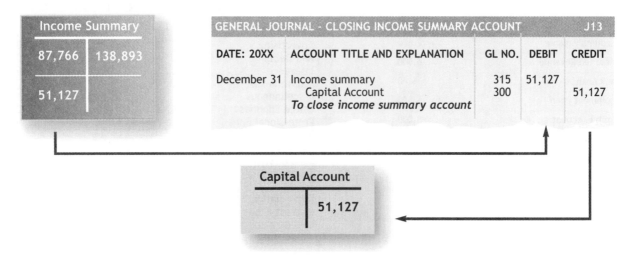

Step 4: Close the Drawings Account

The final step in the closing process is to close the Drawings account. The Drawings account, like revenue and expenses, is a temporary account used so that you can conveniently see withdrawals by the owner during the year.

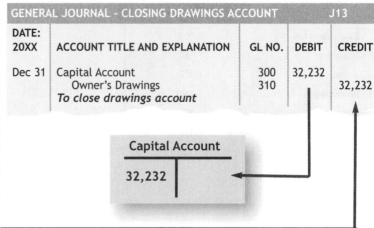

#	ACCOUNT TITLES	DEBIT	CREDIT
	TRIAL BALANCE AS AT DECEMBER 31, 20XX		
101	Cash	10,603	
105	Accounts Receivable	7,100	
110	Prepaid Expenses	3,624	
120	Fixed Assets - Equipment	25,188	
200	Accounts Payable		2,620
205	Unearned Revenue		6,500
210	Bank Loan		0
215	Equipment Loan		5,500
300	Capital Account		36,692
305	Owner's Investment		5,000
310	Owner's Drawings	32,232	

The completed **General Journal** is as follows:

GENERAL JOURNAL				J13
DATE: 20XX	**ACCOUNT TITLE AND EXPLANATION**	**GL NO.**	**DEBIT**	**CREDIT**
December 31	Revenue - Membership Sales	400	138,700	
	Interest on Savings	405	175	
	Discounts Received	410	18	
	Net Income Summary	315		138,893
	To close the revenue accounts			
December 31	Net Income Summary	315	87,766	
	Advertising	500		6,800
	Bad Debts	505		500
	Insurance	510		1,400
	Maintenance	515		4,900
	Miscellaneous	520		410
	Office Supplies	525		1,030
	Professional Fees	530		2,800
	Rent	535		13,800
	Salaries & Bonuses	540		46,400
	Salary Benefits	541		1,000
	Telephone	545		1,160
	Travel	550		1,800
	Depreciation	555		3,280
	Interest & Bank Charges	560		954
	Loss on disposal of equipment	565		1,532
	To close the expense accounts			
December 31	Net Income Summary	315	51,127	
	Capital Account	300		51,127
	To close the Income Summary account			
December 31	Capital Account	300	32,232	
	Owner's Drawings	310		32,232
	To close the drawings account			
December 31	Capital Account	300	5,000	
	Owner's Investment	305		5,000
	To close the investment account			

For this particular Chart of Accounts, the Owner's Investment for the year is recorded in account 305 in order to highlight the amount for management purposes. Not all charts of account will include an account like this. If this is the case, the investment would be recorded directly in the Owner's Equity account.

The following is an example of what your ledgers (the accounts) will look like upon closing. We have selected only four accounts to use as a demonstration:

ACCOUNT: Capital Account **NO.** 300

DATE 20XX		DESCRIPTION	REF.	DEBIT				CREDIT				BALANCE (DR OR CR)				
		OPENING BALANCE										8	0	0	0	CR
Dec	31	Closing income summary	J13					51	1	2	7	59	1	2	7	
Dec	31	Closing drawings account	J13	32	2	3	2					26	8	9	5	

ACCOUNT: Income Summary Account **NO.** 315

DATE 20XX		DESCRIPTION	REF.	DEBIT				CREDIT				BALANCE (DR OR CR)				
Dec	31	Closing revenue account	J13					138	8	9	3	138	8	9	3	CR
Dec	31	Closing expense accounts	J13	87	7	6	6					51	1	2	7	CR
Dec	31	Closing income summary	J13	51	1	2	7								0	

ACCOUNT: Revenue - Membership Sales **NO.** 400

DATE 20XX		DESCRIPTION	REF.	DEBIT				CREDIT				BALANCE (DR OR CR)				
		OPENING BALANCE										138	7	0	0	CR
Dec	31	Closing entry	J13	138	7	0	0								0	

ACCOUNT: Rent **NO.** 535

DATE 20XX		DESCRIPTION	REF.	DEBIT				CREDIT				BALANCE (DR OR CR)				
		OPENING BALANCE										13	8	0	0	DR
Dec	31	Closing entry	J13					13	8	0	0				0	

You would proceed to close EACH and EVERY revenue and expense account as shown above.

Prepare a Post-Closing Trial Balance

"Post" is a Latin word that means "after". So ... a Post-closing trial balance is a trial balance that is prepared after the closing process has been completed.

Since the closing process involves reducing all revenue to zero, reducing all expenses to zero, making the balance in the income summary account a zero balance, and eliminating the drawings account, what is left? Assets, Liabilities and Owners' Equity are the only accounts remaining.

If you have correctly completed the closing process, your post closing trial balance will show only Assets, Liabilities and Owners' Equity.

POST-CLOSING TRIAL BALANCE AT JANUARY 1, 20XX		
ACCOUNT TITLES	DEBIT	CREDIT
Cash	10,603	
Accounts Receivable	7,100	
Prepaid Expenses	3,624	
Fixed Assets - Equipment	25,188	
Accounts Payable		2,620
Unearned Revenue		6,500
Bank Loan		0
Equipment Loan		5,500
Owner's Equity (including Owner's Investment)		31,895
Totals	46,515	46,515

Note: The balance in the Owner's Equity account (Capital Account) is the opening balance at January 1st ($8,000 + Owner's Investment of $5,000) less the total Drawings for the period ($32,232) plus the net income (profit) upon closing all accounts ($51,127):

	$13,000	Owner's Investments
-	32,232	Drawings
+	51,127	Net Profit
	$31,895	Closing Owner's Equity

The post-closing trial balance is a snapshot of all of the Assets, Liabilities and Owner's Equity at the start of the first day of the next accounting period. You will note that on all the balance sheet accounts, the value on December 31st before closing and the value at January 1st after closing are identical. In other words, any assets or liabilities you owned or owed at midnight on December 31st would still be owned or owed by you at 12:01 a.m. on January 1st. The income statement accounts are all at zero as you are starting a new accounting year. All income and expenses on December 31st have been transferred to the Owner's Equity account.

Year-End Summary

Here is a summary of the steps to be taken in completing the accounting cycle:

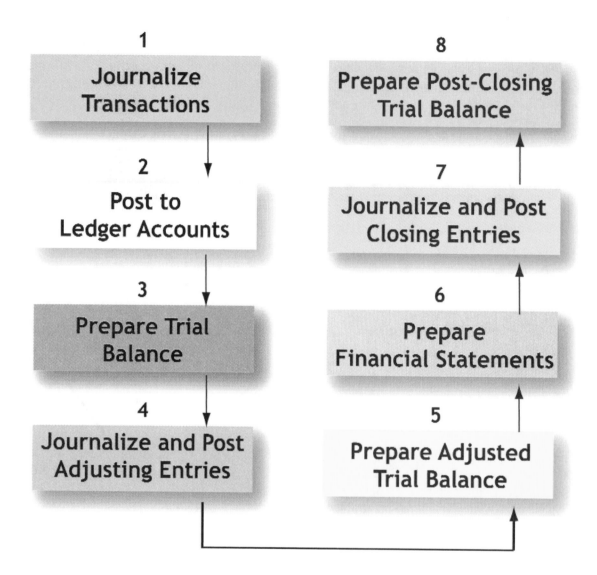

Exercises: Chapter 15

Exercise #1

CLOSING THE BOOKS

Please circle the correct answer.

1. In order to close the books you must clear out the following accounts (circle the correct accounts):
    a. Revenue
    b. Expense
    c. Asset
    d. Liability
    e. Withdrawal

2. Income statement accounts are temporary and are cleared out at the end of an accounting period.
    a. True
    b. False

3. What is the "Net Income Summary" account used for?
    a. To identify the increase in Owner's Equity due to profits.
    b. To record the balances of all balance sheet accounts.
    c. To summarize all the transactions for the past month.

4. The Net Income Summary account is optional when closing the books.
    a. True
    b. False

5. Which of the following procedures are required when closing the books at year end?
    a. Close the revenue accounts
    b. Close the expense accounts
    c. Close the income summary account to the owner's capital account
    d. Close the drawings account

6. In order to clear the expense account (to bring the account to zero) the entry would (generally) be a:
    a. Debit
    b. Credit

7. The total of all expense accounts is recorded on the Net Income Summary as a:
    a. Debit
    b. Credit

8. The closing balance in the revenue account is (generally) a:
    a. Debit
    b. Credit

9. The total of the revenue account is recorded on the Net Income Summary as a:
    a. Debit
    b. Credit

10. Closing the books means:
    a. that you simply start a new year and write zero balances on all GL accounts
    b. that you simply close the books and open them again in the new year
    c. that the income statement starts again in the new year with zero balances

11. The term 'fiscal year' has the same meaning as a 'calendar year':
    a. True
    b. False

12. Different businesses may have different year ends.
    a. True
    b. False

13. The total annual profit is made up of the same profit amount each month.
    a. True
    b. False

14. Profits represent the same amount as cash in the bank at the end of the year.
    a. True
    b. False

15. What does "post" mean in the Latin Language?
    a. Mail letters
    b. Before
    c. After
    d. An amount of money that you owe

16. A Post-Closing Trial Balance is a trial balance that is prepared after the closing entries are prepared.
    a. True
    b. False

17. What is the purpose of a trial balance?
    a. To ensure that every debit has a corresponding credit
    b. To ensure that every debit has a corresponding debit
    c. To ensure that every credit has a corresponding credit
    d. To see if you made a profit
    e. To check if the balance sheet balances

18. If you have correctly completed the closing process, the trial balance will only show Assets, Liabilities and Equity, without Revenue and Expenses.
    a. True
    b. False

Notes

AME | Learning

Chapter 16
Computerized Accounting

Computerized Accounting

Introduction to Computerized Accounting

Making the Invisible Visible

When working with computer software, many of the functions are automatic and *invisible* to the user. For example, when entering a sales invoice or depositing accounts receivable payments, the user does not see the double entry. It's done automatically. However, it's crucial to understand how the system works to enable you to make informed decisions.

Creating financial statements using both T-Accounts or "old fashioned" 3-column ledger accounts can be a painstaking process and it is very easy to make mistakes. It is also time consuming to extract information quickly to enable you to make sound management decisions about your personal life or your business. Welcome to the world of **computerized accounting.**

There are many computer systems that automate the accounting process. Some examples include *Simply Accounting, Quickbooks, MYOB* and *Peachtree*. While each system has its own unique methods of data entry and reporting, they all work according to the same principles. This section will help you understand the basic principles that make computer accounting software operate.

The sequence that we will use in this lesson is typical of most accounting software programs but may change from program to program. For demonstration purposes we will use the name **AME** (Accounting Made Easy) as the software program.

There are a few basic steps to preparing the software for your business. Of course there are many more functions that may have to be completed if you wish to do so. The following, however, are the necessary basic steps. (Remember that the sequence in which these are entered is not consistent with all programs.)

Step 1:

Enter all the details pertaining to the name of your business, address and other details such as phone number, fax number, etc.

Step 2:

You can choose any month of the year for the year-end of the business, however, some businesses are very seasonal. Seasonal businesses (e.g. sports industry) are very busy at certain times of the year so it would not be advisable to end the year during that time.

Another example would be a financial advisory service business whose busiest time is prior to tax season.

All accounting programs require that you enter a conversion month. In other words the month in which you are commencing your new computer software, because the computer will report all transactions from that month onwards.

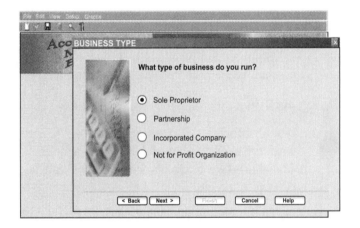

Step 3:

Different types of industries typically would require a different type of layout. For example, a sole proprietary business would record Owner's Equity without the share capital that would be recorded in a corporation.

A partnership would allow for different partners in the equity account.

Step 4:

You do have choices. You can either use the standard Chart of Accounts that is provided with most software packages, import one that is currently in use in a another system that you may be using, or create your own from scratch. You may be able to select a hairdressing salon model, or perhaps an automobile repair shop. Each of these will list different types of accounts which would be typical for that industry. We have chosen a standard health club model for this section.

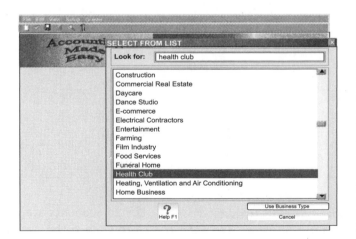

389

Step 5:

Enter the opening balances. If this is the first day of the new fiscal year, then you need to enter the opening balances from the balance sheet accounts because all the revenue and expense accounts would have been cleared out at year-end. If, however, you were to enter on a day *during* the fiscal year, you would need to enter the current balances for each account (including all revenue and expense accounts).

"Header"

"Detail"

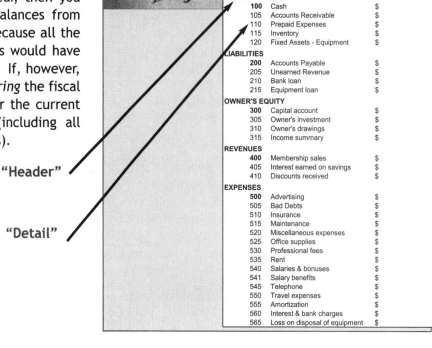

Step 6:

When entering the opening balances, there willl be a choice of the *type* of account. There are two basic choices relating to the type of account:

Header: This type of account is simply a heading, which may or may not show the category total. For example, the heading could be "Assets".

Detail: The type of Asset. In this case it's a "Chequing Account".

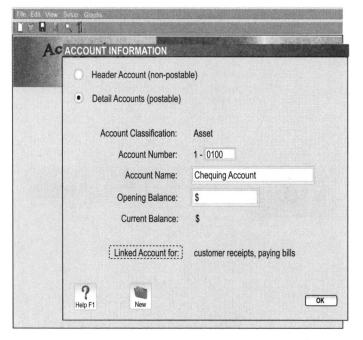

Accounts receivable, for example, can be *linked* to another account such as sales. In other words, every time you make a sale, the other entry will automatically be linked to accounts receivable. If your business worked with cash only then the link would be sales and chequing account. Linked accounts are defaults, which means they are automatic to save time. You always have the choice to change the defaults.

Step 7:

The opening balances for each account will be the same as the closing balances on your manual general ledger accounts (or from another computer system).

Notice that each category of Assets, Liabilities, Equity, Income (sales) and Expenses have a different tab. (Some computer systems may have only one tab and simply list all the accounts.)

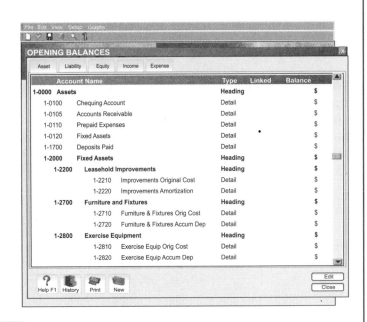

Step 8:

Create your preferences. Typically, the system will allow you to create your own set of preferences. A preference means that you have the choice to use your own *preferred* set of rules. Some examples might include:
· The look of the accounts receivable report.
· Whether you see the account name or the account number when reporting.
· The amount of detail required with the Profit & Loss report.
All these choices can be made at this time or changed later if required.

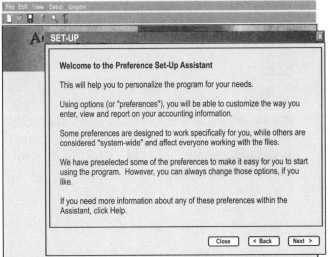

Step 9:

Set up vendor and customer files. All the details pertaining to vendors and customers are stored in these quick-to-access data files. For example, when processing a cheque to a vendor, all you need to do is call up the vendor's name and the address and other details will automatically appear on the cheque.

These details are also important as they provide a quick way to obtain phone numbers, e-mail addresses, etc.

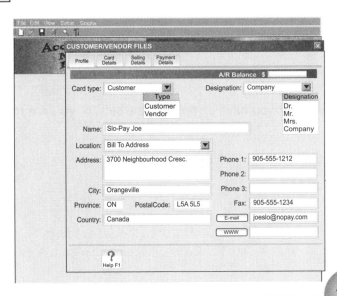

Step 10:

When setting up customer accounts you will specify the payment terms for each customer. For example, whether they will pay cash each month, pay in advance, or you will provide them with payment terms (accounts receivable).

This default can always be changed.

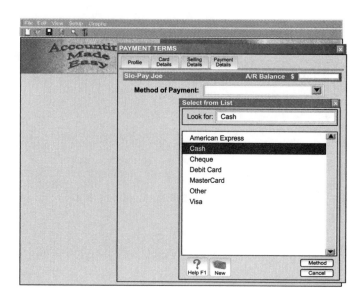

Step 11:

Design your sales layout (invoice style). There are usually standard layouts available that can be used just as they are. Most programs allow you to add your own corporate logo, etc.

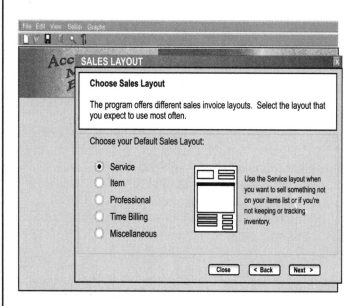

Now that you have completed the set-up, you are ready to start using your accounting system.

Before we show you examples of actual transactions, here is a breakdown of the main *Central Command* computer screen and sub-screens you will use when keying in the transactions:

Accounts

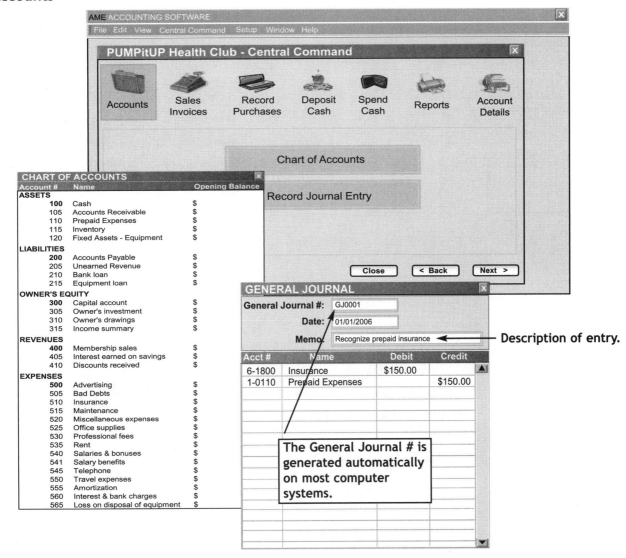

In the **Accounts** screen, our model shows 2 sub-screens:

1. A listing of all General Ledger accounts (chart of accounts), which includes account number, description and current balances.

2. A General Journal, allowing you to create journal entries. These are typically used for month-end adjustments such as to record depreciation and to fix mistakes such as an account entered incorrectly.

Sales Invoices

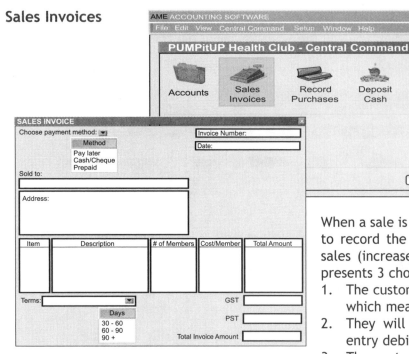

When a sale is made, an invoice must be generated to record the sale. This will automatically credit sales (increase sales). However, the double entry presents 3 choices:

1. The customer will pay by cheque or with cash, which means the other entry debits cash.
2. They will pay later, which means the other entry debits accounts receivable.
3. The customer has already paid, which debits (decreases) unearned revenue.

Record Purchases

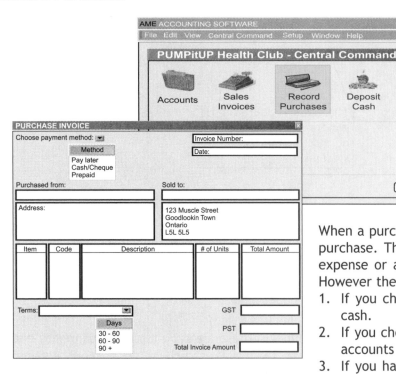

When a purchase is made, you need to record the purchase. This will automatically debit either an expense or an asset (increase expense or asset). However the double entry presents 3 choices:

1. If you choose to pay cash then you willcredit cash.
2. If you choose to pay later then you will credit accounts payable.
3. If you have already prepaid the expense then you will credit (decrease) prepaid expenses.

Deposit Cash

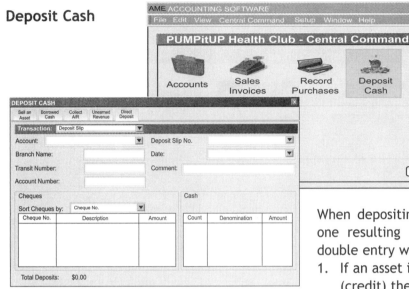

When depositing cash, there are 5 options - each one resulting in a debit (increase) in cash. The double entry will depend on the source of the cash.

1. If an asset is sold the double entry will decrease (credit) the asset that was sold.
2. When borrowing cash, debt will increase (credit).
3. If a customer pays an amount owing, accounts receivable will decrease (credit).
4. When a customer pays in advance, it will increase debt (credit) because you owe them this money if the service is not delivered.
5. A direct deposit such as a cash sale or interest earned on savings will increase (credit) revenue.

Spend Cash

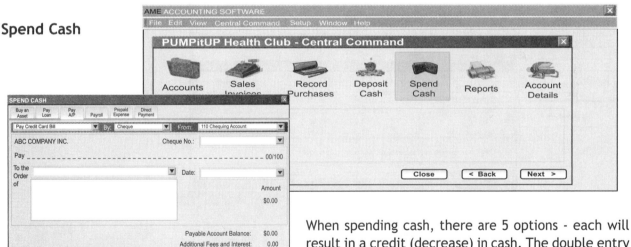

When spending cash, there are 5 options - each will result in a credit (decrease) in cash. The double entry will depend on the use of the cash.

1. If an asset is purchased the double entry will increase (debit) the asset that was purchased.
2. Paying back a loan will decrease (debit) debt.
3. Paying outstanding accounts owing is a decrease (debit) in Accounts Payable.
4. Paying a vendor in advance will increase prepaid expenses (debit) because the vendor will owe this money back if they do not deliver the service.
5. Direct withdrawal from the bank account, such as interest paid or bank charges on account, will increase (debit) expenses.

Reports

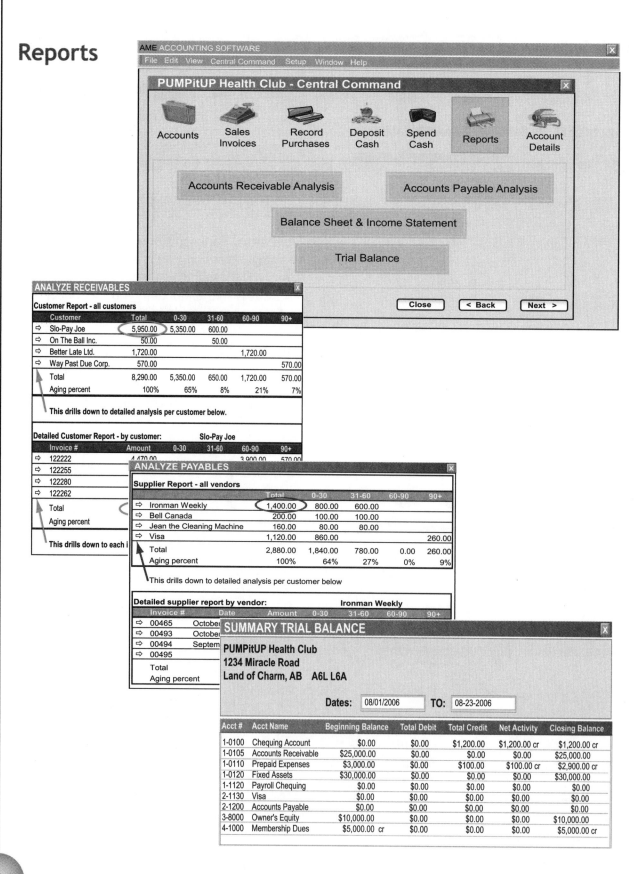

There are literally innumerable reports you can generate from a computer software program. Most programs already have pre-designed reports to select. Here are examples, some of which are illustrated in this chapter:

Accounts
Accounts list summary
Account list with details
Account history

Accounts Receivable
List outstanding account summary for all customers
List detail accounts for each customer

Accounts Payable
List outstanding account summary for all vendors
List detail accounts for each vendor

Balance Sheet
Current balance sheet
Last year versus this year

Profit and Loss
This year
Last year versus this year

Trial Balance
Trial balance summary
Trial balance with details

Taxation
GST and PST return

Transaction Journal
List of all journal entries
List all transactions

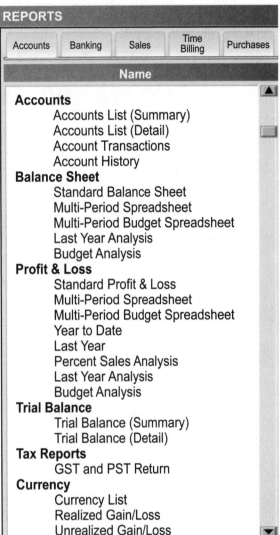

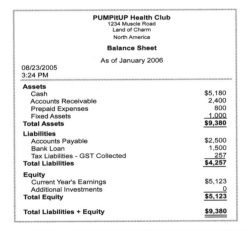

Account Details

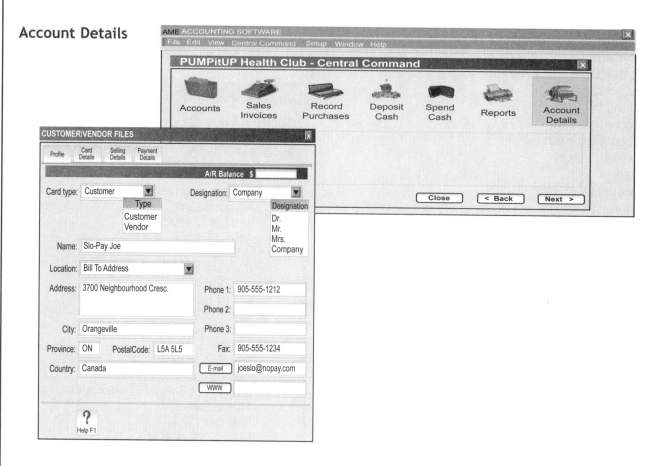

Now it's time to review some transactions. ⟶

Each of the following transactions will be entered into the *AME Software* and compared to the 3-column ledgers.

Transactions

1.	Membership cash sales	$5,000
2.	Advertising billed to you - pay next month to *Ironman Weekly*	800
3.	Pay cash for salaries and bonuses	2,000
4.	Pay bank loan principal	400

Adjustment:

5.	Recognize prepaid insurance	500

Using the opening balances and account codes from the Chart of Accounts:

⟶

CHART OF ACCOUNTS ☒

Account #	Name	Opening Balance
ASSETS		
100	Cash	$2,000.00
105	Accounts Receivable	$3,000.00
110	Prepaid Expenses	$1,000.00
115	Inventory	$0
120	Fixed Assets - Equipment	$8,000.00
LIABILITIES		
200	Accounts Payable	$1,000.00
205	Unearned Revenue	$1,000.00
210	Bank loan	$5,000.00
215	Equipment loan	$4,000.00
OWNER'S EQUITY		
300	Capital account	$3,000.00
305	Owner's investment	$0
310	Owner's drawings	$0
315	Income summary	$0
REVENUES		
400	Membership sales	$0
405	Interest earned on savings	$0
410	Discounts received	$0
EXPENSES		
500	Advertising	$0
505	Bad Debts	$0
510	Insurance	$0
515	Maintenance	$0
520	Miscellaneous expenses	$0
525	Office supplies	$0
530	Professional fees	$0
535	Rent	$0
540	Salaries & bonuses	$0
541	Salary benefits	$0
545	Telephone	$0
550	Travel expenses	$0
555	Amortization	$0
560	Interest & bank charges	$0
565	Loss on disposal of equipment	$0

Transaction #1 - **Membership cash sales:**

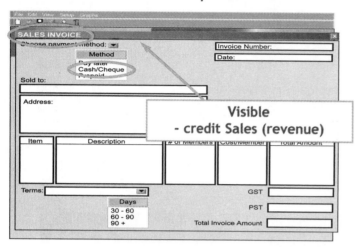

In order to record a sale you would use the **Sales Invoice** screen to enter an invoice. We call this the *visible* transaction because you can see it on the screen. The *invisible* side to the double entry - the part of the transaction that you do not see - is that the program will automatically link the sales (credit) in the sales journal to the cash account (debit). If you were still operating a manual set of financial statements, you would see the two general ledger entries.

Invisible

ACCOUNT: Cash   NO. 101

DATE 20XX		DESCRIPTION	REF.	DEBIT				CREDIT				BALANCE (DR OR CR)				
Jan	01	Membership cash sales	J1	5	0	0	0					5	0	0	0	DR

Transaction #2 - **Advertising billed to you:**

To record a purchase select the **Purchase Invoice** screen. Since this will be paid for at a later date you would select **Pay Later,** which will automatically increase accounts payable. The *invisible* side for this advertising expense is that by entering the advertising account code the program will automatically increase (debit) advertising expenses.

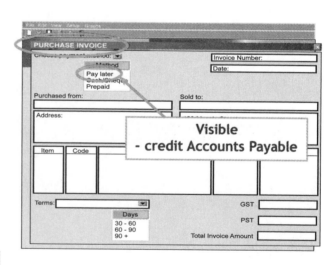

Invisible

ACCOUNT: Advertising   NO. 500

DATE 20XX		DESCRIPTION	REF.	DEBIT				CREDIT				BALANCE (DR OR CR)			
Jan	04	Advertising billed to you	J1		8	0	0					8	0	0	DR

400

Transaction #3 - Pay cash for salaries and bonuses:

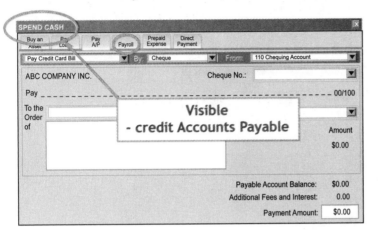

To pay wages using cash, select **Payroll** from the **Spend Cash** screen. By selecting this function, the computer is programmed to automatically decrease (credit) cash and increase (debit) payroll expenses.

This account will also divide the payroll into the various categories such as Gross Pay, Taxes, etc. (Notice the GL account that shows the other side of the transaction in the background.)

Invisible

ACCOUNT: Salaries & Bonuses																NO. 540
DATE 20XX		DESCRIPTION	REF.	DEBIT				CREDIT				BALANCE (DR OR CR)				
Jan	15	Pay cash for salaries	J1	2	0	0	0					2	0	0	0	DR

Transaction #4 - Pay bank loan principal:

To pay back a bank loan, select **Pay Back Loan** from the **Spend Cash** screen. The program will know that cash has to decrease (credit) and the bank loan must also decrease (debit). All you need to select is which account is going to be paid.

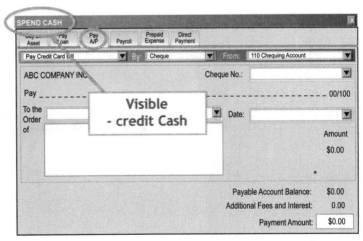

Invisible

ACCOUNT: Bank Loan																NO. 210
DATE 20XX		DESCRIPTION	REF.	DEBIT				CREDIT				BALANCE (DR OR CR)				
Jan	15	Pay bank loan principal	J1	4	0	0						4	0	0		DR

Transaction #5 - **Recognize prepaid insurance (*adjustment*):**

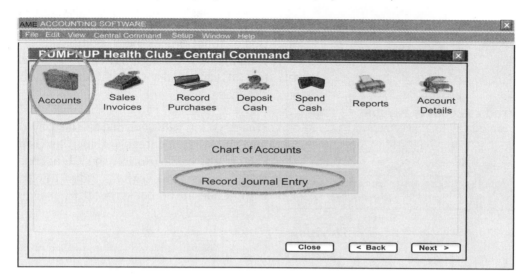

We now record the recognition of prepaid insurance in the amount of $500 - this is a journal entry. Select **Accounts** from the main *Central Command* screen and then select **Record Journal Entry.** You need to decrease prepaid expenses (credit) and increase insurance expense (debit). These are the journal entries you would enter into the system:

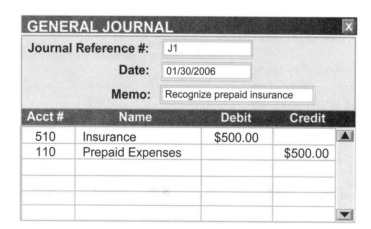

Acct #	Name	Debit	Credit
510	Insurance	$500.00	
110	Prepaid Expenses		$500.00

Summary of the transactions:

TRANSACTION SUMMARY

Acct #	Name	Opening Balance	Trans 1	Trans 2	Trans 3	Trans 4	Trans 5	Assets	Liabilities & Equity	Revenue	Expenses	Closing Balance
ASSETS												
100	Cash	$2,000.00	5,000 Dr		2,000 Cr	400 Cr		$4,600.00				$4,600.00
105	Accounts Receivable	$3,000.00						$3,000.00				$3,000.00
110	Prepaid Expenses	$1,000.00					500 Cr	$500.00				$500.00
115	Inventory	$0.00						$0.00				$0.00
120	Fixed Assets - Equipment	$8,000.00						$8,000.00				$8,000.00
LIABILITIES												
200	Accounts Payable	$1,000.00		800 Cr					$1,800.00			$1,800.00
205	Unearned Revenue	$1,000.00							$1,000.00			$1,000.00
210	Bank loan	$5,000.00				400 Dr			$4,600.00			$4,600.00
215	Equipment loan	$4,000.00							$4,000.00			$4,000.00
OWNER'S EQUITY												
300	Capital account	$3,000.00							$3,000.00			$3,000.00
305	Owner's investment	$0.00										$0.00
310	Owner's drawings	$0.00										$0.00
312	Profit (Loss) this period	$0.00							$1,700.00			$1,700.00
315	Income summary	$0.00										$0.00
REVENUES												
400	Membership sales	$0.00	5,000 Cr							$5,000.00		$5,000.00
405	Interest earned on savings	$0.00										$0.00
410	Discounts received	$0.00										$0.00
EXPENSES												
500	Advertising	$0.00		800 Dr							$800.00	$800.00
505	Bad Debts	$0.00										$0.00
510	Insurance	$0.00					500 Dr				$500.00	$500.00
515	Maintenance	$0.00										$0.00
520	Miscellaneous expenses	$0.00										$0.00
525	Office supplies	$0.00										$0.00
530	Professional fees	$0.00										$0.00
535	Rent	$0.00										$0.00
540	Salaries & bonuses	$0.00			2,000 Dr						$2,000.00	$2,000.00
541	Salary benefits	$0.00										$0.00
545	Telephone	$0.00										$0.00
550	Travel expenses	$0.00										$0.00
555	Amortization	$0.00										$0.00
560	Interest & bank charges	$0.00										$0.00
565	Loss on disposal of equipment	$0.00						$16,100.00	$16,100.00	$5,000.00	$3,300.00	

To review the information entered into the computer system, you would print some reports of the final results by selecting **Reports** from the main *Central Command* screen:

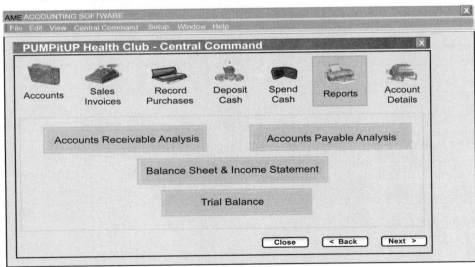

To review the Balance Sheet and Income Statement, for example:

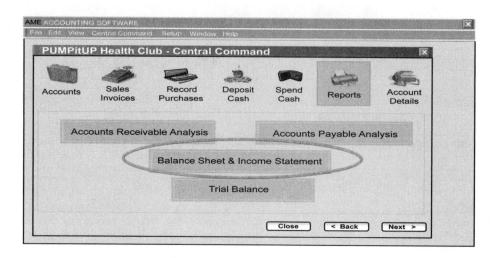

PUMPitUP Health Club
1234 Muscle Road
Land of Charm
North America

Balance Sheet

As of January 2006

01/31/2006
10:45 AM

Assets

Cash	$ 4,600
Accounts Receivable	3,000
Prepaid Expenses	500
Fixed Assets	8,000
Total Assets	**$16,100**

Liabilities

Accounts Payable	$ 1,800
Unearned Revenue	1,000
Bank Loan	4,600
Equipment Loan	4,000
Total Liabilities	**$11,400**

Equity

Capital Account	$ 3,000
Profit (Loss)	1,700
Total Equity	**$ 4,700**
Total Liabilities + Equity	**$16,100**

PUMPitUP Health Club
1234 Muscle Road
Land of Charm
North America

Income Statement

1/1/2006 through 1/31/2006

01/31/2006
11:24 AM

Revenue

Membership Sales	**$ 5,000**

Expenses

Advertising	800
Insurance	500
Salaries & Bonuses	2,000
Total Expenses	**$ 3,300**
Profit (Loss) this period	**$ 1,700**

There are two types of Trial Balance reports:

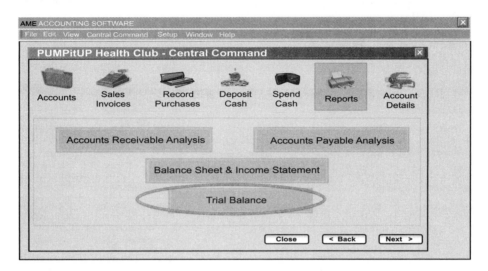

1. **Summary** - reports the total activity of each account.

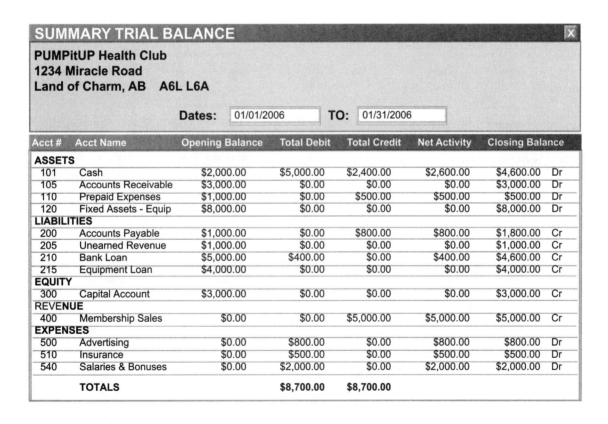

SUMMARY TRIAL BALANCE

PUMPitUP Health Club
1234 Miracle Road
Land of Charm, AB   A6L L6A

Dates: 01/01/2006   **TO:** 01/31/2006

Acct #	Acct Name	Opening Balance	Total Debit	Total Credit	Net Activity	Closing Balance	
ASSETS							
101	Cash	$2,000.00	$5,000.00	$2,400.00	$2,600.00	$4,600.00	Dr
105	Accounts Receivable	$3,000.00	$0.00	$0.00	$0.00	$3,000.00	Dr
110	Prepaid Expenses	$1,000.00	$0.00	$500.00	$500.00	$500.00	Dr
120	Fixed Assets - Equip	$8,000.00	$0.00	$0.00	$0.00	$8,000.00	Dr
LIABILITIES							
200	Accounts Payable	$1,000.00	$0.00	$800.00	$800.00	$1,800.00	Cr
205	Unearned Revenue	$1,000.00	$0.00	$0.00	$0.00	$1,000.00	Cr
210	Bank Loan	$5,000.00	$400.00	$0.00	$400.00	$4,600.00	Cr
215	Equipment Loan	$4,000.00	$0.00	$0.00	$0.00	$4,000.00	Cr
EQUITY							
300	Capital Account	$3,000.00	$0.00	$0.00	$0.00	$3,000.00	Cr
REVENUE							
400	Membership Sales	$0.00	$0.00	$5,000.00	$5,000.00	$5,000.00	Cr
EXPENSES							
500	Advertising	$0.00	$800.00	$0.00	$800.00	$800.00	Dr
510	Insurance	$0.00	$500.00	$0.00	$500.00	$500.00	Dr
540	Salaries & Bonuses	$0.00	$2,000.00	$0.00	$2,000.00	$2,000.00	Dr
	TOTALS		$8,700.00	$8,700.00			

2. Detailed Summary - reports every transaction in each account.

DETAILED SUMMARY OF TRIAL BALANCE ☒

PUMPitUP Health Club
1234 Miracle Road
Land of Charm, AB   A6L L6A

Dates: 01/01/2006   **TO:** 01/31/2006

Bank Account 101

Opening balance: $2,000.00 DR

Reference	Date	Memo	Debit	Credit	Closing Balance
Deposit Slip #7	January 1, 2006	Membership Cash Sales	$5,000.00		$7,000.00 DR
Cheque #26	January 15, 2006	Pay Salaries & Bonuses		$2,000.00	$5,000.00 DR
Direct Deduction	January 15, 2006	Pay bank loan principal		$400.00	$4,600.00 DR

Accounts Receivable 105

Opening balance: $3,000.00 DR

Reference	Date	Memo	Debit	Credit	Closing Balance
					$3,000.00 DR

Prepaid Expenses 110

Opening balance: $1,000.00 DR

Reference	Date	Memo	Debit	Credit	Closing Balance
Direct Deduction	January 30, 2006	Recognize prepaid insurance		$500.00	$500.00 DR

Fixed Assets - Equipment 120

Opening balance: $8,000.00 DR

Reference	Date	Memo	Debit	Credit	Closing Balance
					$8,000.00 DR

Accounts Payable 200

Opening balance: $1,000.00 CR

Reference	Date	Memo	Debit	Credit	Closing Balance
Invoice # 0045	January 4, 2006	Advertising billed		$800.00	$1,800.00 CR

Unearned Revenue 205

Opening balance: $1,000.00 CR

Reference	Date	Memo	Debit	Credit	Closing Balance
					$1,000.00 CR

Bank Loan 210

Opening balance: $5,000.00 CR

Reference	Date	Memo	Debit	Credit	Closing Balance
Direct Deduction	January 15, 2006	Pay bank loan principal	$400.00		$4,600.00 CR

Equipment Loan 215

Opening balance: $4,000.00 CR

Reference	Date	Memo	Debit	Credit	Closing Balance
					$4,000.00 CR

Capital Account 300

Opening balance: $3,000.00 CR

Reference	Date	Memo	Debit	Credit	Closing Balance
					$3,000.00 CR

Membership Sales 400

Opening balance: $0.00 CR

Reference	Date	Memo	Debit	Credit	Closing Balance
Invoice #003	January 1, 2006	Membership Cash Sales		$5,000.00	$5,000.00 CR

Advertising 500

Opening balance: $0.00 DR

Reference	Date	Memo	Debit	Credit	Closing Balance
Invoice # 0045	January 4, 2006	Advertising billed	$800.00		$800.00 DR

Insurance 510

Opening balance: $0.00 DR

Reference	Date	Memo	Debit	Credit	Closing Balance
Prepaid expense	January 30, 2006	Recognize prepaid insurance	$500.00		$500.00 DR

Salaries & Bonuses 540

Opening balance: $0.00 DR

Reference	Date	Memo	Debit	Credit	Closing Balance
Cheque # 26	January 15, 2006	Pay salaries & bonuses	$2,000.00		$2,000.00 DR

Final Thoughts

This chapter dealt with the fundamental principles of computerized accounting and the key information necessary to operate a small business.

For the most part, there is very little information that is entered into the software program that cannot be extracted in one way or another. But beware! Not all information is useful and because it is so easy to extract information from a computer, one tends to produce more reports than are necessary. Be very careful with information overload. Here is a useful tip that will serve you well:

If you did not have a computer and had to produce reports manually, which reports would be your choice? In other words, because manual reports take so long to create, you would only produce those that you REALLY need. Computer reports should be no different. Produce what you NEED, not everything that the computer has to offer.

By now you will have learned about the power of financial knowledge. Information is power and this information will provide you with the knowledge to be successful in both your personal and professional economic lives.

▶ **Use it well.**

▶ **Use it responsibly.**

▶ **Use it morally.**

Notes

AME | Learning

Exercises: Chapter 16

Exercise #1

ACCOUNTING SOFTWARE

Please circle the correct answer.

1. All computer accounting programs are the same.
    a. True
    b. False

2. All computer accounting programs operate from the same principles.
    a. True
    b. False

3. You see the double entry every time you enter a transaction into the computer.
    a. True
    b. False

4. Given that computer accounting is automatic, to a large degree, it means that you do not really have to understand how manual accounting works.
    a. True
    b. False

5. When entering a sales invoice, the first entry would be to Revenue. Which of the following accounts could be the second part of the double entry:
    a. Cash
    b. Accounts Payable
    c. Accounts Receivable
    d. Unearned Revenue

6. When entering a purchase, the first entry could be to Professional Fees. Which of the following accounts could be the second part of the double entry:
    a. Accounts Receivable
    b. Prepaid Expenses
    c. Accounts Payable
    d. Cash

7. When entering a debt reduction, the first entry would be to Cash (Bank Account). Which of the following accounts could be the second part of the double entry:
    a. Accounts Payable
    b. Bank Loan
    c. Car Loan
    d. Prepaid Expenses

8. When depositing cash, the first entry would be to Cash (Bank Account). Which of the following accounts could be the second part of the double entry:
    a. Bank Loan
    b. Collect Accounts Receivable
    c. Record Bad Debt
    d. Loan from Owner
    e. Depreciation

9. When you record GST collected from a customer as part of the sales invoice, which only has to be paid next month, the GST will affect which two accounts:
    a. Cash
    b. Accounts Receivable
    c. GST Owing
    d. Accounts Payable

10. Which of the following transactions should be completed with a journal entry:
    a. Bad Debts
    b. Cash Sales
    c. Buying product on Accounts Payable
    d. Recognizing Unearned Revenue as Earned
    e. Depreciation
    f. Correcting a mistake
    g. Customer paying an outstanding Accounts Receivable
    h. Paying bank debt
    i. Revising an account description

Exercise #2

There are lots of available reports in most computer systems. Name those reports that you think would be most important to you as the owner of a health club.

_____

_____

_____

_____

_____

_____

_____

_____

_____

_____

_____

_____

Exercise #3

If you were running out of cash, what reports do you think you should print and why do you think that these reports will help you find the answer?

_____

_____

_____

_____

_____

_____

_____

_____

_____

_____

_____

Exercise #4

Do you think a computerized accounting system is more efficient than a manual record keeping system? Explain your answer.

_____

_____

_____

_____

_____

_____

_____

_____

_____

_____

_____

_____

_____

_____

_____

_____

_____

_____

_____

_____

_____

_____

_____

Exercise #5

MAKING THE INVISIBLE VISIBLE

For the following transactions, select which *AME Software* computer screen you would use to enter the transaction (the screens are shown with a number and letter reference beside them - **see the last page of this chapter - page 418**).

Then show both sides of the transaction, the visible part and the invisible part, in the table provided for each transaction. (*The first transaction has been done for you as an example.*)

Transaction #1: Membership cash sales ($9,000)   Screen # ___4B___

Description	Debit	Credit
Cash	9,000	
Sales (Revenue)		9,000
Membership cash sales		

Transaction #2: Membership sales - A/R ($5,000)   Screen # _____

Description	Debit	Credit

Transaction #3: Pay cheque for rent for the month ($1,500)   Screen # _____

Description	Debit	Credit

Transaction #4: Advertising billed to you - pay next month ($400)   **Screen #** _____

Description	Debit	Credit

Transaction #5: Deposit payment from customer to settle Accounts Receivable ($1,000)

Screen # _____

Description	Debit	Credit

Transaction #6: Monthly payroll - issue cheques ($6,000)   **Screen #** _____

Description	Debit	Credit

Transaction #7: Office supplies purchased with Debit Card ($200)   **Screen #** _____

Description	Debit	Credit

Transaction #8: Pay bank loan principal ($400)   Screen # _____

Description	Debit	Credit

Transaction #9: Pay bank loan interest ($10)   Screen # _____

Description	Debit	Credit

Transaction #10: Pay Accounts Payable ($1,000)   Screen # _____

Description	Debit	Credit

Transaction #11: Recognize prepaid insurance as expense for this month (150)
          - this is an *Adjustment*   Screen # _____

Description	Debit	Credit

Transaction #12: Depreciate Fixed Assets ($400) - this is an *Adjustment*   Screen # _____

Description	Debit	Credit

Transaction #13: Record bank charges ($20) - this is an *Adjustment*   Screen # _____

Description	Debit	Credit

Transaction #14: Recognize Unearned Revenue as earned for this month ($1,000)
                      - this is an *Adjustment*   Screen # _____

Description	Debit	Credit

Computer Screens

Screen **#1**:
Deposit Cash

Screen **#2**:
Purchase Invoice

Screen **#3**:
Spend Cash

Screen **#4**:
Sales Invoice

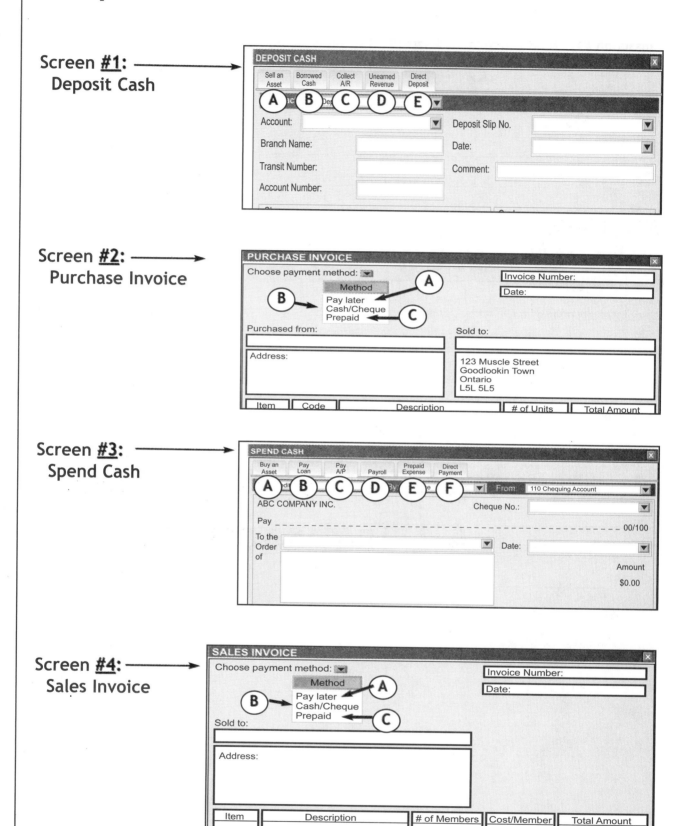

Appendix

Glossary, Index and All Transactions

Glossary

Acid-Test Ratio   A ratio used to assess a company's ability to cover its current debts with existing assets calculated as quick assets (cash, short-term investments and receivables) divided by current liabilities; also called *quick ratio*.

Account   A place or location within an accounting system in which the increases and decreases in a specific asset, liability, or equity are recorded and stored.

Account Balance   The difference between the increases (including the beginning balance) and decreases recorded in an account.

Accounting Cycle   The steps repeated each reporting period for the purpose of preparing financial statements for users.

Accounts Payable   The amount the business has been billed but has yet to pay. This is the money the business owes to its business suppliers from whom it has purchased goods or services.

Accounts Payable Ledger   A subsidiary ledger listing individual credit supplier accounts.

Accounting Period   The length of time covered by financial statements and other reports; also called *reporting periods*.

Accounts Receivable   The amount which is billed to customers and owing from them but has not yet been collected.

Accounts Receivable Ledger   A subsidiary ledger listing individual credit customer accounts.

Accrual Basis Accounting   The approach to preparing financial statements that uses the adjusting process to recognize revenues when earned and expenses when incurred, not when cash is paid or received; the basis for Generally Accepted Accounting Principles. (GAAP).

Accrued Expenses   Costs incurred in a period that are both unpaid and unrecorded; adjusting entries for recording accrued expenses involve increasing (debiting) expenses and increasing (crediting) liabilities.

Accrued Revenue   Revenues earned in a period that are both unrecorded and not yet received in cash (or other assets); adjusting entries for recording accrued revenues involve increasing (debiting) assets and increasing (crediting) revenues.

Adjusting Entry   A journal entry at the end of an accounting period to bring an asset or liability account balance to its proper amount while also updating the related expense or revenue account.

Amortization   The decline of an intangible asset such as a patent (which is only good for 20 years) or a copyright.

Assets   All the items that are owned such as cash, inventory, land, machinery, Accounts Receivable, etc.

Bad Debts   Money owed to the company (Accounts Receivable) that has been proven as non-collectable. This non-collectable money is regarded as an expense.

Balance Sheet   A financial report that shows what a company owns (Assets) and what it owes (Liabilities) the difference between them resulting in the Net Worth at a specific point in time.

Bank Reconciliation   An analysis that explains the difference between the balance of a chequing account shown in the depositor's records and the balance reported on the bank statement.

Bonds   An "IOU" issued by a company. The corporation pays interest on the bond and pays the entire amount (called principal) when due. Corporate bonds are usually traded publicly and they will rise and fall in value on the bond market. These are included in long-term debt on the Balance Sheet.

Book Value of an asset   The cost of the asset less its accumulated amortization.

CA (Canada) CPA (a Certified Public Accountant) (U.S.A)   Chartered Accountant; an accountant who has met the examination, education and experience requirements of the Institute of Chartered Accountants for an individual professionally competent in accounting.

Capital Assets   Include long-term tangible assets such as plant and equipment and intangible assets such as patents. Capital assets are expected to provide benefits for more than one period.

Cash   Either cash in the bank or petty cash.

Cash Based Accounting   Revenues are recognized when cash is received and expenses are recorded when cash is paid.

Cash Disbursement   Cash spent during the reporting (or accounting) period.

Cash Disbursements Journal   The special journal that is used to record all receipts of cash.

Cash Discount   A reduction in the price of merchandise that is granted by a seller to a purchaser in exchange for the purchaser paying within a specified period of time called the discount period.

Cash Flow Statement   A financial report that shows the inflows and outflows of actual cash during a specific period of time; where the company's cash came from and where it was spent.

Cash from Investors   Cash received from investors who have purchased an interest in the business.

Cash Receipts Journal   The special journal that is used to record all receipts of cash.

CGA   Certified General Accountant; an accountant who has met the examination, education and experience requirements of the Certified General Accountants' Association for an individual professionally competent in accounting.

Change in Cash   The net increase or decrease in the cash owned by the business measured in the beginning of the reporting period to the end of the reporting period. Cash receipts less disbursements for the period.

Chart of Accounts   A list of all accounts used by a company; includes the identification number assigned to each account.

Closing Entries   Journal entries recorded at the end of each accounting period that transfer the end-of-period balances in revenues, expenses, and withdrawals accounts to the permanent owner's capital account in order to prepare for the upcoming period and update the owner's capital account for the events of the period just finished.

CMA   Certified Management Accountant; an accountant who has met the examination, education and experience requirements of the Society of Management Accountants for an individual professionally competent in accounting.

Common Shares   The name for a corporation's shares when only one class of share capital is issued.

Common Stock   Shares of the company that have a claim on the assets of the company AFTER preferred shareholders.

Compound Journal Entry   A journal entry that affects at least three accounts.

Consignee   One who receives and holds goods owned by another party for the purpose of selling the goods for the owner.

Consignor   An owner of goods who ships them to another party who will then sell the goods for the owner.

Consistency Principle   The accounting requirement that a company use the same accounting methods period after period so that the financial statements of succeeding periods will be comparable.

Contra Account   An account linked with another account and having an opposite normal balance; reported as a subtraction from the other account's balance so that more complete information than simply the net amount is provided.

Corporation   A business that is a separate legal entity under provincial or federal laws with owners that are called shareholders.

Cost of Goods Sold   The cost to directly produce the product or deliver the service. In the case of retail the "Cost of Goods" is the cost that the store paid for the goods. In manufacturing the "Cost of Goods" is the material cost, labour overheads, supervision or any other cost attributing to produce the product.

Credit   An entry that decreases asset, expense, and owner's withdrawals accounts or increases liability, owner's capital and revenue accounts; recorded on the right side of the T-account.

Credit Period   The time period that can pass before a customer's payment is due.

Credit Terms   The description of the amounts and timing of payments that a buyer agrees to make in the future.

Current Assets   Cash and those assets which in the normal course of business can be turned into cash typically within one year. Examples are: Inventory and Accounts Receivable.

Current Liabilities   All liabilities that are due within the next 12 months.

Current Ratio   Current Assets divided by Current Liabilities. This is used to measure the company's ability to pay its current debts in the short term.

Days of Inventory on Hand   An estimate of how many days it will take to convert the inventory on hand at the end of the period into Accounts Receivable or cash; calculated by dividing the ending inventory by the cost of goods sold and multiplying the result by 365.

Debit   An entry that increases asset, expense and owner's withdrawals accounts or decreases liability, owner's capital and revenue accounts; recorded on the left side of a T-account.

Debt to Equity Ratio   Total liabilities divided by total Shareholders Equity. This ratio indicates how much has been borrowed versus how much has been invested by the shareholders. This ratio is helpful in determining whether or not the company has too much debt.

Deferred Taxes   The amount of tax that must eventually be paid.

Deposit Slip   Lists the items such as currency, coins and cheques deposited along with each of their dollar amounts.

Depreciation   Depreciation is the decline in the useful value of a tangible asset due to its use over time.

Discount Period   The time period in which a cash discount is available and a reduced payment can be made by the buyer.

Dividends   The amount paid to the shareholders from the profits of the company.

Double-entry Accounting   An accounting system where every transaction affects and is recorded in at least two accounts; the sum of the debits for all entries must equal the sum of the credits for all entries.

Earning per Share   Net income divided by the total number of shares of the company owned by the shareholders. (See Net Income). This gives a good indication of the earning ability of the company relative to the number of people who may at some point share in the benefit of those earnings.

Equity   The interest that the shareholders own in the company. This is also known as Net Worth (Assets minus Liabilities).

External Auditors/Auditing   Examine and provide assurance that financial statements are prepared according to Generally Accepted Accounting Principles (GAAP).

Financial Statement   Written record of the financial status of an individual, association or business organization. It usually includes a Balance Sheet, Income Statement and Cash Flow Statement.

First In First Out Inventory Pricing (FIFO)   The pricing of an inventory under the assumption that inventory items are sold in the order acquired; the first items received were the first items sold.

Fiscal Year   A fiscal year is defined as a period consisting of 12 consecutive months. A fiscal year does not necessarily start and end in a calendar year.

Fixtures and Fittings   The furniture and any fixture owned by the company.

FOB   The abbreviation for *free on board*; the designated point at which ownership of goods pass to the buyer. FOB shipping point (or factory) means that the buyer pays the shipping costs and accepts ownership of the goods at the seller's place of business. FOB destination means that the seller pays the shipping costs and the ownership of the goods transfers to the buyer at the buyer's place of business.

Full Disclosure Principle   The GAAP that requires financial statements (including footnotes) to report all relevant information about the operations and financial position of the entity.

GAAP   Generally Accepted Accounting Principles are the rules that indicate acceptable accounting practice.

General and Administrative Expenses   Expenses that support the overall operations of a business and include the expenses of such activities as providing accounting services, human resource management and financial management.

General Journal   The most flexible type of journal; can be used to record any kind of transaction.

Gross Margin   Gross Profit (the difference between revenues and COGS) divided by revenues; also called *Grosss Margin Ratio*.

Gross Profit   Net sales less the cost of goods or the cost of sales. It is called "gross" because it does not take into account other types of expenses which must still be deducted from sales before the Net Income (or profit) is calculated, e.g. operating expenses.

Income Statement   The financial statement that records the sales and expenses thereby calculating a profit or loss for the accounting period.

Income Summary   A temporary account used only in the closing process to which the balances of revenue and expense accounts are transferred; its balance equals net income or net loss and is transferred to the owner's capital account.

Income Tax   The amount of money the government charges the company for making money. The more the profit, the more the tax.

Income Taxes Payable   Money owed to various tax agencies but not yet paid. This is a liability to the company.

Intangible Assets   Long-lived (capital) assets that have no physical substance but convey a right to use a product or process, eg. patents, copyrights and goodwill.

Interim Financial Reports   Financial reports covering less than one year; usually based on one-month, three-month, or six-month periods.

Internal Controls   Procedures set up to protect assets, ensure reliable accounting reports, promote efficiency and encourage adherence to company policies.

Inventory   Inventory is composed of three classes of material: raw material used in making goods; work in progress, which is goods in the process of being manufactured; and finished goods ready to be shipped to customers. In a retail store or distribution business the value of the inventory would generally be what the company was charged for it plus the shipping costs.

Invoice   An itemized statement of goods prepared by the vendor that lists the customer's name, the items sold, the sales prices and the terms of sale.

Journal   A record where transactions are recorded before they are recorded in accounts; amounts are posted from the journal to the ledger; also called the *book of original entry*.

Journalizing   The process of recording transactions in a journal.

Last In First Out Inventory Pricing (LIFO)   The pricing of the inventory under the assumption that the most recent items purchased are sold first and their costs are charged to cost of goods sold.

Ledger   A record containing all accounts used by a business.

Liabilities   All the debts and legal obligations that the business owes and must pay.

Limited Liability   The owner's liability is limited to the amount of investment in the business.

Limited Liability Partnership   Restricts partners' liabilities to their own acts and the acts of individuals under their control.

Limited Partnership   Includes both general partner(s) with unlimited liability and limited partner(s) with liability restricted to the amount invested.

Liquid Assets   Assets that can be easily converted to cash or used to pay for services or obligations; cash is the most liquid asset, eg. Accounts Receivable and inventory.

Liquidation   The sale of the assets of the company. This is done when the business goes broke. The assets are sold and the proceeds are used to pay the creditors.

Liquidity   The ability to pay day-to-day obligations (current liabilities) with existing liquid assets.

Long-Term Investments   Assets such as notes receivable or investments in shares and bonds that are held for more than one year, or the operating cycle.

Long-Term Liabilities   All debts that are due by the company that are payable after 12 months.

Lower of Cost or Market (LCM)   The required method of reporting merchandise inventory on the balance sheet, where market value is reported, when market is lower than cost; the market value may be defined as net realizable value or current replacement cost on the date of the balance sheet.

Market Value of an Asset   The amount that an asset can be sold for; market value is not tied to the book value of an asset.

Matching Principle   The broad principle that requires expenses to be reported in the same period as the revenues that were earned as a result of the expenses.

Materiality Principle   This GAAP states that an amount may be ignored if its affect on the financial statements is not important to their users; also called *cost-to-benefit constraint*.

Merchandise   Products, also called goods, that a company acquires for the purpose of reselling them to customers.

Merchandise Turnover   The number of times a company's average inventory was sold during an accounting period, calculated by dividing the cost of goods sold by the average merchandise inventory balance; also called *inventory turnover*.

Net Income   The excess that is left after all expenses have been paid; also called Profit.

Net Realizable Value   The expected sales price of an item minus the cost of making the sale.

Net Sales   The amount of sales billed, less any refunds, returns or bad debts.

Notes Payable   Money owed to the bank, an individual, corporation or other lender.

Note Receivable   An unconditional written promise to pay a definite sum of money on demand or on a defined future date(s); also called a *promissory note*.

Operating Expenses   Total expenses incurred in promoting and selling the product or services and running the operation that makes and sells the product or service; they are different from direct expenses such as material and labour; they are usually divided into selling expenses and general administration expenses.

Operating Income   Gross profit minus the operating expenses. This figure shows what a company is making or losing when it produces and sells the product or service.

Other Income/Expenses   Money earned or expenses incurred not directly involved in making and selling the product or service. For example, interest earned on bank deposits or paid for bank loans.

Owner's Equity   Everything that the company owns, less what it owes, belongs to the owner(s).

Plant and equipment   Tangible long-lived assets used to produce goods or services.

Permanent Accounts   Accounts that are used to report on activities related to one or more future accounting periods; their balances are carried into the next period and include all balance sheet accounts; permanent account balances are not closed as long as the company continues to own the assets, owe the liabilities and have owner's equity; also called *real accounts*.

Periodic Inventory System A method of accounting that records the cost of inventory purchased but does not track the quantity on hand or sold to customers; the records are updated at the end of each period to reflect the results of physical counts of the items on hand.

Perpetual Inventory System A method of accounting that maintains continuous records of the cost of inventory on hand and the cost of goods sold.

Post(ing) Transfer journal entry information to ledger accounts.

Posting reference (PR) Column A column in *journals* where individual account numbers are entered when entries are posted to the ledger; a column in *ledgers* where journal page numbers are entered when entries are posted.

Prepaid Expenses Payments for items that will not immediately be used and are therefore not charged immediately as an expense. For example, 6 months worth of office supplies are purchased and at the end of the reporting period only 2 months worth of supplies have been used. The additional 4 months that are unused are considered as prepaid expenses.

Preferred Stock Shares of the company that have preference with respect to dividends and distribution of assets in case of liquidation.

Price/Earnings Ratio Current market price of a company whose shares are publicly traded divided by the earnings per share. This is an indicator of how the company is valued by the public stock market relative to its ability to earn.

Promissory Note An unconditional written promise to pay a definite sum of money on demand or on a defined future date(s); also called a *note receivable*.

Purchase Discount A term used by a purchaser to describe a cash discount granted to the purchaser for paying within the discount period.

Purchases Journal A journal that is used to record all purchases on credit.

Quick Ratio The total of cash, marketable securities and Accounts Receivable divided by the total of current liabilities. In other words, those items that can be rapidly converted into cash with which the current liabilities can be paid. Another way of calculating the quick ratio is simply to add cash plus Accounts Receivable divided by current liabilities.

Sales Journal A journal used to record sales of merchandise on credit.

Replacement Cost Current cost of purchasing an item.

Report Form Balance Sheet A balance sheet that lists items vertically with assets above the liabilities and owner's equity.

Retail Inventory Method A method for estimating an ending inventory cost based on the ratio of the amount of goods for sale at cost to the amount of goods for sale at marked selling prices.

Retained Earnings Retained earnings accumulate as the company earns profits and reinvests or "retains" the profits in the company rather than paying out the profits to the shareholders in the form of dividends.

Return on Equity Net Income divided by total Shareholders Equity. This is an indicator of how well the company is using the money invested in it so that it can bring a return to the investors. Investors can place their capital in alternative places so it is important that this ratio is attractive.

Revenue   Also referred to as sales.

Reversing Entries   Optional entries recorded at the beginning of a new period that prepare the accounts for simplified journal entries subsequent to accrual adjusting entries.

Sales Discount   A term used by a seller to describe a cash discount granted to the purchaser for paying within the discount period.

Selling, General and Administrative Expenses   Advertising and promotion costs, sales, staff salaries and commissions, travel, executive salaries and office expenses needed to sell the product and operate the company, but not directly related to making the product.

Shrinkage   The cost of goods "not sold", which is typically caused by theft, goods signed for and not received, spoilage, reject production, etc.

Single-Step Income Statement   An income statement format that includes cost of goods sold as an operating expense and shows only one subtotal for total expenses.

Special Journal   Any journal that is used for recording and posting transactions of a similar type.

Straight-line Amortization Method   Allocates equal amounts of an asset's cost to amortization expenses during its useful life.

Source Documents   Documents that are the source of information recorded with accounting entries; can be in either paper or electronic form.

T-Account   A simple characterization of an account form used as a helpful tool in showing the effects of transactions and events on specific accounts.

Temporary Accounts   Accounts that are used to describe revenues, expenses, and owner's withdrawals for one accounting period; they are closed at the end of the reporting period; also called *nominal accounts*.

Time period principle   A broad principle that assumes that an organization's activities can be divided into specific time periods such as months, quarters, or years.

Total Assets   The total of current assets, property, plant and equipment (less accumulated depreciation) and intangibles (such as goodwill) = the total assets of the company.

Total Debt   Current and long-term debt added together.

Total Equity   The total of the Shareholders Equity including the stock.

Total Liabilities   The total of all Current and Long Term Liabilities.

Trade Discount   A reduction below a list or catalogue price that may vary in amount for wholesalers, retailers and final consumers.

Trial Balance   A list of accounts and their balances at a point in time; the total debit balances should equal the total credit balances.

Unearned Revenue   Liabilities created when customers pay in advance for products or services; created when cash is received before revenues are earned; satisfied by delivering the products or services in the future.

Weighted Average Inventory Costing   An inventory pricing system in which the unit prices of the beginning inventory and of each purchase are weighted by the number of units in the beginning inventory and each purchase. The total of these amounts is then divided by the total number of units available for sale to find the unit cost of the ending inventory and of the units that were sold.

Wholesaler   A middleman that buys products from manufacturers or other wholesalers and sells them to retailers or other wholesalers.

Working Capital   Current Assets less Current Liabilities; it is called "Working Capital" or "Operating Capital" because it is capital that has been put to work in the business and has taken the form of inventory, Accounts Receivable, cash etc.

All Transactions

The following is a list of all the possible transactions in accounting:

#	Transaction		Debit		Credit
1	Use cash - purchase an asset	Increase	Asset	Decrease	Cash
2	Use cash - reduce debt	Decrease	Debt	Decrease	Cash
3	Use cash - owner's drawings (dividends)	Decrease	Owner's Equity	Decrease	Cash
4	Use cash - lend money	Increase	Loans Receivable	Decrease	Cash
5	Use cash - pay cash for expenses	Increase	Expense	Decrease	Cash
6	Use cash - buy shares back	Increase	Owner's Equity	Decrease	Cash
7	Receive cash - revenue	Increase	Cash	Increase	Revenue
8	Receive cash - accounts receivable and loans payable	Increase	Cash	Decrease	Accounts Receivable
9	Receive cash - borrow cash	Increase	Cash	Increase	Debt
10	Receive cash - sell shares/increase capital account	Increase	Cash	Decrease	Owner's Equity
11	Receive cash - refund of expense	Increase	Cash	Decrease	Expense
12	Receive cash - unearned revenue	Increase	Cash	Increase	Unearned Revenue
13	Receive cash - sell an asset for cash/refund for a expense	Increase	Cash	Decrease	Asset
14	Refinance debt	Increase or vice versa	Debt	Increase or vice versa	Debt
15	Record sales on account	Increase	Accounts Receivable	Increase	Revenue
16	Expenses on account	Increase	Expense	Increase	Accounts Payable
17	Purchase an asset on account	Increase	Asset	Increase	Accounts Payable
18	Recognize unearned revenue	Decrease	Unearned Revenue	Increase	Revenue
19	Recognize any asset to expenses	Increase	Expense	Decrease	Assets
20	Corrections/adjustments expenses	Increase or vice versa	Expense	Decrease or vice versa	Expense
21	Corrections/adjustments revenue	Increase or vice versa	Revenue	Decrease or vice versa	Revenue
22	Corrections/adjustments assets	Increase or vice versa	Asset	Increase or vice versa	Asset
23	Corrections/adjustments liabilities	Increase or vice versa	Debt	Increase or vice versa	Debt
24	Corrections/adjustments owner's equity	Increase or vice versa	Owner's Equity	Increase or vice versa	Owner's Equity
25	Allow for doubtful debts (contra account)	Increase	Expense	Decrease	Allowance for doubtful accounts
	Record accumulated depreciation (contra account)	Increase	Expense	Decrease	Accumulated depreciation
26	Offset account	Increase	Expense	Decrease	Revenue
27	Discounts received for assets	Decrease	Accounts Payable	Decrease	Asset
28	Discounts received for expenses	Decrease	Accounts Payable	Decrease	Expense
29	Discounts allowed	Decrease	Accounts Receivable	Decrease	Revenue

Notes

Notes

Notes

Notes

Notes

Notes

Notes

The Accounting Map™

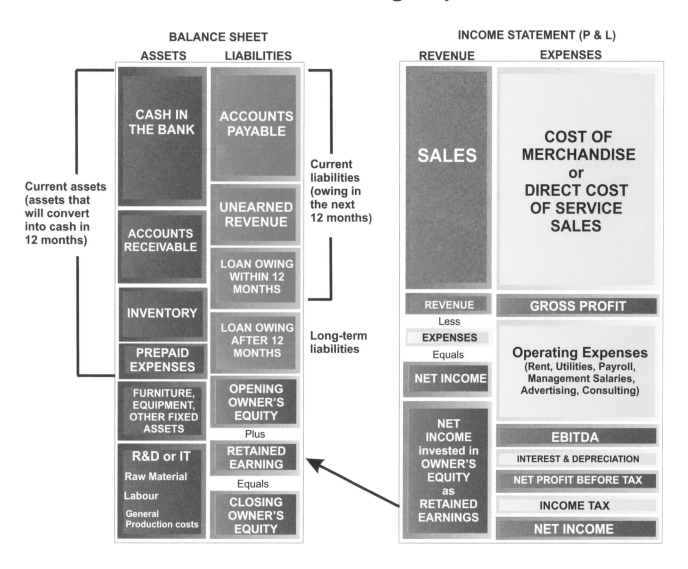

BALANCE SHEET

ASSETS | LIABILITIES

INCOME STATEMENT (P & L)

REVENUE | EXPENSES

Current assets (assets that will convert into cash in 12 months)

- CASH IN THE BANK
- ACCOUNTS RECEIVABLE
- INVENTORY
- PREPAID EXPENSES
- FURNITURE, EQUIPMENT, OTHER FIXED ASSETS
- R&D or IT
  - Raw Material
  - Labour
  - General Production costs

- ACCOUNTS PAYABLE
- UNEARNED REVENUE
- LOAN OWING WITHIN 12 MONTHS
- LOAN OWING AFTER 12 MONTHS
- OPENING OWNER'S EQUITY

  Plus
- RETAINED EARNING

  Equals
- CLOSING OWNER'S EQUITY

Current liabilities (owing in the next 12 months)

Long-term liabilities

SALES

COST OF MERCHANDISE or DIRECT COST OF SERVICE SALES

REVENUE
Less
EXPENSES
Equals
NET INCOME

GROSS PROFIT

Operating Expenses (Rent, Utilities, Payroll, Management Salaries, Advertising, Consulting)

NET INCOME invested in OWNER'S EQUITY as RETAINED EARNINGS

EBITDA

INTEREST & DEPRECIATION

NET PROFIT BEFORE TAX

INCOME TAX

NET INCOME

Navigating The Accounting Map™

BALANCE SHEET ACCOUNTS:

ASSETS (blue)	-	what the company **OWNS**
LIABILITIES (red)	-	what the company **OWES**
EQUITY (grey)	-	what the owners (shareholders) **INVESTED**
OWNER'S EQUITY	=	**ASSETS less LIABILITIES**

INCOME STATEMENT ACCOUNTS:

REVENUE (green)	-	what the company **GENERATES IN REVENUES**
EXPENSES (yellow)	-	what the company **USES IN EXPENSES**
NET PROFIT (LOSS)	=	**REVENUE less EXPENSES**

Other than investing more money into a company, **EQUITY** will only increase if the company can manage to create a **NET PROFIT**. It is therefore everyone's responsibility to maximize **REVENUE** while minimizing **EXPENSES**, without compromising **QUALITY** or **SERVICE**, in order to maintain profitability that in turn builds the company's Net Worth.

AME | Learning

© AME Learning Inc. Phone (905) 731-2408 or 1-888-401-3881 Fax (905) 731-8120
www.amelearning.com

Quick Reference Sheet

1. Revenue is not profit and profits do not guarantee cash in the bank.

2. Net Worth (Owner's Equity) can only increase if revenue exceeds expenses.

3. Buying or selling assets (according to the value on the balance sheet) has no impact on Net Worth.

4. Assuming or reducing debt has no impact on Net Worth.

5. GAAP rules require that revenue and expenses be MATCHED to each other in the same period. The word *cash* does not exist in the world of accruals.

6. Budgets:
   a. There is a difference between a cash flow budget and an operating budget.
   b. If you experience a negative or positive variance, ensure that your expenses have been accrued appropriately.
   c. Do not *sweep negative variances under the carpet*. Understand your business case and explain the variance.

7. Three ways to recognize revenue:
   a. Receive cash when delivering the service.
   b. Receive payment after the fact (accounts receivable).
   c. Receive the cash before the fact (unearned revenue) and recognize the revenue when delivering the service.

8. Three ways to recognize expenses:
   a. Pay cash when the service is delivered.
   b. Pay after the fact (accounts payable).
   c. Pay cash before the fact (prepaid expenses) and recognize the expense when the service has been delivered.

9. Three ways to increase or decrease cash:
   a. *Operations* - revenue exceeds expenses or vice versa (ultimate reason for being in business).
   b. *Investment* - buy or sell assets, such as equipment, or build/ sell technology.
   c. *Financing* - borrow or repay loans, or deposit cash from new investors or divest.

10. *Revenues are Vanity, Profits are Sanity and Cash flow is Reality.* A business can fail due to cash starvation despite being profitable.

11. Three ways to create a viable business:
    a. *Profitability* - you are in business to make a profit.
    b. *Liquidity* - you can fail despite your success by making a profit and running out of cash.
    c. *Sustainability* - the business is only viable if the business case can be sustained.

12. Three documents to monitor your business:
    a. *Income Statement* - compare profits from month-to-month.
    b. *Balance Sheet* - monitor liquidity ratios and management ratios monthly.
    c. *Cash Flow Statement* - ensure that cash flow is being generated from operations.

13. POPPEN: If your **P**rocess **O**r **P**roposed **P**lan does not improve **E**quity, then the answer is **N**o. Create a business case to ensure that a new initiative can either increase revenue, decrease expenses or both.

14. Analyze Key Performance Indicators and financial ratios each month to assess if your performance is in harmony with the corporate financial objectives.

15. If you cannot measure it, you cannot manage it.